SOFTWARE ENGINEERING SERIES

A UML Pattern Language

Paul Evitts

MACMILLAN
TECHNICAL
PUBLISHING
U·S·A

A UML Pattern Language

By Paul Evitts

Published by:
MTP
201 West 103rd Street
Indianapolis, IN 46290 USA

Copyright © 2000 by MTP

Printed in the United States of America

First Printing: February, 2000
03 02 01 00   7 6 5 4 3 2 1

Library of Congress Cataloging-in-Publication Number 98-87412

ISBN: 1-57870-118-X

Trademark Acknowledgments

All terms mentioned in this book that are known to be trademarks or service marks have been appropriately capitalized. MTP cannot attest to the accuracy of this information. Use of a term in this book should not be regarded as affecting the validity of any trademark or service mark.

Warning and Disclaimer

This book is designed to provide information about UML pattern language. Every effort has been made to make this book as complete and as accurate as possible, but no warranty or fitness is implied.

The information is provided on an "as is" basis. The author and MTP shall have neither liability nor responsibility to any person or entity with respect to any loss or damages arising from the information contained in this book or from the use of the discs or programs that may accompany it.

Feedback Information

At MTP, our goal is to create in-depth technical books of the highest quality and value. Each book is crafted with care and percision, undergoing rigorous development that involves the unique expertise of members from the professional technical community.

Readers' feedback is a natural continuation of this process. If you have any comments regarding how we could improve the quality of this book, or otherwise alter it to better suit your needs, you can contact us at www.newriders.com/contact. Please make sure to include the book title and ISBN in your message.

We greatly appreciate your assistance.

Publisher
David Dwyer

Associate Publisher
Brad Koch

Executive Editors
Linda Ratts Engelman

Product Marketing Manager
Stephanie Layton

Development Editor
Thomas Cirtin

Managing Editor
Gina Brown

Project Editor
Laura Loveall

Copy Editor
Nancy Sixsmith

Indexer
Joy Dean Lee

Editorial Coordinator
Jennifer Garrett

Manufacturing Coordinator
Chris Moos

Book Designer
Gary Adair

Cover Designer
Aren Howell

Composition
Amy Parker

About the Author

Paul Evitts is a systems and management consultant from Toronto, and he is the President of neoLogistiks, Inc. He has more than 20 years of experience in systems integration, technology planning and implementation, and software methodology/lifecycle development. Paul's clients have included dozens of private sector and government organizations across North America, including insurance and manufacturing companies, real estate and retail organizations, educational institutions, and financial sector firms.

Over the last 10 years, Paul has successfully crafted custom use-case driven development approaches for clients, acted as business architect and project manager for individual projects, and provided strategic planning support for clients migrating to new technologies.

His consulting activities have not been limited to traditional applications development and system integration. He has also evaluated business opportunities for systems technology in the Third World (Africa, Latin America, and the Caribbean), acted as technical producer for a commercial CD-ROM published by The Voyager Company, assisted a startup multimedia media company in business planning, and worked as a system architect for one of the significant successes in business re-engineering.

Paul's methodology consulting practice has not been limited to object-oriented development. He spent many years in the 1980s providing clients with Rapid Application Development and event-based development approaches, coaching and mentoring modeling using a variety of CASE tools.

Before getting into Information Technology, Paul was involved in community development and the use of emerging technologies to promote social change. As a socio-economic consultant, he was an early part of the Inuit Land Claims effort in the Canadian Arctic, which recently culminated in the establishment of a new Canadian Territory called Nunavut. Paul helped the Inuit use video and other media in the process of initial consensus-building across the North, and he provided advice on housing and community planning. His first exposure to the ideas of Christopher Alexander came about earlier as a result of work with a legalized squatting community in London, England—where he was involved in the cooperative rehabilitation of abandoned neighborhoods.

Paul studied community development, politics, and advanced technology at Rochdale College in Toronto. Rochdale is an experimental educational community that he helped establish. It is an alternative to traditional universities. His experiences at Rochdale were recently made into a very popular television documentary in Canada, which aired a number of times by the Canadian Broadcasting Corporation and is available as a video from the National Film Board of Canada. Please refer to Paul's Web site, www.umlpatterns.com, for further materials related to this book.

About the Technical Reviewers

These reviewers contributed their considerable, hands-on expertise to the entire development process for *A UML Pattern Language*. As the book was being written, these folks reviewed all the material for technical content, organization, and flow. Their feedback was critical to ensuring that *A UML Pattern Language* fits our readers' needs for the highest quality technical information.

David G. Lewis is a technology consultant in the Washington D.C. area, specializing in enterprise software development and technology management. He has been active in the design, development, and management of distributed object-oriented technology for more than 10 years. David began his career working on an object-oriented point-of-sale system in C on a DEC Rainbow running Venix in 1986. The company failed, but the product's successful use of object-oriented principles, reusable frameworks, and thoughtful design demonstrated the merits of this approach. Thus began a career-long commitment to object-oriented design and software reuse.

David's contributions in this area included a persistence framework for the GenBank project at Los Alamos National Laboratory; file-system technology licensed for the NeXTSTEP operating system; and key roles in the development of object-oriented systems, reusable frameworks, and technology adoption at Washington-area companies—including Fannie Mae, MCI, and T. Rowe Price. He is currently involved in developing and promoting CORBA technology at a start-up company in northern Virginia. David graduated from the Great Books Program at St. John's College in Santa Fe in 1985.

Mark Sandberg has been developing software for over 14 years for a wide variety of industries, including financial, telecommunications, and healthcare businesses. Currently, Mark is the e-commerce development manager for HealthObjects Corporation, where he is managing the design and development of a healthcare portal product.

From 1995 to 1999, Mark was a consultant with Object Systems Group, for which he concentrated on technical and process mentoring on application development teams. From 1989 to 1995, he worked at Campbell and Co., developing proprietary trading systems for the options and futures markets. From 1985 to 1989, Mark worked at Electronic Data Systems, implementing and supporting client/server applications for the US Army's Housing Management System. He received his B.S. degree in Mathematics and Economics from Wake Forest University in 1985.

Dedications

I want to dedicate this book to four people who have made this book possible on a personal level. My son, Jesse, contributed an occasionally inscrutable sense of humor whenever humor disappeared. My brother, Chris, nagged me to do something over a few beers. My wife, Lyne, knew when to disappear, and when not to. Last but not least, my father-in-law, Eugene Cote, whose sparkling faith in the book's inevitability got me over many rough spots. This book would not have been finished without him. And, as a lagniappe, I also want to thank my Mom, without whom I wouldn't have been possible. She's number five, but also number one.

Acknowledgments

I have to acknowledge the determination and god-like patience of Tom Cirtin, my development editor at MTP, and Jen Garrett, our editorial coordinator. On a professional level, they made me do it. And do it. And do it. The reviewers, David Lewis (Mr. SoapBox) and Mark Sandberg (Mr. Laconic), played complementary (if not always complimentary) roles in keeping me honest and real. Dion Hinchcliffe, a senior architect at T. Rowe Price in Baltimore, provided the original version of a large percentage of the more technical patterns here, as well as the initial idea for the book, although one I've deviated from enormously.

Contents at a Glance

Table of Contents

Introduction

Arma virumque cano.

I sing of tools and the man.

—*Virgil's introduction to the Aeneid, freely translated*

This book is about how to model software systems and how to use those models. It is rooted in that emerging intellectual "ecosystem" comprising the various networks (the Internet, intranets, extranets, and so on), distributed objects, piecemeal development based on short development cycles, and something called *patterns*. It is aimed at developers, designers, and architects of software systems and the ways they practice their craft.

It proposes that the convergent appearance of patterns and the Unified Modeling Language (UML) is no accident. Patterns are a way of documenting collective, timeless ways of thinking about designing and building software systems. The UML is a way of documenting the specifics of a system for a particular time to support a development effort as the system evolves and changes. Both are exercises in eliminating the ephemeral quality of process and product that has bedeviled our profession.

The two are manifestations of a basic shift in the way systems are designed and built—one that software professionals are just beginning to grapple with. This shift is indicative of a broader trend in the way professionals work and the way they work with the people they are supposed to help, which is beginning to be felt in the software community.

At its simplest, the change for software developers represents a shift away from an immature vision of software development as a field dominated by solitary coders. It moves toward a more mature vision of a collaborative nature of software development—one that is typical of genuine professional practice. But it also challenges the traditional views that software developers have about their profession.

In a sense, the emergence of patterns and the UML also symbolizes a shift away from a systems culture, in which programming defined the core of the discipline and coding defined the core of its practice. Design and modeling have become equal partners with programming and coding in the enterprise of software development.

The pattern language in this book is a practical adjunct to this shift. Its goal is to provide a toolset that software professionals can use, one that is fitted to the dimensions of the work to be done in modeling systems and is equally fitted to the needs of real practitioners and craftspeople engaged in software development.

This book's audience is neither hackers (in the original sense of cowboy programmers), engineers, nor academics; rather it is software developers. Its readers are literate, not just in software languages, but also in software ideas. They have a professional need to understand the exciting new ideas that are emerging, as well as a need for the tools they generate. And they have a professional curiosity about the origins of the ideas that shape their work.

The pattern language itself—the core of this book—reflects the importance of being practical. Patterns are inherently practical. By keeping faith with current notions of practicality (in particular, the need to avoid creating a methodology), however, this book is not intended to end up as "shelfware." Nor is it courseware. It isn't intended to be read from cover to cover as a unified learning experience. Rather, it's meant to be applied, used, and shaped by the user.

Patterns and the UML

At their simplest, patterns are structured, packaged problem solutions in literary form.

Patterns are a new literary form, the first to originate from the software community. As you will see, this form has its roots in architecture—especially in the work of Christopher Alexander, a visionary architect who first achieved prominence for his work on architectural design in the 1970s. In systems development, the idea of patterns is very much a "bastard stepchild" appropriated by software developers in response to communication frustrations and to the need for a medium that goes beyond objects as a way of organizing the complex thinking behind design.

Pattern languages are collections of related patterns that have a common domain. They have many advantages over methodologies and courses for explaining how to go about modeling software today. They are descriptive, not prescriptive (the bane of methodologies). Although they capture experience, pattern languages are not didactic nor the expression of a single perspective. They are loose and open-ended.

At their best, patterns enhance creativity. At their worst, they allow for interpretation, and thus support agility and grace in decision-making. They facilitate structured learning through links that are "hypertextual" and dynamic, not sequential. The learning they support is better suited to the "just in time" approach that many find more sensible for software work than traditional training.

The domain for the pattern language in this book is system modeling— *software-intensive system modeling*, as the UML puts it. Although patterns are becoming the conceptual *lingua franca* of the software world, this book focuses not on patterns per se, but rather on the emerging operational lingua franca of the shop floor: the UML.

The UML is as revolutionary in its way as patterns, and not as just another modeling facility. Its importance for the software practitioner is as much a result of its role and how it evolved as it is a result of what it provides.

Up until recently, software modeling has been a Balkanized domain, in which the intellectual and practical cost of entry was determined by proprietary and often conflicting standards. Tools and training were expensive, and a typical software developer had to gain useful experience doing work on big projects for big organizations.

This cost of entry was affordable for big organizations focused on internal standardization. They paid because it was in their interest to use standardized models internally. These models helped to establish a common corporate picture of their information technology assets, both for control and planning. The results of modeling were, frequently, of questionable value to users and of limited utility for programmers.

Then, client/server, a variety of new programming languages, and finally the Internet entered the picture. The old ways of modeling—structured modeling and information engineering, for example—ceased to be relevant. They were aimed at building internal, self-contained operational systems residing on mainframes in one form or another—the so-called monolithic or stovepipe systems—in a relatively homogeneous computing environment. They didn't scale up well to a more complex world of dynamic interactions between organizations and interactions with customers, suppliers, competitors, and partners.

Meanwhile, the new environment of objects and components was immature. It had captured most of the elusive "mindshare," (the intellectual equivalent of market share) among software developers that so often determines what happens next in information technology. Development approaches that made models a critical element in the development process were being seen as essential if object technology was to mature. But object modeling was as much of a dog's breakfast as mainstream modeling.

The UML emerged from this combination of opportunity and need. Unlike previous efforts to define a toolset for software modeling, the UML has been a group effort. So, it has escaped the dead end of being proprietary. It is intentionally built to evolve and respond to new needs as they emerge. These differences reflect the different landscape that software modeling has to fit into today and that the UML serves.

The notion of model-driven development has taken hold for all sizes and types of software projects. Iterative, incremental development that is planned with the help of models is replacing the all-at-once crapshoot of mainframe style development. The availability of inexpensive personal productivity software has nurtured expectations among developers for development tools that are personally affordable. The mantra of reuse has encouraged the notion of sharable solutions, which is documented in models and implemented in components. The Iron Curtains and Berlin Walls around organizations are being replaced by firewalls with interfaces, responsibilities, and collaborations that need to be modeled.

Modeling is now at center stage, and the UML is perhaps the lever that is needed to move the world. It provides the starting point for inexpensive tools, shareable models, and a manageable development process. It has been shaped or embraced by all the significant players in the systems industry.

And with a focus on modeling using the UML, I specifically chose patterns as media because they fit the dynamic landscape of software development in the same way as the UML. The two are complementary, not orthogonal, artifacts of the same culture.

Patterns compress experience, whereas models filter and abstract relationships and conceptual structures. Patterns are literary; models are architectural. Both are ways of managing complexity. Both emerged out of a volatile consensus that reflects a bigger tendency away from the proprietary and the closed, and toward the standard and the open. Both reflect the success of a philosophy of piecemeal growth, team-based development, and what might be called *permeable organizations*: organizations without walls.

Levels and Shared Idioms

The patterns included in this book are all derived from *pattern-mining*, a term coined by the self-described patterns community that surfaced in the last few years among software developers. Pattern-mining is a variation on the original approach taken by Alexander and his colleagues when they created the first set of architectural patterns.

I use patterns to document the successful approaches to working with the UML from the existing literature. The software literature was scoured for repeated examples of good modeling and good uses of models. These examples were evaluated, validated, filtered, factored and refactored, and then documented.

Some patterns are reworked versions of existing patterns; some are first drafts that are based on proven practices or common approaches to solving modeling problems. Some patterns are stronger than others. All of them are open to further evolution.

The pattern language has multiple dimensions and levels. I loosely follow the example set by Alexander. His patterns for building human structures range from the level of the region to that of the components of a house. The subtitle of Alexander's *A Pattern Language* identifies the three key organizing ideas he uses: towns, buildings, and construction (1977).

I've taken the liberty of adopting and freely adapting three of the key organizing ideas that are becoming important in quality software development: domain, products, and components. These are the levels in our pattern language network; they provide the context for the work of modeling.

For the purposes of this book, a *domain* is the combination of technical and business constructs and concepts that provides the immediate context for software development. It brings together a high-level business model with a high-level technology architecture. Domain is the highest level of modeling for this pattern language. Domains define the context, scope, and business vocabulary for engineering, modeling, and management. For a software developer, a domain may be a "family of systems" (Jacobson, Griss, and Jonsson 1997, 19), that is, a collection of *products*; for someone doing business re-engineering, it may be the overall enterprise.

Products are what are planned, managed, and delivered to the end user as a unit. They have a life and a lifecycle that is separate from the development lifecycle, especially now with iterative design and incremental delivery. They are born, introduced, evolved, matured, and theoretically have a sunset. Whether internal to an organization or sold on the open market, products need to managed and modeled beyond the boundaries of a single development project, and they provide the context for each development spurt.

For the purposes of this book, a product goes beyond just the software itself. It is the total package, what Geoffrey Moore, the technology marketing guru, called a "whole product": the supporting services, the documentation, and the ongoing management (1991, 110–35).

As short-cycle development replaces the protracted development style of the mainframe era, products become the ongoing reality of software development, replacing projects as the collective fetish in the management heart of darkness. The UML is especially endowed with artifacts to support the modeling of products.

Components are what is deployed. To start with, they are the executables delivered to the end user on processors and devices. In the UML, they are also the documentation, the source code, the help files, and any other supporting artifact needed to make the executable solution useful and maintainable.

This interpretation straddles the definition gap between *everything is a component*, with its emphasis on reuse, and *components are parts* (that is, only binary code—a portion of a system). As with products, the pattern language looks not just at all the things that make up a component, but it also covers problems that are not strictly development issues (although they are critical for long-term success).

I don't limit these patterns to the problems faced by a developer. I also include patterns useful to management, to operations, and to the deployment team— although they are patterns that an architect and designer should keep in mind because they provide a basis for communication with management.

Some patterns are idiomatic, specifically about making diagrams and creating UML artifacts. Others are more concerned with packaging, making choices about artifacts, and management and organizational considerations that are critical to modeling success.

Most, but not all, of the idiomatic patterns are separated from the pattern language levels described previously. These are the *patterns of style* and *patterns of substance*, addressed to any UML modeling effort. For anyone new to modeling or the UML, they provide some basic guidelines for formatting models and using the UML artifacts effectively. Look there for guidance on the best way to set up a diagram or model a particular situation with the UML. They also help explain how to make use of some of the specific features of the UML that differentiate the UML from other modeling languages, past or present. These patterns can be applied at any level of modeling, from the conceptual to the detailed.

Using This Book

The core of this book is Part II, "The Pattern Language." This is a language for building, planning, and using models of software-intensive systems. The rest of the book can be considered the theory and instructions for using the language, or for using it more efficiently. There's no need to read the book or major parts of it sequentially. The route you take should depend on what you need.

Those unfamiliar with patterns should at least read Chapter 1, "Pattern Essentials," which is an introduction to patterns. Those unfamiliar with the UML should read Chapter 2, "The Unified Modeling Language," which is an introduction to the UML, and Chapter 3, "UML Essentials, Elements, and Artifacts," which is an overview of the elements and artifacts of the UML from a modeling perspective.

Following the pattern language is Part III, "Another Starting Point." These chapters provide context and enrich the use of both the UML in particular and patterns in general. They are meant to be glosses for the main body of the book, the pattern language itself. They are both introductory and *extensive*— providing links to other works. They can provide a starting point for exploring both patterns and the UML further.

Neither the UML nor patterns are fixed or simple. In order to make maximum use of either, move from being a user to a practitioner and eventually become professional, a lot of further work is required beyond what I offer here.

The UML received a great deal of attention as it formed and is a natural extension of previous efforts to define a modeling language. As a result, not only is the important information needed to become a serious practitioner readily available, but most of the skills needed will be extensions of existing skills for anyone with modeling experience.

In the case of patterns, there's history and background to get acquainted with as well because patterns are much more than just a form. They are also very different from anything most developers will be familiar with. Also, patterns have not been well documented for the beginning user. Very little outside attention was paid to them as they emerged, and the background material critical to working with and using patterns effectively is skimpy at best. For anyone getting involved with patterns now, the results can be confusing—even frustrating.

Therefore, I dwell a bit more on patterns and provide otherwise unavailable information in the hopes that those readers looking to move beyond the limited scope of the pattern language will be armored effectively to deal with the pattern's labyrinth itself.

Because it is not a simple topic, the background to the pattern format I use is discussed in detail in Chapter 1. However, for the user of this book, the critical parts of each pattern that will help determine the applicability of a pattern and its potential as a starting point are the *context* and *problem* statements. These parts should be looked at first and looked at together. Applicability can be further refined by reading the *forces* statement, which details the pressures, tendencies, needs, and constraints that the *solution* needs to resolve.

A number of patterns within a chapter will have overlapping contexts and/or forces. Neither is meant to be necessarily unique for each pattern. There may be related patterns to look at, especially among the patterns of usage. The pattern names are intended to be meaningful and may also provide a hook when scanning for one that is useful. And because the patterns are meant to be the basis for creative solutions, some patterns that do not specifically fit the context and forces at hand may be worth considering.

Resources, Sources, and References

Both patterns and the UML emerged in the last half-dozen years, when the Internet made such a big impact on the way people in the systems world communicate. Much of what is here is culled from publicly available sources; most is available on the World Wide Web. The Internet's mailing lists and e-mail facilities were also critical for supporting the research that went into this book. To a significant extent, this book would not have been possible before the Internet.

The most notable source for material on patterns is the WikiWikiWeb site (www.c2.com), also known as the Portland Pattern Repository. Started by Ward Cunningham, a pioneer of patterns, CRC cards, and other such tools for connecting systems to people, this site is a fascinating and idiosyncratic glimpse at the patterns community, perhaps as seen by the multifaceted eye of a spider.

Using a technology that exploits the mostly neglected hypertext capabilities of the Web, it combines snippets of patterns, longer rambling observations and personal anecdotes, and freeform commenting. The results are unique. Anyone can contribute. Each contribution can be added to, edited, erased, and connected to other contributions in a free-form fashion—by anyone. It results in the Web being what it should be: a tool for supporting what I will explain is a very vital and virtual community of practice.

I used the various patterns' mailing lists, magazine Web site articles, and patterns books for details on changing ideas, changing attitudes, and as sources for specific material. The mailing lists provided pointers to sources that I quote and reference and are otherwise useful as an archive of the recent evolution of the patterns community.

The handful of good books that have been published have provided frozen-in-time snapshots of ideas and intensive examples of real patterns. In keeping with the philosophy of patterns, many of the best patterns in the patterns books are also available on the Web, where they are subject to ongoing criticism, evolution, and reflection. Software development magazines have articles and columns that are both less immediate than the lists (and WikiWikiWeb) and more accessible than the books. They provide an additional invaluable source of critiquing and insight.

The UML sources are a mirror image of those for patterns, as they reflect the difference between organizational "official" initiatives and those that emerge from a community. Material directly meant for the Web is secondary, although much of the material is available on the Web.

Because the UML is an initiative driven by organizations (in particular, the metaorganization known as the Object Management Group and the commercial development tools organization known as Rational Software), official and anonymous UML pronouncements have substituted for the give-and-take of WikiWikiWeb as a central source. However, the mailing lists dedicated to dissecting the UML and castigating its authors (especially the OTUG mailing list and its variants that are maintained by Rational) have been most useful as sources of attitude and altitude, that is a higher-level perspective.

Other, non-system works have contributed directly to my book. In particular, Donald Schon's *The Reflective Practitioner* (1983) and Thomas Kuhn's *The Structure Of Scientific Revolutions* (1970) provide some intriguing insights into how professional practitioners work and think that elucidate aspects of both patterns and the UML. And, naturally, all of Christopher Alexander's works have been critical.

The various Web sites and collections of magazines and books reflect the new intellectual culture we're living in. For example, many of the quotes are deliberately taken from secondary sources (references provided by email messages, Web papers, and WikiWikiWeb material). They show the quotes that developers feel add meaning to what they do. Still, it must be said, much of what I write about is based on my own very general experience. In selecting from this public storehouse, I've been deliberately personal, selective, and perhaps idiosyncratic—the better to tell the story well.

PART I

Getting Started

CHAPTER 1

Pattern Essentials

What's new here is that there's nothing new here. Patterns are about what works. Patterns give us a way to talk about what works.

—*Brian Foote, pattern writer (1997, ix)*

What are patterns? Why are patterns important, and why are they useful? These are the questions answered in this chapter.

Although an explanation of understanding patterns is given, using patterns well requires an understanding of the background to the form itself—more so than for any other tool in the software development arsenal.

Patterns hide a lot of cultural and conceptual "baggage," providing a compressed intensity and an economy of expression in return. Patterns users who experience the power of patterns have acquired this baggage, either tacitly (through repeated use) or explicitly, by studying the literature. This is the opposite of models, for which syntax and semantics act as decoder rings for the model message. But it also explains the complementarity of models and patterns as tools for successful and quality-focused software development.

So, this chapter introduces the baggage as part of how to use the book. Later on, there is a more personalized account of a technical subject(see Chapter 9, "Patterns in Context"). But be warned. This book is conceived as a starting point for a journey, and if you want to make that journey, both chapters are necessary. Fortunately, unlike in real life, the baggage gets lighter along the way.

1.1   Patterns and Paradigms

In his now-classic book, *The Structure of Scientific Revolutions*, Thomas Kuhn appropriated the word *paradigm*, twisting the meaning to suit a new need. Kuhn used it to mean significant achievements that share two characteristics:

- They are "sufficiently unprecedented to attract an enduring group of adherents away from competing modes of activity."

- They are "sufficiently open ended to leave all sorts of problems for the redefined group of practitioners to resolve" (1970, 10).

Kuhn's appropriation was so successful that *paradigm* has now been even further appropriated to the point of becoming jargon.

His meaning, his associated notions of *revolution*, and the change in world-view that results are the most useful starting points for understanding patterns and the Unified Modeling Language (UML). Kuhn's analysis of the way that a *paradigm shift* reshapes the workings of the normal world is the best explanation for events that have taken place in the last half-decade in software development.

Kuhn explained how a new paradigm emerges from a revolution in ideas. This makes it possible afterwards for scientists to engage in what he called *normal science*: a scientific practice in which the definition of what constitutes a problem and what is acceptable in arriving at a solution are both provided by the significant achievements that constitute the paradigm shift. Seen this way, new paradigms are not about revolution, but rather about getting the job done. After a new paradigm is established, sensible and conventional people rush in. The new paradigm provides the tools and examples that everyone else can use in figuring out what the revolution means and in applying the revolution.

The normal world Kuhn describes was, until the advent of the information age, limited to the only real *knowledge workers* that existed before the computer: scientists and academics. Now, what Peter Drucker calls *knowledge workers* and Robert Reich calls *symbolic analysts* are the people who are problem-solvers in the new knowledge-based economy (Nonaka and Takeuchi 1995, 7).

Ironically, the conventional meaning of paradigm that Kuhn reworked, which has now almost disappeared as a result, is that of an *accepted model* or *pattern*. In later revisions of his book, Kuhn accepted that the multiple meanings he attached to paradigm were confusing. He responded by suggesting that *exemplar* might be a good term to add to paradigm. By suggesting this term instead, he meant the patterns of experience that science students were exposed to in their studies, expressed as problems that had to be solved in the course of mastering science. This is very much like one of the intentions of software patterns: to provide examples of problems, as solved by the masters, which can be learned from by the inexperienced.

The new paradigm in software development, which is reshaping the world of both software developers and users, is substantially based on patterns and models. The patterns movement and the accepted approach for software documentation that is embodied in the UML are both critical elements in a revolution that is transforming software development at the end of this millennium—a revolution that is finally starting to live up to the hype of what computers can do *for the rest of us.*

1.1.1   The Idea of a Pattern

Defining a pattern is one of those deliciously difficult exercises that challenges the easy boundaries we all usually want to place around ideas. According to the *Oxford English Dictionary*, a pattern is "a regular or logical form," "a model, design or instructions for making something," or "an excellent example." In software development, all of these meanings apply.

As "a regular or logical form," patterns are now an accepted way of packaging software design experience (specifically, object-oriented software design experience). Even with the variety of formats that have been used by pattern writers, there's an underlying similarity that binds all software patterns together.

The simplest way of explaining the usefulness of patterns is embodied in the second definition, especially the idea of instructions for making something. Fundamentally, patterns are about crafting things—think of sewing patterns and recipes, each of which are open to adaptation by experienced users. Patterns are not about engineering, which requires blueprints, building plans, and other conventional documents that are specific and (ultimately) legally binding. Instead, they enlighten the normal processes of designing and building—the ways ordinary craftspeople make things.

However, as I suggested earlier, they complement models and other engineering tools in two very practical ways. First, they explain the logic of the problem being solved, and then they provide the guidelines for solving the problem. Used properly, patterns help ordinary craftspeople to do extraordinary things.

For this book, I'm concerned with crafting software and the organization, architecture, and processes needed to craft it—the infrastructure that makes such building possible. But, unlike a methodology, these instructions are not hard and fast rules in a logical sequence of well-defined activities. Rather, they're closer to cooking recipes—open to experimentation—to be combined in creative ways to make a meal.

An understanding of the power of patterns comes from the third definition—patterns as "an excellent example," providing a non-prescriptive source for initiating and guiding the creative aspects of software development. They provide starting points for novice developers, reminders for experienced developers, and a way of sharing lessons learned.

There are other informal definitions that also help round out an understanding of why patterns are so important in software development:

- From a broad perspective, a pattern can be seen as a form for documenting *best practices*. In a profession that lacks centuries of experience and scientific underpinnings of engineering or architecture, best practices have become a touchstone for ensuring that risks are understood and that commonly accepted techniques and technologies are used. Patterns provide a standard format and repository for them—replacing what has been, until now, anecdotal reporting and documentation of the best ways to do things.

- From a narrower perspective, a pattern can be seen as a *rule of thumb*: a heuristic—quick way of providing a starting point for solving a problem. The craft of software development has generated many rules of thumb in its brief history. Patterns can provide a home for them that is formalized without being fussy.

- Finally, and even more narrowly, a pattern can be viewed and used as a template. This definition captures a critical aspect of patterns: they can be applied over and over again, in different situations. They are not specific solutions, but rather the basis for a solution. And, in software development, they derive from the fact that software solutions themselves tend to be repetitive. There is only a small set of solutions for any design problem in information systems, whether the problem is in software architecture or in development organization.

These definitions are drawn directly from the systems community. They suggest that patterns, in many ways, provide a more organized and consistent way of communicating by replacing previously existing methods for sharing experience and knowledge. In short, they suggest that patterns are simply a more effective way of capturing and expressing the developer's *tacit knowledge* than, for example, traditional methodologies, by making such knowledge explicit and available for all in a convenient and general form.

Of course, there are more comprehensive and formal definitions of a pattern that come out of the work done in the patterns community. I'll discuss these in detail in Chapter 9. The more formal definitions and associated philosophies have a place, but they are not critical to evaluating and applying patterns for the average user.

In this book, I don't slavishly support any one definition of a pattern. I consider all of the informal definitions to be useful, because they can provide a way to start thinking about and using patterns. However, there needs to be a more rigorous working definition to help make this book useful.

1.2   Elements of Patterns

Patterns as rules of thumb and model solutions for guiding design and development could be found in the systems community before objects appeared and long before any disciplined consideration of patterns.

In activities such as structured analysis and design, concepts such as coupling and cohesion, the visual rule of *Seven Plus or Minus Two*, or the notion of a program architecture based around a main module all provided the kind of packaged insight that patterns offer. However, the special notion of patterns that formed the basis for software patterns came out of another field: architecture and the work of Christopher Alexander in the '60s and '70s.

While trying to establish a mathematical basis for design, Alexander started using diagrams to capture the relationships between forces that a good design solution should resolve. Although these diagrams, which he later dubbed *patterns*, were only a small part of the resulting book, he decided afterward that they, not the mathematics, were the key ideas.

He saw that the independence, modularity, and abstractness of his diagrams enabled them to provide a starting point for a variety of designs by themselves, in particular, by combining them as needed. And they did this in a simple, easy to use, and easy to understand way.

Subsequent books by Alexander and his partners switched the focus to patterns. They established the conceptual basis for a formal definition of patterns in architecture and the core of the idea of patterns for software development. Each pattern in the language:

> ...describes a problem which occurs over and over again...and then describes the core of the solution to that problem in such a way that you can use this solution a million times over, without doing it the same way twice. (Alexander, Ishikawa, and Silverstein 1977, x)

By the way, this is *not* Alexander's formal definition of a pattern, but it is a working description that lives and breathes. Alexander's definitions of pattern have a minimalist character. The one most often quoted is this:

> Each pattern is a three-part rule, which expresses a relation between a certain context, a problem, and a solution. (1979, 247)

Short, sweet, simple…and it identifies the basic elements. What's noticeable is the idea that a pattern has three parts, not just two. The added part—the context—is critical for fitting a solution to a problem. The context contains a *system of forces* that is unbalanced until the problem is resolved.

In Alexander's patterns, the solution itself is a balancing act. It becomes a way of structuring the components of what has to be crafted so that the forces that affect them and that they affect in turn are harmonized. A real solution takes into account these forces—pressures, trends, needs, and constraints—and balances them all in the end result.

Finally, Alexander saw that individual patterns by themselves were not enough; what was needed was a language woven of patterns. This special language would be a distillation of the experience that he and his fellow authors acquired in planning and building. And, it would be practical—providing guidance and a common vocabulary for planning, designing, and building at a variety of levels, from local neighborhood improvement to constructing a house.

With these concepts, Alexander identifies all the critical elements of a pattern—what they're made of and how to organize them. Software developers have taken his concepts, elaborated them, enhanced them, and argued about them. The key concepts remain the same. In most ways, only the elements and packaging are different from what Alexander described.

Before getting into a more substantial description of the essential structure of patterns and the way patterns are organized, let's look at an example of a pattern, given the information available so far. For a more detailed and colorful account of the birth of patterns and the variety of software patterns, see Chapter 9, "Patterns in Context."

1.2.1   A Simple Example

The following example is closely related to modeling, and it illustrates how a rule of thumb can be interpreted as a pattern. The rule of thumb is *Seven Plus or Minus Two*. Interestingly, it translates nicely into not one pattern, but two patterns that are tied together, like a miniature pattern language. It illustrates how modeling is a fundamental human activity.

Here's an informal description of the problem, context, and solution(s).

From the earliest days of software modeling, it was obvious that diagrams loaded down with many elements were not easy to understand and did not communicate well. Anyone who's seen the typical Enterprise Data Model from the halcyon period of information engineering will remember diagrams that were virtual self-parodies, on which seemingly numberless geometric shapes, lines, and squiggles seemed to be fighting for survival.

The standard way of resolving the problem of diagram overload was (and still is) to break down the model itself into a set of digestible pieces. This approach reflected a known cognitive strategy among humans, which is called chunking: organizing logically related items into groups based on patterns (cognitive patterns this time), and thinking about the groups rather than the individual items.

Model elements are chunks themselves. They abstract the multiple properties associated with each element. But this strategy creates another problem: how to chunk?

This is where Seven Plus or Minus Two comes in. Pattern recognition is itself dependent on the capabilities of human short-term memory. Individual elements in a potential cognitive pattern can be related and organized only if they are in short-term memory, and short-term memory can manage only a limited number of items. It turns out that this number, which varies only slightly— depending on the circumstances, is (of course) Seven Plus or Minus Two (7 ± 2).

So, the ideal model should consist of a number of diagrams, each of which has 7 ± 2 main elements. In fact, the model should itself be organized into a number of levels so that each level has 7 ± 2 diagrams. Of course, a modeling language such as the UML adds semantic and syntactical rules that can stretch the limits of the rule, but only to an extent—and only within an appropriate context.

So, how does all of this look expressed as one or more patterns? I'll start with one pattern, which we can name Seven Plus or Minus Two.

The *context* is building diagrams of software. Within this context, we have a variety of *forces* that we have to balance, such as the following:

- Models are made up of diagrams.

- Diagrams have to communicate useful views of the real world.

- A model must be comprehensive but focused.

- The real world can be complex, messy, and unfocused.

- Diagrams are not inherently limited in the number of elements they can contain.

- Human understanding of diagrams is constrained by the limits of human cognitive capabilities, such as short-term memory. Humans have limited cognitive resources. That is, they can attend to only so many things and perform only so many activities at once.

In this context, the problem is how to make diagrams that can be grasped easily.

The solution is to limit the number of elements in any given diagram to the magic number of seven, give or take two elements. These elements should be logically related; the diagram structure should express a sensible pattern connecting the diagram elements.

There's actually another pattern, at a different level, in this miniature pattern language. One level up from that of *building diagrams* is *building models*. Although many of the same forces are present at this level, the specific problem of how to make models that work adds a few others that have to be resolved. Look at the pattern called Digestible Chunks as one solution to this problem.

The context this time is building models (as opposed to diagrams). Within this context, most of the forces will look familiar:

- A model must be comprehensive but focused.

- The real world can be complex, messy, and unfocused.

- Models have to communicate useful views of the real world.

- Human understanding of diagrams and models is constrained by the limits of human cognitive capabilities, such as short-term memory.

- Models are made up of one or more connected diagrams that have to be organized.

- Human ability to organize models is also constrained by the limits of human cognitive capabilities.

The significant difference is that I've added *organizing needs* to our list.

The solution is to chunk the models into diagrams that are digestible bits, which are individually meaningful and connected in a sensible fashion. A related pattern useful for figuring out how to build these digestible bits is, of course, Seven Plus or Minus Two.

Naturally, there are other patterns that I could define that solve problems related to modeling software, and later on I will present some of these that are more specific to modeling with the UML. However, these two patterns illustrate not just the basic elements of a pattern, but also some of the distinctive and necessary characteristics of patterns.

1.3 Interpreting the Patterns in This Book

The way I formatted the two previous example patterns, which I squeezed out of the idea of *Seven Plus or Minus Two*, is a version of the way Alexander formats and writes patterns. However, the software developers who first popularized patterns didn't adopt his format. They opted for a form that was more formal and more precisely attuned to what they were trying to accomplish. The book, *Design Patterns: Elements of Reusable Object-Oriented Software* by Erich Gamma and others helped to popularize their format as well as patterns for software (1995). For simplicity, I'll call the format *GammaForm* after one of the book's authors and the originator of this type of pattern.

Since the publication of *Design Patterns*, Jim Coplien (another patterns guru and object-oriented expert) has become the most visible spokesperson for a looser format, which I'll call *CoplienForm* (1995). Although more extended than a minimal format would be, it is still succinct; the results tend to be less verbose and less didactic than GammaForm patterns. Many software patterns follow some version of this generic format or the GammaForm format.

An extended explanation of the GammaForm format can be found in Chapter 9. My pattern language uses a slight modification of CoplienForm. Here's how Seven Plus or Minus Two (one of the example patterns above) would look expressed this way. I've included this pattern in the body of the language. An explanation of the pattern's sections follows the pattern.

SEVEN PLUS OR MINUS TWO (FORMALIZED)

NAME	Seven Plus or Minus Two
PROBLEM	How to make diagrams that can be grasped easily.
CONTEXT	Building diagrams that are themselves part of an overall model. In this case, we are specifically concerned with software models, but the pattern could apply to any type of potentially complex model using standardized modeling elements and syntax.
FORCES	• Models are made up of diagrams. • Diagrams have to communicate useful views of the real world. • A model must be comprehensive but focused.

- The real world can be complex, messy, and unfocused.
- Diagrams are not inherently limited in the number of elements they can contain.
- Human understanding of diagrams is constrained by the limits of human cognitive capabilities, such as short-term memory.

SOLUTION

Limit the number of elements in any given diagram to the magic number of seven, give or take two elements. These elements should be logically related; the diagram structure should express a sensible pattern connecting the diagram elements.

RESULTING CONTEXT

Diagrams that are easy to understand at a glance and can be organized in a logical fashion into more complex models.

DISCUSSION

Humans have limited cognitive resources. That is, they can only attend to so many things and perform a limited amount of activities at once. Too many elements in a diagram can be confusing and are hard to retain in short term memory all at once. This pattern provides a simple way of ensuring that the number of elements is reasonable for most people. The related pattern, Chunking, explains how and why the process of decomposing a model into logical diagrams works.

1.3.1 This Book's Pattern Format

Coplien suggests that the *name* for a pattern should be chosen with as much care as the name for a first born child. Pattern names should be succinct, memorable, and relevant. Naturally, this is much more difficult to do than to say. At the very least, I've tried to make the names of the patterns in this book expressive of their possible usage.

The *problem* is the easiest statement of what the pattern is a response to, providing the potential user with a quick way of assessing the usefulness of the pattern. (Remember that the kind of problems this language deals with are those connected with modeling, using models, or managing models.)

The *context* provides more help in determining the applicability of a pattern. It situates the pattern, providing information about where the results might fit into a typical UML-based development effort.

Forces are where any remaining uncertainties about the applicability of a pattern may be resolved. I've tried to be explicit about the conditions, constraints, and considerations that the pattern tries to resolve.

The *solution* is a straightforward explanation of how a modeler using the UML would solve the modeling problem that the problem, context, and forces present. It leads to the *resulting context*, summarizing the effects of applying the pattern, and it is explained in more detail in the *discussion*, which may also provide additional pattern and/or literature references.

Where appropriate, example diagrams will be provided to clarify a pattern. However, in the same way that the UML is *not* only about diagrams, some UML patterns do not lend themselves to diagram examples.

This format is meant to be useful with a minimum of overhead. As with the UML, which the next chapter introduces, it (and the patterns in this book) is a convenient compromise between the theoretical and the practical.

CHAPTER 2

The Unified Modeling Language

Who controls the past commands the future.
Who commands the future conquers the past.

—attributed to George Orwell

The UML has resurrected modeling as a respectable practice within software development. Indeed, it has moved modeling back into the development spotlight and made it an equal player with coding as an essential skill.

The UML has done this by providing a comprehensive language for modeling. It is every bit as expressive, flexible, and useful as programming languages are for coding—and it is at least as complicated in a similar way. More to the point, the UML has made it possible to see object-oriented models as having a legitimate existence outside of the realm of code-production—in business modeling, workflow design, and enterprise architecture, for example. These are realms that have been dominated by other modeling approaches until now.

Despite its evolutionary nature, the UML is very different from the modeling tools and languages that preceded it. These differences are what make UML so important to understand (not to mention the reasons why the UML is superseding them all).

This chapter will explore the roots of the UML within the traditions of software development. It will show how the UML is part of those traditions with appropriate history to justify a patterns-based approach for describing good UML modeling practices—using patterns based on practical traditions and rules of thumb and allowing for the beneficial inclusion of selected UML-specific idioms.

Chapter 10, "The UML in Context," will explore modeling and the UML (the nature of models and modeling), and Chapter 3, "UML Essentials, Elements, and Artifacts," will provide an introduction to the basic elements and artifacts of the UML and the connections between the UML and patterns. Essentially, it discusses how patterns can contribute to working with the UML in a way that fits the new kind of modeling the UML makes possible.

So, rather than seeing the UML as just another tool, you will be able to see how it can affect the way you work as a software developer—how it makes possible a new way to think about modeling.

Just to be clear, the intention of these few chapters is not to provide the ultimate guide to the UML. They will only provide enough context to make the pattern language useful and meaningful. Unlike the built world from which Alexander wove a pattern language, the UML is new fabric. So, we all need a little help with the basics.

Note

I use the terms *methodology, process,* and *method.* For this book, the meanings are as follows:

- A *methodology* is a formal packaging of a set of activities, techniques, and end products. It typically has an underlying theoretical basis and an associated modeling language.

- A *method* is a smaller and less-comprehensive version of a methodology. It focuses on the techniques and engineering elements, and it puts less emphasis on the sequencing of specific activities.

- A *process* is like an instance of a methodology with less emphasis on techniques, more emphasis on sequencing of activities, and elements added to support the practical needs of using the methodology (such as management, metrics, and deployment).

2.1   The UML, Briefly Put

With some sensitivity to the needs of the busy reader, I'll start with a shorthand version of a definition that can be used to consider the flavors and variations that will follow.

Briefly, the UML is a formally defined, object-oriented development notation. The formal definition is complete and consistent enough to qualify the UML as a type of language, but it is a formal one (as opposed to a natural language). The object-oriented aspect is a horse-and-cart situation; in many ways, the effort to specify the UML is to provide new ways to think about object-orientation itself.

The UML encompasses the entire scope of a typical development process— from requirements to deployment planning. In addition, it offers the basis for documenting the releases of a software product and is the basis for a repository of critical knowledge about the domain.

It unifies the modeling approaches of the three key players in the area of contemporary software: Grady Booch, Jim Rumbaugh, and Ivar Jacobson (the self-described "Three Amigos" of Rational Software) and adds substantial chunks from a number of other major players who are currently active. It aims to provide a standard notation for modeling systems—in particular, software-intensive systems where an object-oriented implementation is anticipated.

It is the first successful unification of its kind, not just in object-oriented development, but within the larger arena of information technology. Its status as a standard comes from the institutional imprimatur of the Object Management Group (OMG), an industry consortium and self-appointed standards body in the area of object technology.

UML is a standard modeling language, not a standard modeling method. It is independent of programming language and development techniques and processes. As a result, it *is* dependent for its usefulness on how it is implemented within a methodology and/or a development process.

On the other hand, UML allows (and perhaps encourages) tool and methodology/process vendors to step up to the plate to support it, and it competes in providing features and services that will differentiate their product offerings. The notation standards envisage tool vendors having some flexibility in implementingthe specifics; the language itself assumes that modern tool software will be available to make it work.

Whatever the variations provided by the supporting vendors, UML allows users of whatever method, process, and tool set to communicate and interchange models by using a consistent set of model elements and concepts.

Finally, UML is collaboratively developed, extensible, scalable, and flexible—and, most important, it is evolving. Nothing is carved in stone.

2.2 Roots

A little history is needed as a preamble to understanding the UML and as a way to introduce a cast of characters.

The context for the development of the UML was the increasing complexity of software as the 1990s began. Mainstream technology couldn't cope with a networked and information-driven world. Rigid organizational boundaries started to leak like the proverbial dike in the face of desktop interactions, virtual connections, and an event-driven competitive environment that demanded more, faster.

In 1991, Thomas Malone and John Rockart provided a picture of the expectations that were beginning to appear everywhere:

> The industrial economies are now in the early stages of another transfor-
> mation that may ultimately be at least as significant as the Industrial
> Revolution…The revolution underway today will be driven not by
> changes in production but by changes in coordination. Whenever people
> work together, they must somehow communicate, make decisions, allo-
> cate resources, and get products and services to the right place at the right
> time…These new technologies will enable people to coordinate more
> effectively, to do much more coordination, and to form new, coordination-
> intensive business structures. (1991, 92)

Malone and Rockart focused on what they called the "networked computer"
as the basis for the revolution-in-progress. They emphasized that the term
computer was becoming misleading because it suggested a machine for
calculating and processing information:

> [T]his image of computing does not capture the essence of how comput-
> ers are used now and how they will be used even more in the future…
> computers and computer networks may well be remembered not as
> technology used primarily to compute, but as coordination technology.
> (1991, 92)

Meanwhile, the object-oriented approach was sputtering at the starting gate—
it was the little engine that could, but usually didn't. The object-oriented languages scene was a gang war landscape, cluttered with acronyms. Compared to
their structured brethren, object-oriented methods and development processes
were skeletal at best—blinkered, inconsistent, and shallow.

Members of the object-oriented fraternity like to see the success of objects as
fated, and they view the UML as an element of that inevitable success. From the
broader perspective of mainstream computing as defined in the *Fortune 500*, the
picture is a little different. For most big organizations, object-orientation
has been an alien force.

As recently as the early years of the '90s, big organization managers were
used to the comforts of a few common languages, a relatively homogeneous
technology, and a semi-standard development process (the "waterfall"), which
was manageable even if spectacularly unsuccessful.

Objects provided none of these comforts, and the perception was that few of
the significant object-oriented development efforts demonstrated any real

advantages for object-orientation over other, more mainstream approaches. As late as 1993, the *Sloan Management Review* from MIT had a paper that proclaimed: "(O)bject orientation has low prospects for becoming dominant in large in-house IS organizations" (Fichman and Kemerer 1993, 21). Only a major upheaval would change their world.

The distribution of applications and information in the guise of the Internet phenomenon—Rockart and Malone's "networked computer"—was, of course, the comet that disturbed the evolutionary equilibrium of the development world. It created what paleobiologist Elizabeth Vrba calls a "turnover pulse" (discussed in Eldredge 1999), which shattered the static rut that information technology had settled into. It also provoked the "speciation" of new technologies, including languages and methods. It created the need and the opportunity: customers wanted the capabilities promised by the new, but the old ways of development couldn't do the job.

Of course, the old ways included the old ways of doing object-oriented development. Change affected the object-oriented community just as much as the mainstream. However, the opportunistic speciation of object-orientation was profoundly advantageous and has resulted in real benefits. The meteoric rise of Java, the standardization of C++, components, the birth and rebirth of CORBA, and the emergence of pattern languages for software design are all results of the changed technological and business ecosystem that dawned with the '90s—as is the UML.

2.2.1 Key Players

Another way to understand the development of the UML is in terms of the key players and their roles. Unlike the development of patterns, commercial rather than personal interests drove the development of the UML. Therefore, the personal interactions that formed the backdrop are less significant for our purposes. (For anyone interested, *UML Distilled*, by Martin Fowler, Kendall Scott, and Ivan Jacobson [1997] has a terrifically wry, wonderfully personalized account of the way the UML emerged from its cocoon.)

There is one personal factor that warrants mentioning, though. It incidentally provides a further comparison with the mainstream. Structured Methods, plus its competitors and variants, resulted from the growing maturity of both the technology and the people in the computer industry in the '60s and '70s. By then, the mainframe world had its own period of heroic hacking and cowboy programming. When software design was a back-of-the-envelope affair, having a personal coding style was a matter of pride; amphetamine-driven, all-night work sessions got the code out; and documentation was non-existent.

The work of Edgar Djykstra in combating the results—spaghetti code and unmaintainable programs—and the notion of structured programming were milestones in the maturing of mainframe software development. The industry discovered that cowboy programming produced downstream maintenance costs, which were all out of proportion to the original development costs.

As with nuclear power, the initial infatuation with a new technology was replaced by a more seasoned assessment of the long-term costs and benefits. At the same time, as programming and programmers matured, the population of programmers grew and broadened; and communication, training, and control became concerns for business management. The need for a more disciplined approach to development encouraged the creation of methodologies and modeling systems—but not yet modeling languages.

Similarly, through the '80s, object-oriented development was dominated by a cowboy mentality, which was further emphasized by the availability of interactive programming tools and the lack of a workable, consistent development process that could provide discipline. Young "techies," pioneering in unknown terrain dominated object-oriented development.

But, as happened in the mainframe world, the commercial realities of development, combined with an increasing personal maturity on the part of the high-profile players in the field, provoked a sea change in attitude. And, as was the case with Structured Methods, a few key players personified the change and provided its leadership. The three players who are most visible in all this are, of course, the "Three Amigos" of the UML: Grady Booch, James Rumbaugh, and Ivar Jacobson. Booch is arguably the methodology granddaddy of the bunch. (I have already mentioned him as a force in the emergence of patterns.)

In the early '80s, Booch introduced the phrase "object-oriented design," notably in his book called *Software Engineering with Ada* (Booch, Bryan, and Petersen 1993). The book also introduced many of the themes that later object-oriented methods would mine and refine. Based on training courses, which *then-Captain* Booch and a fellow member of the US Air Force Major Dick Bolz developed for the Air Force Academy in 1979, the book was primarily aimed at programming-language issues rather than system design, but it had a software engineering flavor.

Even then, Booch combined many of the better ideas, which were floating around about how to develop software-using objects, and packaged them with a notation and guidelines into a "lifecycle process." His models were the newly minted Structured Design approaches, which were becoming popular (Berard 1998).

By the late '80s, Booch had left the Air Force and eventually joined Rational Software Corporation. He brought an evolved Booch Method with him, along with his understanding of a need for a formalized approach to design that included a consistent notation.

Ivar Jacobson surfaced publicly a little later than Booch. In 1986 and 1987, he presented papers on object-oriented design at OOPSLA, based on his experience in developing real-time systems in Sweden. A key to his thinking was the notion of taking a black-box approach to design—hiding the complexities of the system as a design technique. In his technique, use cases provided the ultimate black box, allowing for a specification of behavior that didn't get muddled by a description of how the behavior was implemented. Instead, the view of the user drove the modeling. They also provided a real way to document requirements and discipline the development so that it was traceable back to what the user wanted.

By the early 1990s, Jacobson's use cases were already being incorporated into a variety of methods, filling a gap that was perceived to exist in the standard design approaches (such as the Booch Method). Jacobson was also contributing an emphasis on models as the core of systems development. As Jacobson put it, "System development is a process of model building" (1995, 309).

James Rumbaugh was, in some ways, the latecomer to the party. While working for General Electric during the '80s, he authored a number of papers that were typically concerned with a data-centric view of object-oriented design. His influence was substantial, however. In 1991, he published (along with the inevitable *et. al.*) what became *the* book on object-oriented development, *Object-Oriented Modeling and Design* (Rumbaugh et al. 1991). The book was the basis for the Object Modeling Technique (OMT), which Rumbaugh popularized. It provided more of a middle ground between Structured approaches and object-oriented design, compared to Booch or many of the other object-oriented methods that were around at the time.

Efforts to reach some sort of unification or standardization of methods had been attempted occasionally during the early '90s but without success. In 1993 and early 1994, the OMG tried to standardize the methods but was roundly criticized for the attempt. Booch even attempted an informal rapprochement but was also unsuccessful. He felt the time was ripe:

> Is standardization desirable? Standardization is relevant to consider in the domain of object-oriented methods for two reasons. First, the existing diversity fragments the market and is a barrier to entry by all others than the usual early adopters and is a barrier to creating an industry of third-party vendors that help feed the core industry. Second, even given the

diversity of object-oriented methods, there is apparent consensus in what should be modeled during analysis and design. (Booch and Rumbaugh 1996)

He threw in a couple of significant caveats, though:

> What than can be standardized? The most obvious target of opportunity is a common object-oriented analysis and design notation. It is entirely inappropriate to try to standardize upon process. How should standardization proceed? The right way to consummate a standard is through a formal standards body, but using that body to hammer out a standard is entirely wrong. Standards wrought by such impersonal bodies are often entirely void of relevance to the real problems of software development. (Booch and Rumbaugh 1996)

Just before that OOPSLA, Rumbaugh made the dramatic announcement that he was leaving General Electric to work with Booch at Rational. He did this, as he explained, to unify their two methods—and despite the apparent qualms expressed by Booch.

Rumbaugh expressed his own version of qualms about standardization at OOPSLA: "I am 'for' convergence and 'against' standardization. I think 'standardization' of object-oriented methodologies now is undesirable and unnecessary." He felt the marketplace would sort out the methods wars and added, "In two years the dust will have settled, a few methods will be clear leaders, and there will be a general (if not universal) consensus about certain core modeling concepts" (1996). He was particularly critical of anything done via committee, which he said would "likely produce an inelegant hodgepodge that cuts the heart out of each methodology. Even a panel of methodologists is still a committee subject to the same pressures" (1996).

Rumbaugh admitted that the differences between the two methods were in no way as great as their own self-interests had made them appear (Rational Software Corporation 1995). And their self-interests were substantial. Booch and Rumbaugh had the majority (possibly 85 percent) of the object-oriented method market share by 1994, with Rumbaugh's OMT being the clear leader. However, Jacobson also had a method, and his popular and influential use cases were being adopted by a number of methods, Booch and OMT included.

Their initial Unified Method, identified as version 0.8 of the unified process, was released at OOPSLA. Then, Jacobson joined the unification effort because Rational purchased his Objectory process. So, in a typical act of male bonding, the Three Amigos were born (named after a forgettable comedy of the late '80s and an earlier Disney cartoon).

Difficulties in merging the three processes and time pressures resulted in a switch from producing a Unified Method to the easier target that Booch proposed at OOPSLA: a UML. With this new rubric, Rational released the 0.9 revision in June 1996. After another six months of intense effort involving public feedback, the 1.0 spec of the UML was released for publication in January 1997.

At this point, the final character in the UML drama emerged: the OMG returned to active status. Independently, they formed a task force for standardizing a method and a notation, and several organizations submitted proposals. A consortium of key object technology users and vendors was formed to define a 1.0 specification.

In the end, a UML proposal was hammered out, combining the September 1997 release of Rational's UML 1.1 and some revisions by the OMG. Confusingly enough, the final product was named UML 1.0.

In an ironic twist, the ongoing evolution of the UML is now in the hands of a number of OMG Committees, one of which—the Revision Task Force, has Jim Rumbaugh as a very visible and active participant.

2.3   Understanding the UML

According to the UML Specification, the UML is a language

> ...for specifying, visualizing, constructing, and documenting the artifacts of software systems, as well as for business modeling and other non-software systems. (Object Management Group 1999, xi)

This official description, which appears right at the beginning of both the Preface and the Summary of the *UML Specification* document, emphasizes a couple of key qualities that a prospective user of the UML has to keep in mind.

First of all, it is confusing. The intended reading of this definition is that *artifacts* really refers to modeling artifacts, and that the UML is about modeling and building models; it is not about constructing code, project management, or production support. But appropriating the term *constructing* this way and abusing the term *artifacts* provide little mental hiccups instead of a strong declaration. The official prose of the UML frequently has a committee-built quality (sometimes resulting in unclear intentions and inconsistent interpretations). For example, more than one book on the UML has stumbled on this particular definition: the second key quality is that it is somewhat muddy and fuzzy.

Specification is a well-understood activity within software development. Visualization is a little soft, well known only as a technique. Constructing is, as I explained previously, a little confusing in this context and is typically a process. Documenting seems prosaic at best and, given the reluctance of almost anyone in software development to actually do documentation, has a well-earned last place in the list. Adding to the lack of focus is the direction that the UML can and should be used for business modeling and for creating models for systems that are not software systems.

So, aside from being an obvious result of "committee-think," the shortcomings in this section suggest that it was composed in haste, perhaps to be reworked at some future date.

What all of this textual nitpicking underlines is that the UML itself is first and foremost an evolving project with muddy areas. It has a formal specification written to accommodate the wide variety of interests that have been part of its birthing, and so it is occasionally fuzzy.

The formal specification is critical to understanding what the UML is about, especially when faced with contradictory and dated interpretations. And yet, it can itself be infuriatingly circular, self-referential, opaque, obscure, and possibly wrong-headed in spots.

Given all of this, a cautious but flexible interpretation of the specification is the best way to approach defining the UML. Too many of the books and articles that have been written about the UML mix in information about, for example, Rational Software's development process, the author's methodological biases, or specific uses—without being clear about the boundaries of the UML itself.

2.4   Unification: The Methods Wars Are Over

In a widely read column in the April 1998 issue of *Object* magazine, Ivar Jacobson declared that "the methods war is over" after a period of confusion and uncertainty that accompanied the transition from a world dominated by structured approaches to one in which the object paradigm became champion (1998, 72).

Ivar was actually repeating in a (hopefully) tongue-in-cheek fashion a comment that Booch and Rumbaugh made publicly a couple of years earlier—one that prompted sizeable dissent in the object-oriented community.

The earlier war cry predated Jacobson's conversion to Rational, and so it was definitely premature because Jacobson's Objectory had substantial mind-share even then. However, the methods being replaced, aided, and abetted by a unified approach to modeling aren't just the object-oriented ones. Rather, as Jacobson explained it in the article, "all the different methods in the software industry are now moving to one modeling language: UML" (1998, 72).

Although Jacobson's observation may have been premature (and certainly self-serving), it points to the most significant meaning behind the UML: It unifies everything under one flag. The UML Specification makes it clear that:

> [T]he UML is the proper successor to the object modeling languages of three previously leading object-oriented methods (Booch, OMT, and OOSE). The UML is the union of these modeling languages and more... (Object Management Group 1999, xi)

Beyond the ideal of convergence, *unified* has other levels and shades of meaning, all of which contribute to a better understanding of the purpose of the UML.

With the UML, all of the hidden non-engineering purposes of modeling are brought to the forefront and made connectable, consistent, and applicable. UML models can be used to help conceptualize the context for an application. They can organize the requirements and package the work. They can, of course, embody the design. After that, they can provide the basis for generating usable results and the means to package the end result for deployment. Software architects and managers can use the same set of notations and conventions as designers and programmers to suit their purposes, as well as the purposes of engineering.

So, the UML helps to unify the practices of developing, planning, and managing software development by making modeling a pertinent part of all these activities.

2.4.1   Best Practices: In the Eye of the Beholder

Essentially, the UML brings together the *best practices* of an increasingly mature software development community. In a phrase used over and over again in books and articles about the UML, the introduction to the specification claims that it "represents the convergence of best practices in the object-technology industry" (Object Management Group 1999, xi).

Of course, as with all best practices, many are most notably so in the eyes of the beholder. They are beliefs rather than empirically substantiated reality and meant to be taken with a grain of salt. And, as with beliefs of any kind, they are subject to the usual "religious" squabbles and/or interpretations.

The idea of best practices emerged in the manufacturing world. There, it is tightly coupled to benchmarking processes and measured performance. As an idea, it was adopted in software development with none of the rigor of manufacturing management. There is little benchmarking (more in Europe than North America) and, given the churn of technologies and processes within software development, there is little likelihood of any meaningful benchmarks for awhile. In IT, *best practices* is an inherited management idea with many meanings.

Shoshanna Zuboff described the evolution of management ideas in her book, *In the Age of the Smart Machine*. She uses a geological metaphor that adds some useful nuances to Kuhn's notions of the way a paradigm shift works. Zuboff suggests that "each period leaves a layer of sedimented beliefs," like the eons of previous geologies that can be seen in layered cliff walls (1988, 233). A paradigm shift is not a complete change. It encapsulates the beliefs of previous generations, but then moves on.

The evolution of software engineering ideas can be viewed the same way. The UML brings with it a great deal of baggage from earlier periods in software development (in particular, Structured Analysis and Design) and from the beginnings of object-oriented analysis and design. Not all of this baggage is excess baggage.

The gurus of previous modeling approaches articulated a number of sound, valuable insights into their work. The best results have a resonance that transcends their packaging, becoming *best practices* in the informal way that the software community thinks of such things.

I attempted to capture as many of them as possible in the patterns themselves. In some cases, because these insights have been translated directly into the UML, the patterns are specifically about using the UML. In other cases, I use patterns to show how these insights shape the practice of modeling in general, and how they work in the UML.

2.4.2   An Independent-Minded Modeling Language

The miracle of the UML is that it unifies without being tied to a prescriptive methodology or process. This is the second significant characteristic of the UML: its independence of process, programming language, and technique.

By being process-independent, it is unique among modeling languages. All of the structured modeling techniques and object-oriented modeling languages that existed previously were extensions of a methodology or process.

Originally, the creators of UML wanted to unify their different object-oriented development methods into one process. Initial discussions showed the task to be more difficult than they imagined. Booch, Rumbaugh, and Jacobson determined that merging their notations was the best thing to do first. One of the insights that the creators of the UML had was the notion that a one-size-fits-all *process* wasn't possible or even desirable. They intentionally left the choice of process up to the individual users of UML. Therefore, the UML is deliberately process-independent.

Although there is now a Unified Process available from Rational that exemplifies the type of process that maps well to the UML, it does not have to be the process that you use. The process chosen for a particular development project is determined by a variety of factors such as project size, organizational standards, tool support, architectural goals, and so on. It isn't likely that a single process can satisfy the requirements of all possible variations of these factors, and there is any number of processes available to a developer that all use the UML as their modeling language. Examples include *Objects, Components and Frameworks with UML: The Catalysis Approach* from Desmond D'Souza and Alan Wills (1998), with its emphasis on component-based development and the offerings of Sally Shlaer and Ward Mellor, with their slant toward real-time systems (1999).

The UML is also programming-language-independent, which has a number of dimensions. On the one hand, the UML is not unnecessarily biased toward any implementation via a particular programming language, so it can reflect the generic needs of programmers for a standard way of communicating the blueprint for a system.

On the other hand, a number of the constructs in the UML do not map to *any* programming language. They are modeling abstractions that always need translation.

On top of this, although it is language-independent, the UML does reflect the underlying conceptual framework of object-orientation. As has been acknowledged in some small ways already, it will need to be reworked to accommodate more recent approaches, such as component-based development. But, to its credit, the UML has already accommodated patterns and frameworks during its brief evolution.

Finally, the UML is technique-independent. For example, a process that calls for use cases as the primary vehicle for communicating functional requirements may describe techniques. However, the streetwise practitioner recognizes that prescribed techniques work well in some circumstances...and not in others. In situations where they don't, the end result is what's important. The UML does not tie artifacts to techniques any more than methods or processes.

The agile modeler will appreciate the UML's independence. Process, language, and technique neutrality make it a relatively easy task for designs to be communicated across the boundaries of projects, environments, and tools. Instead of notational factions and models separated by walls of incompatibility, the UML provides a generalized language for modeling that eliminates artificial boundaries and permits the free flow of models and design information in a way that wasn't previously possible.

CHAPTER 3

UML Essentials, Elements, and Artifacts

There aren't enough symbols to cover all the subtly different things we want to say.

—Desmond D'Souza and Alan Wills (1998, 371)

This chapter provides you with a high-level summary of the main elements and artifacts of the UML—enough to get started with the pattern language.

Obviously, a single chapter is scarcely adequate to even begin the exercise of learning about the UML. But there are many good books out there that can provide an introductory service for those not already using the UML, and this book isn't meant to cover their territory. Anyone with a working knowledge of the UML can skim this chapter with the proviso that it provides information based on the 1.3 beta version of the *UML Specification* (Rational Software Corporation 1999), and so it may be useful as an update.

Also, I take a somewhat different approach than is typical for introductions. One difference is that this chapter, like this book and the UML itself, is process-independent. And, where it's important to illustrate anomalies and differences that come from the different ways that processes can interpret the UML, I use Rational's Unified Process and Desmond D'Souza and Alan Wills' book, *Objects, Components and Frameworks with UML: The Catalysis Approach* (1998) as examples of almost orthogonal processes. I've tried to distinguish between process-specific uses and notations and those that are "vanilla" UML. Where there are notable anomalies, I draw attention to them.

The other way that this chapter is different is that I focus on the packaging and notational side of the UML rather than the detailed semantics of the UML constructs. I do this for two reasons:

- The packaging, organizing, and drawing side of the UML seems to be underrepresented in the literature. How to go about making a model has taken a back seat to using the UML in creating development artifacts—a subtle but significant difference.

- For a book like this, which is aimed at modeling rather than programming, understanding packaging and notation is crucial to using the UML effectively as a tool, just as knowing the syntax is crucial to using a programming language effectively. This chapter aims to clarify what has been a notable amount of confusion in this area, in writings about the UML.

For the most part, the semantics of the UML are sufficiently object-oriented to present little difficulty to anyone with a programming background in any of the object-oriented languages. Of course, some aspects of the UML semantics that are specific to modeling or that are idiomatic to the UML need to be explained, and I'll cover these as well.

Like patterns, a summary such as this one doesn't benefit from inspired originality or novel insights. So, I relied on tried-and-true sources, and I reworked existing material, rather than providing a new way of looking at the innards of the UML. The description that follows is primarily drawn from the *UML Specification, Version 1.3* (Rational Software Corporation 1999), fleshed out by readings from *UML Distilled: Applying the Standard Object Modeling Language* (Fowler, Scott, and Jacobson 1997) and *Objects, Components and Frameworks with UML: The Catalysis Approach* (D'Souza and Wills 1998).

3.1   Elements, Viewpoints, and Views

The idea of a *view* is a key one in the UML: It provides the basis for the UML notion of a model. However, it is *not* a formal construct in the UML (although it *is* in the Rational Unified Process [RUP], a distinction that is typically muddied by writers about the UML). Instead, it acts as an informal concept that helps situate the role—and responsibilities—of the modeler.

In the UML, a model is a complete representation of a system from a particular viewpoint (that is, an aggregation of a set of views from specific perspectives). At the same time, systems are logically composed of many nearly independent models, representing many different viewpoints; and they can be physically composed of many independent subsystems, each of which can also be treated as a system for modeling purposes.

A system itself is implicitly represented by a top-level model with subsidiary models representing specialized views. Each model is made up of diagrams and text. The *UML Specification* describes diagrams as "views of a model," each representing a particular perspective that the overall model aggregates and integrates (Rational Software Corporation 1999). All of this applies recursively to subsystems as well.

The perspective that a model represents is a combination of the model's purpose and the level of detail it provides. Any system can contain a myriad of viewpoints and models, which depend on the role of each viewer, the conceptual stance he or she brings to the viewing, and the ultimate purpose of the view. Any viewpoint can be expressed by a myriad of views and diagrams, depending on the interests of the audience being addressed.

The modeler represents these views, wearing different hats in turn, and adopting different viewpoints. A user's view will end up being expressed differently depending on whether the audience is senior management or a technical person. A management perspective might result in a management model that emphasizes architecture and minimizes technical detail.

At the most abstract, a system should be modeled from at least two viewpoints:

- Looking at the outside world—an interpreted reality

- Looking at the product—a constructed reality

As modelers, in order to build a system, we model our understanding of the context, requirements, practices, and constraints to ensure that we have the problem and problem setting right. We then model the architecture, specifications, design, implementation, and deployment of what the builders should build. The second viewpoint provides a blueprint that builders can work from and the documentation that management needs to get the product built, keep it working, and make it useful.

The advantage an object-oriented approach brings to modeling is that it allows a modeler to "bridge the chasm" (Jacobson, Booch, and Rumbaugh 1998a, 7) between the analysis and design models by providing a semantically consistent conceptual framework, regardless of the viewpoint involved. Things in the real world are represented as objects, in the same way that things in the constructed world are. The modeling modes are still distinct, but the language is very much the same.

Naturally, in an iterative development process, even the barrier between modeling modes is permeable, and there's a constant to-and-fro, as opposed to rigid distinctions. In fact, as I will discuss in Chapter 11, "Putting It All Together: Reflecting on the Work of Design," proper design practice requires the interweaving of these two modes.

Beyond the simple need for a minimum of two viewpoints, additional viewpoints can be added to the picture, depending on the expressive granularity the modeler feels is warranted. Individual processes will treat the idea of views differently, making them formal constructs (for example, RUP) or leaving them as informal concepts (for example, *Objects, Components and Frameworks with UML: The Catalysis Approach* [D'Souza and Wills 1998]). The UML also assumes that you may want to create your own kinds of diagrams and your own kinds of models, and you may want to extend the UML in various ways to establish your own local modeling dialect.

3.1.1 Models and Model Elements

To repeat: A UML model is an abstraction, a complete representation of a physical system. Models are about things, relationships, behaviors, and interactions in a system. Equally important, models are about how to organize this information because conceptual chunking is an important tool for successful abstracting.

The UML itself distinguishes two types of models:

- *Structural models*—Represent the pieces of a system and their relationships.

- *Dynamic models*—Represent the behavior of the elements of the system and their interactions.

Models are made up of model elements. Model elements are named uniquely in the context of a given namespace (usually a package) and have *visibility*, which defines how they can be used (and reused) by other model elements.

Visibility determines the way individual elements can connect with each other. Therefore, it is a critical part of managing the complexity of models via information hiding. Decisions about visibility can be powerful factors influencing decisions about the logical organization of models. It is one of the ways in which the UML is distinctly different from previous generations of modeling languages and tools—by leveraging and extending the notion of visibility from object-oriented languages themselves.

In the UML, model elements may be visible in one of three ways:

- *Public*—Any outside model element can see the model element.

- *Protected*—Any descendent can see the model element.

- *Private*—Only the model element itself, its constituent parts, and the model elements nested within it can see it.

Note

Individual parts of the UML adjust this general notion of visibility to suit specific circumstances. See the discussion of package visibility in Section 3.2, "Packages," later in this chapter.

Models and model elements are rendered graphically in diagrams and textually in specifications, and they are organized in packages.

In UML notation, model things are expressed as symbols or icons, and relationships and interactions are typically expressed by using various kinds of adorned lines. The lines themselves aren't just passive, decorated connectors; in the UML, they're also symbols with semantic content and underlying rules. And, as organizational elements, neither models nor diagrams have a specific notational form (that is, the UML symbol)—only packages do.

Of course, it's not the rendering of the individual elements that provides the meaning and meat to a model, but the way they all connect. The connection between a model, its diagrams, and their parts—the connection between a viewpoint and expressed views—is almost rhetorical. Intention, attention, and focus provide differences in level of detail, formality, content, and manner of presentation.

Models aren't just diagrams; in the UML, the diagrams are only the visual rendering of the model. Underlying the graphics of a model are the specifications of the model elements. These are composed in text, and may be a mix of the formal and the informal. The text is as important as the diagrams and in some cases more so: use cases are an example (see Section 3.6.2, "Use Case Diagram," later in this chapter). The *UML Specification* itself is an example of a model (although not a good one, if judged by its clarity and communicative effectiveness).

3.1.2   Diagrams

Semantically, *diagrams* express views of a model (that is, subsets of the viewpoint that each model represents). An individual model element can be presented in one or many of the diagrams for a model; in other words, a model element can be presented in many different ways and in many diagrams—but it must be presented in at least one diagram in one way.

Diagrams don't have any special shape assigned to them; they can be free-floating, bounded by a box, or contained within a package. Some other considerations are as follows:

- Neither geometry nor "geography" has much significance in a UML diagram. For the most part, a symbol's size or relative location generally has no semantic content, except for diagrams that have a time dimension.

- Diagrams are all two-dimensional because of the current limits imposed by available technology and tools, although some shapes are nominally three-dimensional, rendered in two dimensions (cubes, for example).

- Text can be used liberally within a diagram. Examples include expressing rules and, within symbols, identifying attributes.

Finally (for this introduction), the *UML Specification* (Rational Software Corporation 1999) highlights three kinds of visual relationships in diagrams:

- *Connection*—Lines connect icons and symbols, forming connecting paths. Paths are *always* attached to symbols at both ends (that is, no dangling lines are allowed).

- *Containment*—Boxes, circles, and other fully enclosed shapes contain symbols, icons, and lines.

- *Visual attachment*—Elements that are close together may have a relationship suggested by their proximity. For example, a name above a line or next to a box may be interpreted as applying to the line or box.

3.2   Packages

A *package* is a grouping of UML elements, which can include diagrams and may include subordinate packages and other kinds of model elements. According to the *UML Specification*, packages "can be used for organizing elements for any purpose; the criteria to use for grouping elements together into one package are not defined within UML" (Rational Software Corporation 1999). Packages are probably the most important aspect of the UML from a modeling perspective; they play a role in UML modeling that is similar to the role classes play in programming.

Most UML books treat packages lightly. Because of their importance and this lack of attention elsewhere, I'll provide more details on them here than I will for the other UML symbols and artifacts.

Packages can be nested and can reference other packages. They provide the basis for configuration control, storage, and access control. They also provide the basis for *naming* model elements. They define the namespace for model elements; nested packages create a naming hierarchy. Because packages can't be instantiated, nominally their only formal function (in a system) is to provide this name space.

Each element in a package must be uniquely named. Elements in different packages may have the same name, but they are differentiated by the package name as an additional identifier. This capability becomes significant with components, with reuse, and as systems grows larger. A name collision between components can be resolved by placing them into separate packages and referencing their fully qualified name:

```
packageName::elementName
```

Individual packages *own* model elements directly; an element can belong only to one package. If the owning package is removed from the model, the owned model elements are removed as well. A package is "the basic unit of development product—something you can separately create, maintain, deliver, sell, update, assign to a team and generally manage as a unit" (D'Souza and Wills 1998, 285).

Elements contained in the same package can be related, and can be related to elements in a containing package at any level. Elements in contained packages are not visible; "packages do not see inwards," as the *UML Specification* puts it (Rational Software Corporation 1999). Elements in other packages (contained or separate) can be made available by importing or accessing the package(s) or by generalization.

Packages can import or access the contents of other packages. When one package imports another, it imports all those elements that are visible in the second package. Imported elements become part of the importing package's namespace (that is, they can be referenced without the qualification of a pathname), and may be used in relationships owned by the package. An access relationship keeps the namespaces separate, requiring that the accessing package reference elements in the accessed package use fully qualified names (ones that include the pathname). Packages can also "specialize" other packages in a generalization relationship that parallels inheritance among classes.

Containment and visibility are key characteristics of model elements in packages. Packages encapsulate the model elements they contain and define their *visibility* as private, protected, or public:

- *Private*—Elements that are not available at all outside the containing package

- *Protected*—Elements that are available only to packages with generalizations to the package owning the elements

- *Public*—Elements that are available also to importing and accessing packages (see the following sections)

Package visibility is a variation on the standard approach that the UML provides for the visibility of model elements. Martin Fowler rightly cautions against using the UML's standard version of visibility too glibly because it is a mishmash of compromises that don't necessarily correspond to the way visibility is used in your programming language. For object-oriented development, he suggests relying on the flavor of visibility supported by the language you're using (1997, 99). For component-based development, on the other hand, especially where packages form the basis for working with components (as in D'Souza and Wills' book), UML package visibilities are a critical tool. For components, UML visibility is a significant modeling concern, not just one that has a transitive interest, as a reflection of programming concerns. See *Objects, Components and Frameworks with UML: The Catalysis Approach* for an example (D' Souza and Wills 1998, 259–296).

Although *package* can be mapped to programming constructs, the UML version is far richer and more nuanced than any of the available programmatic translations. It is the core-modeling concept that distinguishes the UML from previous programming-oriented modeling approaches. Reflecting its importance, the idea of a package has undergone significant shifts during the brief life of the UML, contributing to user confusion.

UML 0.8 did not include packages; instead, *category* and *subsystem* provided logical and physical organizing mechanisms. UML 0.9 combined categories and subsystems into an all-purpose construct called *package*, initially limited to grouping classes. With *UML Specification, Version 1.3*, packages can be used to group a much broader range of model elements. It seems likely that package, as a modeling construct, will continue to be refined and refactored, especially given its utility in managing the complexity of components.

The downside of all this is that the literature on the UML varies in its treatment of packages, depending on the vintage of the *UML Specification* being referenced. However, the evolving notion of a package and its evolving usage is probably a key to understanding the changing environment of modeling (and development), and it is a key to the success of the UML in the post-object-oriented world of systems development.

3.2.1   Models: Packages of Views

Models are one type of package explicitly identified in the UML metamodel. Therefore, it is a good example of how to use packages. Conceptually, packages provide a way of organizing models that is analogous to a hierarchic directory structure of folders and files.

With the UML, the process you use (and the toolset) will dictate the structure you use to organize your models. Generally, a single top-level package provides the starting point for a hierarchy of views and models (organized in packages and expressed as diagrams). Rational's Rose CASE tool is organized this way, but its approach is at best a useful convention that reflects the RUP. D'Souza and Wills' book incorporates a more imaginative approach that leverages packaging to the hilt, based on factoring the system in a variety of ways (1998). These can accord with the categories of user, express the different architectural layers in a system, contain the rules that constitute a system's architectural style, hold the patterns that drive the design, and provide the means of organizing work and configuring the work products.

3.2.2   Subsystems: Packages of Behavior and Operations

Subsystems are the other type of package explicitly identified in the UML metamodel. Subsystems decompose systems, whereas models partition the logical abstractions that describe a system. Models should be "nearly independent," whereas each subsystem should be independent and complete—there should be a minimum of coupling between the parts of different subsystems.

The notion of subsystems that has been incorporated in the 1.3 version of the *UML Specification* has an enhanced flavor that hints at a cross between model and class. A subsystem is no longer a collection of modules or classes as it was for Grady Booch in *Object-Oriented Analysis and Design with Applications* (1994, 221) or Ivar Jacobson in *Object-Oriented Software Engineering* (1994, 148). Now, a *subsystem* is a means of representing "a behavioral unit in the physical system" and a collection of model elements. It is fundamentally a way of partitioning the system-to-be-implemented, and so is more physical than logical or conceptual.

Although it is a chunking mechanism like a model, at its simplest it is meant to address the organization of executables and production artifacts rather than ideas.

A model can be divided into subsystems; subsystems can include one or more models. Conceptually, the whole physical system is represented at the top level by a single model. This model can then be subdivided as needed to suit the purposes of the modeling exercise. Ordinary subordinate models that are packaged as models are logical conveniences. Subsystems are miniature systems themselves, ones that do not overlap. In the course of development, as the focus of modeling shifts towards construction and the physical architecture becomes stabilized, subsystems provide a way of organizing work products that can be translated into real physical implementations.

A subsystem inherits all the naming, access, and dependency properties of a package. However, like a class and unlike a model, a subsystem provides interfaces and has operations. Its contents can be separated into specification and realization subsets:

- *Specification*—Operations and/or features, together with such elements as use cases and state machines

- *Realization*—Identifies those elements that physically implement the specification

Subsystems are one of those areas in the UML that are notably inconsistent and muddy. For example, on page 2-180, the *UML Specification* declares that a subsystem "may or may not be instantiable." On page 2-181, however, it says that subsystems "cannot be instantiated" while declaring that an instantiable subsystem has some of the semantics of a composite class, whereas one that is not instantiable has the semantics of a package (Rational Software Corporation 1999).

Subsystems are probably going to become much clearer when the next major revision happens. Meanwhile, the importance of subsystems is very much a matter of the process that you're using. The RUP relies on subsystems heavily; for D'Souza and Wills' book, they're mostly a convenient way to package infrastructural services.

3.2.3   Frameworks: Packages of Patterns

A framework can also be expressed by using a package, one "consisting mainly of patterns, where patterns are defined as template collaborations" (Rational Software Corporation 1999, 2-174). The generic package acts as a template with some elements parameterized (that is, acting as placeholders for elements in what amounts to a software pattern) such as the Gang of Four patterns or Martin Fowler's analysis patterns.

Although not high-profile members of the UML (that is, they don't have a specification as a separate ModelElement, such as Model and Subsystem), *frameworks* are the third legitimate use for packages.

D'Souza and Wills' book uses frameworks as a way of providing a consistent mechanism for organizing and reusing model elements across all stages of development (1998). An implementation model can be composed of code frameworks that reflect the frameworks that emerged in the analysis model and were refined in the design model. Seeing components as collaborations and systems as collaborations between components makes the use of patterns that are instantiated as frameworks an effective alternative to the models-and-subsystems approach of traditional object-oriented design.

In the same way that packages have evolved from groupings of classes, in D'Souza and Wills' book, a framework provides a more refined means of using patterns, especially as a way of enhancing reuse. Although collaboration remains the core of patterns and frameworks in D'Souza and Wills' book, catalysis frameworks go beyond the simplistic understanding of patterns as a collaboration between objects that underlies the way patterns are currently embodied in the UML (1998).

3.3   Extensions

One of the key capabilities of the UML is that it can be customized and tailored as needed with a number of *extension mechanisms*. Extensions aren't just a means of localizing the UML to provide a dialect for a project or organization. They also provide a means of cautiously evolving the language.

Extensions can be added to the language as a whole as an informal solution to a general need, and later (possibly) being translated into a full and distinctive member of the language. For example, Framework is currently handled by means of an extension, rather than having the full blessing associated with being a ModelElement, the way Model and Subsystem are handled.

There are three extension mechanisms currently available, and one way of packaging extended dialects of the UML in standardized form. The following is a basic introduction.

3.3.1 Tagged Values

Tagged values are properties of elements that are explicitly defined. They are information about the model or model element, not the system itself. The tag and its associated value are defined using the following form:

```
{tag = "value"}
```

For example:

```
{modeler = "L. DaVinci"}
```

with braces surrounding the tagged value. The tagged value can be placed inside a container or in close proximity to the model element being tagged. There are some predefined tags in the UML, such as *invariant*, *precondition*, and *postcondition*, which can be used (for example) to support the use of contracts.

3.3.2 Constraints

Constraints are semantic restrictions on a model element—essentially, rules or conditional statements. They can be user-defined or part of the UML generally. Like tagged values, they appear within braces, typically contained within the model element they relate to, or appear close by. For example:

```
{age >= 21}
```

There are a substantial number of UML-provided constraints.

3.3.3 Stereotypes

Stereotypes are the most powerful and used of the extension mechanisms. They provide the means to specialize existing ModelElements—in effect, by creating new ones. This way, limitations or special needs can be addressed without having to get an official change to the UML itself (although, as with tagged values and constraints, the UML includes a number of official stereotypes, and local stereotype generation needs to be handled with caution).

Currently, for example, framework is a stereotype of package, and actor is a stereotype of class. A stereotype is expressed by adding the name of the stereotype to the model element being extended. The name is enclosed in guillemets. Therefore, the framework looks like Figure 3.1.

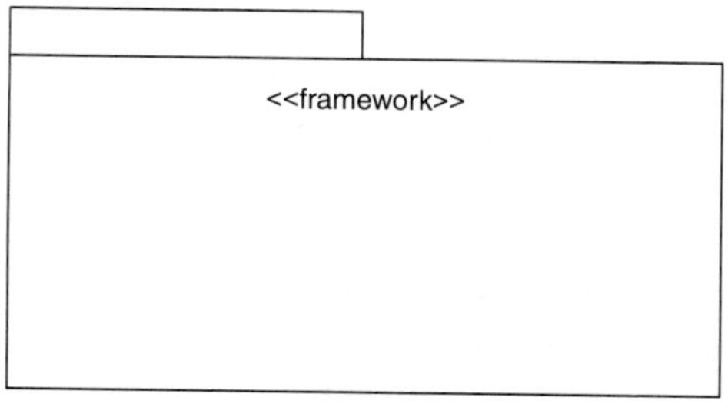

FIGURE 3.1   *A package stereotyped as a framework.*

3.3.4   Profiles

The UML provides a mechanism called a *profile* to act as a way of packaging a predefined set of stereotypes, tagged values, constraints, and notation icons to customize the UML for a specific domain or process. Because they are extensions, profiles don't alter the basic UML. Instead, they are intended to help in the creation and management of dialects that can be more or less local.

Two samples are included in the 1.3 Specification; one for the RUP (referred to as the Unified Process), and Business Modeling a la the Three Amigos: Ivar Jacobson, Grady Booch, and James Rumbaugh. Others have been proposed, notably for workflow and process modeling, and to handle persistence.

Although not intended this way, an organization or process profile might also be a way to document which of the UML's copious supply of formal constraints, tags, stereotypes, and keywords are legal—providing a filtering capability as well as an extending capability. A profile would then be included as part of the documentation of the architectural style for a development effort.

3.4   Symbols

The authors of the UML have made an effort to avoid overwhelming the user with too many distinctive symbols, and have also tried to provide notational similarities among conceptually related symbols (packages and classes, for example).

UML symbols can have content or just be iconic. Actually, the UML distinguishes between what it calls, awkwardly, two-dimensional symbols and icons:

- *Icons*—Fixed in size and shape, icons do not have to be attached to paths (but can be *terminators*: icons on the end of a path that qualify the meaning of the path symbol). They may be located within symbols.

- *Two-dimensional symbols*—Having the capability to shrink or grow, two-dimensional symbols can have compartments as well. Some two-dimensional symbols are also graphs—they contain nodes connected by paths.

3.4.1 Actor

An *actor* is something or someone outside the system that interacts directly with it—typically, a user of the system or another system/subsystem (see Figure 3.2). An actor participates in use cases and may be represented in other types of diagrams anywhere in the system model.

Waiter

FIGURE 3.2   *Actor.*

3.4.2 Use Case/Collaboration

A *use case* is a sequence of interactions by an actor with the system, which yields observable value to the actor (see Figure 3.3). By the way, this is not the UML definition, which is deplorably fussy and technical, and seems to be an effort to make use cases into a type of class and what the UML calls a "behavioral thing."

take order

FIGURE 3.3   *Use case.*

A *collaboration* a collection of objects that interact to implement behavior (see Figure 3.4). Typically, a collaboration can be used to specify the realization of a use case or an operation. A collaboration can also be used to specify a software pattern, and a *parameterized* collaboration (that is, one with abstract participants that are replaced when the pattern is used) can specify an architectural pattern.

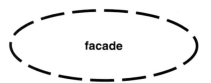

FIGURE 3.4 *Collaboration.*

3.4.3 Class/Object/Type/Active Class

A *class* is an abstraction of a set of possible objects that share the same attributes, operations, methods, relationships, and semantics (see Figure 3.5). A class may use a set of interfaces to specify collections of operations it provides to its environment. A *type* is a representation of a collection of objects without specifying the physical implementation as a class. Class and type use the same symbol in the UML.

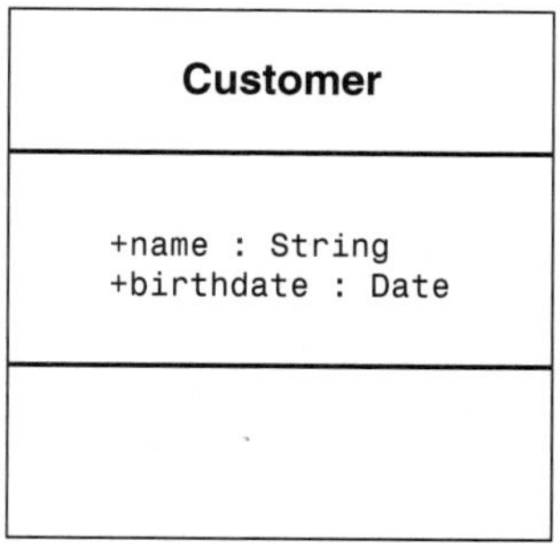

Customer
+name : String +birthdate : Date

FIGURE 3.5 *Class.*

An *object* is an instance of a class or an example of a type—the same symbol as class, but with the name underlined (see Figure 3.6).

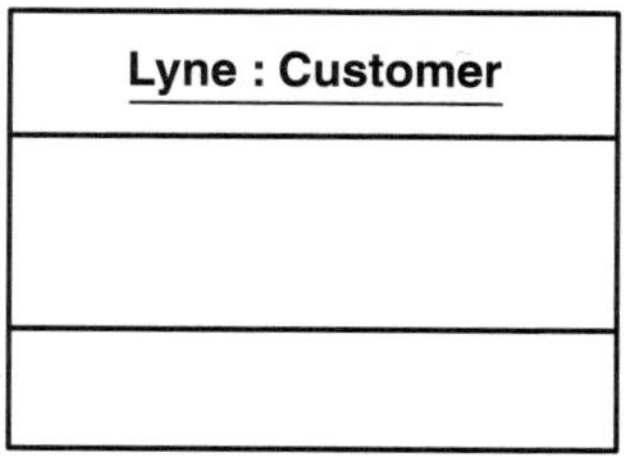

Lyne : Customer

FIGURE 3.6 *Object.*

An *active class* is a set of objects, each of which owns a thread of control (that is, it can initiate, control, and terminate a process or thread). (See Figure 3.7.)

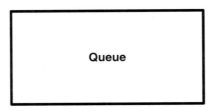

FIGURE 3.7   *Active class.*

3.4.4   Interface

An *interface* describes the visible operations of a class, component, or package (see Figure 3.8). It defines the services available from the implementing element.

FIGURE 3.8   *Interface.*

3.4.5   Component

A *component* is a physical, replaceable part of a system that packages implementation and provides the realization of a set of interfaces (see Figure 3.9). A component represents a physical piece of implementation of a system, including software code (source, binary, or executable) or equivalents such as scripts or command files (Rational Software Corporation 1999, B-5).

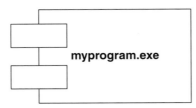

FIGURE 3.9   *Component.*

3.4.6   Node

A *node* represents a processing resource that exists at run time, with at least a memory and often processing capability as well (see Figure 3.10). Nodes comprise computing devices and any other physical resources used in a system, such as people or machines.

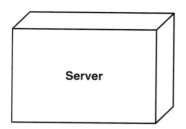

FIGURE 3.10   *Node.*

3.4.7   Package

A *package* (see Figure 3.11) is a UML container used to organize model elements (refer to Section 3.2, "Packages," earlier in this chapter).

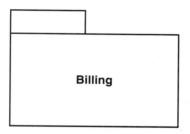

FIGURE 3.11   *Package.*

3.4.8   State

A *state* is the condition, status, or situation of an object as part of its lifecycle and/or as the result of an interaction (see Figure 3.12). A state may also be used to model an ongoing activity.

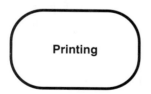

FIGURE 3.12   *State.*

3.4.9   Note

A *note* is used to provide explanatory text, such as comments in a model (see Figure 3.13). A note can also be used in specific ways, depending on the modeling dialect you adopt (requirements are a good example).

Figure 3.13   *Note.*

3.5   Lines

In the UML, *lines* are used to express messages (dynamic connections between model elements), "links" (relationships between model elements—the term *link* also has a formal meaning within the UML), and interactions. Generally, messages don't appear in structural models; links don't appear in dynamic models. But this, too, can be varied within a dialect. A basic set of line-based UML notation is explained in the following sections.

> **Note**
>
> Remember (as I mentioned when discussing visual relationships in Section 3.1.2, "Diagrams"), lines must be terminated in some fashion in the UML, either with a model element graphic or an icon.

3.5.1   Messages

Messages are used in interactions between model elements in *dynamic models*, those that represent the behavior in a system. Messages convey information between objects, for example, and trigger activities. There are four types of messages (as shown in Figure 3.14):

- *Simple message*—Control is passed from one object to another without providing details.

- *Synchronous message*—The sending object pauses to wait for results.

- *Asynchronous message*—The sending object does not pause to wait for results.

- *Return message*—This message indicates a return from a procedure call.

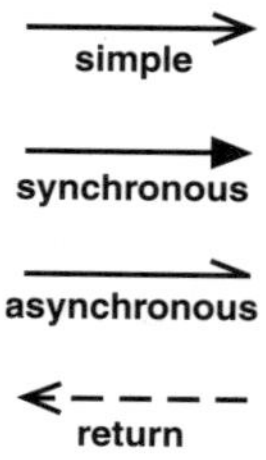

FIGURE 3.14 *The four types of messages.*

3.5.2   Relationships in General

Relationships are used in *structural models* to show semantic connections between model elements.

A *dependency* is what *The Unified Modeling Language User Guide* calls a "using" relationship (Jacobson, Booch, and Rumbaugh 1998a), one in which the connection between two things means that if one changes, it affects the other (see Figure 3.15). Dependencies can be used to identify connections between a variety of model elements, packages being a notable example. These are unidirectional relationships.

FIGURE 3.15 *Dependency.*

A *generalization* is a relation between two elements, in which one is a more general form of the other (see Figure 3.16). Class inheritance is represented this way, but generalization can be used more generally. Again, packages are an example.

FIGURE 3.16 *Generalization.*

An *association* is what the UML calls a *structural relationship*, mapping one object to another set of objects (see Figure 3.17). It is also used to identify the communication path between an actor and a use case. *The Unified Modeling Language Reference Manual* describes associations as "the glue that ties systems together" (Jacobson, Booch, and Rumbaugh 1998b, 47). In the UML, an association has a navigational sense to it as well (you can get there from here, from one object to another), which can cause heartburn among some object methodology purists.

FIGURE 3.17 *Association.*

A *realization* is a type of dependency relationship that identifies a *contractual link* between elements—a realizing element. For example, a class implements the behaviors in a specifying element; in this case, it is an interface (see Figure 3.18). A realization also links use cases and collaborations. (See Section 3.5.4, "Relationships: Some Uses of Dependency.")

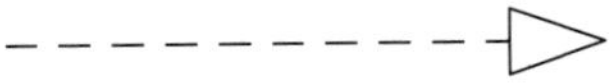

FIGURE 3.18 *Realization.*

3.5.3 Relationships: Some Types of Associations

The UML considers aggregations and composites to be special forms of association with distinctive notations. Needless to say, the semantics of aggregates and composites is subject to much debate.

A *qualified association* is a plain association with an indication of what information to use when identifying a target object in the set of associated objects. In Figure 3.19, bank account # is used to identify the customer it belongs to.

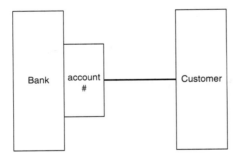

FIGURE 3.19 *Qualified association.*

An *aggregation* represents a whole-part relationship. This contrasts with a plain association, which shows a relationship among/between peers, depending on the number (see Figure 3.20). In an aggregation, one element is the *whole* and the other(s) are the *parts.*

FIGURE 3.20 *Aggregation.*

A *composition* is an aggregation that has strong ownership of its parts.
Therefore, if the whole element disappears, the parts do, too (see Figure 3.21).

FIGURE 3.21 *Composition.*

3.5.4 Relationships: Some Uses of Dependency

Dependency relationships are frequently stereotyped in the UML to support
the needs of particular types of diagrams or model elements. The following are
some examples:

Extends provides a way of handling behavior that is optional in a use case (see
Figure 3.22). The optional behavior is packaged in an extending use case and
connected via an <<extends>> dependency.

<<extends>>

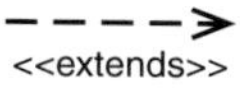

FIGURE 3.22 *Extends dependency.*

Includes provides a way of handling behavior that is common to a number of
use cases (see Figure 3.23). The optional behavior is factored out, packaged in
an included use case, and connected via an <<includes>> dependency.

<<includes>>

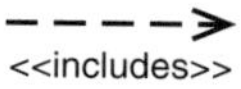

FIGURE 3.23 *Includes dependency.*

Imports is a dependency between packages (see Figure 3.24). A receiving package can access the publicly visible elements of the package being imported.

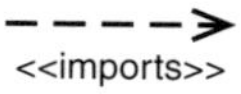

<<imports>>

FIGURE 3.24 *Imports dependency.*

3.5.5   Abstraction: Other Uses of Dependency

The UML includes a variety of explicit expressions of abstraction:

Refinement indicates a dependency between two elements at different levels of abstraction (see Figure 3.25). An example of this is related elements in different types of models, such as an analysis model and a design model, which are very important in D'Souza and Wills' book, but are hardly mentioned in the RUP.

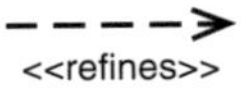

– – – –▶
<<refines>>

FIGURE 3.25   *Refinement.*

Realization was introduced earlier as a full-blown significant relationship meriting its own line symbol. It can also be indicated by using a stereotype (see Figure 3.26). The *UML Specification* says, "Realization can be used to model stepwise refinement, optimizations, transformations, templates, model synthesis, framework composition, and so on" (Rational Software Corporation 1999).

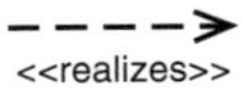

– – – –▶
<<realizes>>

FIGURE 3.26   *Realization.*

Derivation indicates that an instance of an element (the derived element) can be computed from the other element in the relationship (see Figure 3.27).

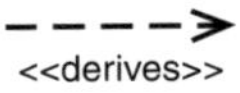

– – – –▶
<<derives>>

FIGURE 3.27   *Derivation*

A *trace* relationship shows connections between model elements or sets of model elements representing the same concept in different models (see Figure 3.28). Traces are mainly used for tracking requirements and changes across models.

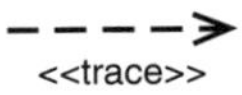

– – – –▶
<<trace>>

FIGURE 3.28   *Trace.*

3.6   Diagrams

UML diagrams are where it all comes together. As I already mentioned, in the UML there is no formal way of bounding or containing a diagram (that is, no notation for the diagram itself), so there are no relationships between diagrams. Instead, diagrams are the graphical presentation vehicles for aspects of a model. They don't stand alone, but are meant to be part of the textual narrative that provides the model specification.

The UML specifically includes nine different diagrams in its documentation, which I'll discuss briefly here. However, these diagram types are process-dependent and suggestive, rather than prescriptive. The UML allows the modeler to combine any and all elements into diagrams, depending on the modeling needs at hand. In practice, of course, only certain combinations of elements are sensible, and these nine types are pretty much the "canonical" ones for object-oriented programming.

However, all of this really needs to be considered in the context of the process and the tool being used. Although the RUP includes all of these diagrams, D'Souza and Wills' book (for example) doesn't.

Detailing these diagrams and the alternatives can be a book by itself. Most of the literature on the UML focuses on these diagrams, so there are already many good books to choose from. Because this book is as process-independent as the UML, I'll leave detailed discussions of these diagrams to the many other more programming-oriented, books out there and to come.

3.6.1   Class Diagram

For traditional object-oriented development, the class diagram is the keystone for the system model. In UML terms, it is a view of the static structural model. It is *not* a formal partitioning of the model; therefore, individual class diagrams "do not represent divisions in the underlying model" (Rational Software Corporation 1999, 3-33).

Aside from classes, a class diagram can also contain interfaces, packages, relationships, and instances (such as objects and links). The *UML Specification* suggests that "a better name would be *static structural diagram*," but bows to tradition and brevity in sticking with *class diagram* (1999).

The UML recognizes the distinction between *class* and *type*; the nature of what is meant by *class* changes conceptually, depending on the development stage that the modeling effort is in. For those interested, Martin Fowler, Kendall Scott, and Ivar Jacobson do an admirable job of capturing and explaining the modeling nuances of class, type and object in *UML Distilled: Applying the Standard Object Modeling Language* (Fowler, Scott, and Jacobson 1997).

3.6.2 Use Case Diagram

For use case-driven development, the *use case diagram* is the keystone of the modeling effort. Use case diagrams show actors and use cases, together with their relationships. These include the following:

- *Associations* between the actors and the use cases
- *Generalizations* between the actors
- *Generalizations*, *extends*, and *includes* relationships among the use cases

The use cases may be enclosed by a rectangle to show the boundary of the containing system, and so on. As will be evident in the UML patterns, use case diagrams by themselves are essentially trivial. The real substance of a use case is in the text (narrative).

A use case captures the significant parts of an interaction with the system or some part of the system by the actor(s) defining the scope, context, and requirements. Use cases can be used in a variety of ways throughout the development effort (for example, as the basis for setting up the test environment and as a starting point for a user manual).

The following is an example of a basic use case, which describes making a phone call, in text format first and then the diagram (see Figure 3.29). The caller initiates the use case, and the receiver is a secondary actor. The system that the caller and actor interact with is, of course, the phone system. The alternate flows aren't completely described, but indicate the kind of conditions that alternate flows handle.

Actors:

Caller
Receiver

Normal Flow:

The use case begins when Caller picks up the handset of telephone.

> Caller listens for dial tone.
> (Alternate flow: no dial tone)
> Caller dials a phone number.

> Phone System rings Receiver's phone.
> (Alternate flow: Wrong number)
> Receiver answers.
> (Alternate flow: no answer)
> Caller conducts conversation.

The use case ends when Caller hangs up phone.

Alternate Flows:

No dial tone
Wrong number
No answer

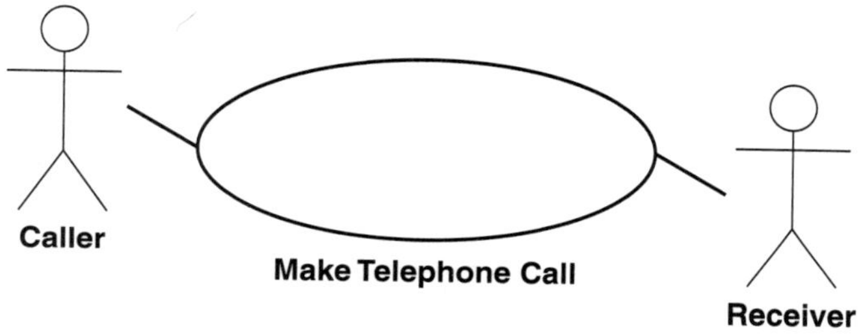

Caller

Make Telephone Call

Receiver

FIGURE 3.29   *Telephone call use case diagram.*

3.6.3   Interaction Diagrams

Interaction diagrams are used in the dynamic modeling of the system. There are two kinds: sequence diagrams and collaboration diagrams.

Sequence Diagram

A *sequence diagram* shows an interaction arranged in time sequence: the objects (*not* classes) and the messages that pass between them when an interaction occurs. These are what Ivar Jacobson used to call interaction diagrams.

A sequence diagram has a list of participating objects across its top, shown as rectangles. Each object rectangle contains at least a name, always underlined to indicate that the rectangle is an object and not a class. Below each object rectangle, shown with a dotted line, is the object *lifeline,* the time-ordered visual framework for message exchanges between the objects (and with the system). A narrow vertical rectangle called the *activation* represents the period of time an object is actually performing an action (directly or through an intermediary, such as another object). Object messages appear as arrows with a text description. Figure 3.30 shows the basic elements of a sequence diagram.

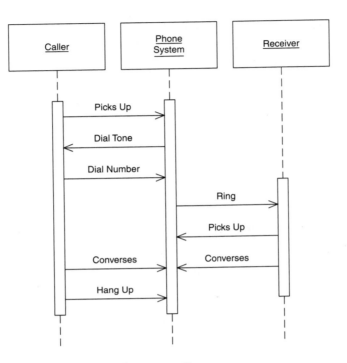

FIGURE 3.30 *Simple sequence diagram.*

Collaboration Diagram

A *collaboration diagram* also shows the passing of messages between objects, but focuses on the objects and messages and their order instead of the time sequence. The sequence of interactions and the concurrent threads are identified using sequence numbers. A collaboration diagram shows an interaction organized around the roles in the interaction and their links to each other, and shows the relationships among the objects playing the different roles. The *UML Specification* suggests that collaboration diagrams are better for real-time specifications and for complex scenarios than sequence diagrams.

Figure 3.31 shows the telephone call example expressed as a collaboration diagram.

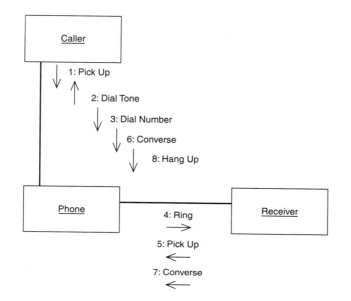

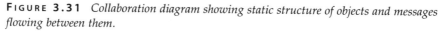

FIGURE 3.31 *Collaboration diagram showing static structure of objects and messages flowing between them.*

3.6.4 State Diagrams

State diagrams show the states, events, transitions, and activities for the system, depicted as *state machines*. They're part of dynamic modeling rather than structural modeling. They are used to describe the behavior of a model element such as an object or an interaction, describing "possible sequences of states and actions through which the element can proceed during its lifetime as a result of reacting to discrete events (for example, signals, operation invocations)" (Rational Software Corporation 1999, 3-131).

The official name in the UML is *statechart diagram*, but *state diagram* pops up all over the place in the *UML Specification* and in much of the literature. The term *statechart* reflects its origins in Harel Statecharts, a long-used tool for modeling real-time systems, which the UML has modified to fit object-oriented development.

A state diagram is typically used to model the behavior of an object that needs a complete description of its discrete states. Many objects in standard business systems may not have significant states, in which case they will not need state diagrams. (On the other hand, for those developing real-time systems, a discussion of state diagrams and state modeling can be a book by itself.) A state diagram is typically associated with one and only one class, and lists all the states that a particular object can have during system operation.

Each rounded rectangle represents one state that an object can be in. A state diagram must represent all the states in which an object can find itself, as well as define an initial state the object will be in. An *initial state* is shown as a filled-in black circle. The *final state* of an object is not required if the object has no final state, such as in a system that is always running.

An object passes from one state to another following a *transition* triggered by an event within the system (typically, a method invocation). A transition is shown by drawing an arrow from one state to another and is associated with an event that triggers the transition.

Figure 3.32 shows the state diagram for a light switch that shows both transition lines and events.

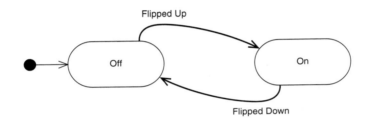

FIGURE 3.32   *State diagram showing the two states of a light switch.*

3.6.5   Activity Diagrams

An *activity diagram* is a "special case of a state diagram in which all (or at least most) of the states are action or subactivity states and in which all (or at least most) of the transitions are triggered by completion of the actions or subactivities in the source states" (Rational Software Corporation 1999, 3-151). In fact, they're basically sophisticated versions of flowcharts. They're intended to cover workflows and processes, and have much of the flavor of flowcharts without the negative "baggage." Their depiction as versions of state diagrams is subject to much criticism, but at least it helps to make them a consistent member of the UML family.

An activity diagram is attached to a class (which includes a use case for the UML), to a package, or to the implementation of an operation. The *UML Specification* says that they "focus on flows driven by internal processing (as opposed to external events)" (1999, 3-151). It recommends using them where the events involved represent the completion of internally generated actions (for procedural flow of control).

In an activity diagram, *swimlanes* are used to package the organizational boundaries within an activity model: they are used to show *who* is doing *what* in an activity model.

When it is necessary to indicate that two or more actions occur in parallel, a line called a *synchronization bar* shows where each thread in the parallel actions halts, waiting until the other threads reach the same point.

Figure 3.33 shows an activity model for the workflow of an order system. Organized around the responsibilities of the customer, sales, and the warehouse, swimlanes are the vertical lines partitioning the diagram and identifying the responsibilities for each activity.

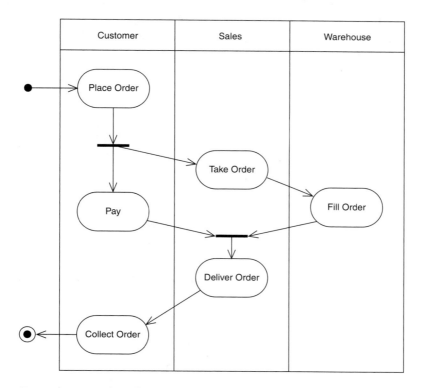

FIGURE 3.33 *An order process with three swimlanes, each showing the responsibility of the business unit during the process.*

3.6.6   Implementation Diagrams

Implementation diagrams model implementation artifacts and considerations, including how the source code is structured and how (and where) the executables are made available. The *UML Specification* suggests that they also can be applied in a broader sense to business modeling. *Components* are the business procedures and documents, and the *run-time structure* is the organization units and resources (human and other) of the business (1999, 3-165). There are two types of implementation diagrams: component diagrams and deployment diagrams.

Component Diagrams

Component diagrams show the structure of the code (see Figure 3.34). According to the *UML Specification*, they are "the dependencies among software components, including source code components, binary code components, and executable components" (1999). The nuances of *component* are such that it seems to be as malleable a term as *architecture* and *abstraction*.

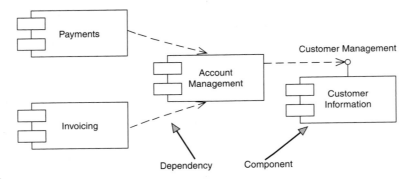

FIGURE 3.34 *Component diagram showing the dependencies between components of a payment-processing system*

Deployment Diagrams

Deployment diagrams show the structure of the runtime system (see Figure 3.35), including the "configuration of runtime processing elements and the software components, processes, and objects that live on them" (Rational Software Corporation 1999, 3-166). For business modeling, the *UML Specification* says runtime elements include workers and organizational units, and the software components include procedures and documents used by the workers and organizational units.

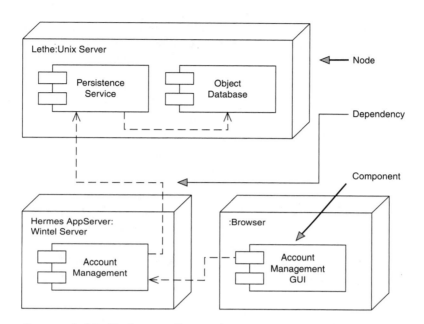

FIGURE 3.35 *Deployment diagram showing run-time nodes and components for a browser-based three-tier account management system*

3.7   Further Reading

Martin Fowler, Kendall Scott, and Ivar Jacobson's book, *UML Distilled: Applying the Standard Object Modeling Language* (1997), is still the best practical introduction to the UML, despite having been pretty much the first out of the chute. It shows its age in spots, but combines modeling and programming concerns and cuts the huge beast down to a digestible size.

All of the UML books by the Three Amigos are useful, although with varying degrees of often-unstated bias towards the RUP. The *Unified Modeling Language User Guide* seems badly organized when you try to actually use it, but has a wealth of real-life, useful suggestions and ideas, a number of which provided the starting point for patterns in this book (Jacobson, Booch, and Rumbaugh 1999a). The *Unified Modeling Language Reference Manual* is occasionally idiosyncratic in content, at least when compared with the *UML Specification, Version 1.3*, but it is the most up-to-date and least influenced by the RUP (Jacobson, Booch, and Rumbaugh 1998b). With its encyclopedia/dictionary-type approach, it sometimes provides the only way to get the right information on nuances of current meaning that end-run some of the inconsistencies in the *UML*

Specification. The Unified Software Development Process is the best of the bunch, but, of course, is even more biased toward Rational's process than the other two… but at least it's meant to be (Jacobson, Booch, and Rumbaugh 1999a).

Objects, Components and Frameworks with UML: The Catalysis Approach by Desmond D'Souza and Alan Wills (1998) is the best antidote to the bias towards the RUP that shows up not just in the Three Amigos books, but in almost all the UML books. The first chapter is almost impenetrable, but gradually you get the sense of the catalysis approach and why it (and component-based development) really is different from traditional object-oriented thinking.

One of any number of short articles by D'Souza is probably required reading as a preamble to undertaking the book, though. Alternatively, try the patterns first and then read the rest of the text. I've reworked a number of the patterns from catalysis in this book because they express real best practices from mainstream modeling. Although the rest of the book requires a real paradigm shift in thinking to absorb properly, the patterns are good fundamental ideas expressed simply and well.

Finally, the *UML Specification, Version 1.3* (released in July 1999) is a necessary part of the library, although not one meant to be read. Because of the changes that have been made and some that are presaged, the 1.3 version needs to be available for occasional consultation. The language is frequently impossible, the odd inconsistencies are frustrating, but it *is* the source of final judgment. And it's free for downloading from the OMG and Rational Software Web sites.

PART II

The Pattern Language

CHAPTER 4

Patterns of Style

Catalogue

Context

This chapter provides the modeler with a set of UML style idioms that will contribute to the graphical quality of UML diagrams. They were gleaned from a careful examination of many UML diagrams. The idioms presented here are the ones that most clearly stood out, represented approaches that had enduring traits, were clearly effective in their solutions, and recurred across many different types of models and modelers.

Fortunately, the UML has been around long enough for stylistic approaches to begin emerging in informal, clearly observable ways. Style is more than cosmetic—it combines intelligence with personality. Effective style adds timeless qualities such as grace, taste, and a sensitivity to the user.

Diagrams are the heart of UML models; visual appeal and expressiveness are critical qualities. An effective diagramming style makes the difference between diagrams that work and those that don't.

Common Forces

- Too much detail can be blinding.

- Clutter confuses.

- Diagrams abstract by using semantic information, not syntax.

- A good diagram is as simple as possible, but no simpler.

- Standard visual conventions are easily understood.

- Obscure conventions and unusual layouts in diagrams make them more difficult to understand.

- Surprises in design or presentation should be pleasant.

- Creativity and novelty are valuable for creating better solutions.

- Diagrams adhering to well-known standards and using orthogonal presentation rules are more comprehensible.

- Standards, clarity, and usability are driving forces for integrating work and group collaboration.

- Occam's Razor says that the simplest explanation is usually the right one (a version of Keep It Simple, Stupid—KISS).

Discussion

Exercising creativity and ingenuity is one of the essential tasks of a software development team. The creativity and ingenuity should be limited to the product being developed, however, not the diagrams.

The UML modeler is faced with the responsibility of creating models that are easily accessible by the average person who is expected to use them. Indulging in excessively original but unfamiliar presentation practices, or using obscure UML model elements when well-known ones can work, results in UML models that aren't as usable as they can be. Esoteric design and presentation choices can also cause confusion in the development team, and they will inevitably result in wasted time and resources as the models are changed or the approach is explained.

4.1   ATTRIBUTES AS COMPOSITIONS TO TYPES

PROBLEM

A large or important class has key attributes whose significance needs to be obvious or clear.

CONTEXT

A UML class diagram, especially one that depicts a complex or central class in a system whose attributes are contained as line items in the class's attribute compartment.

FORCES

- Excessive detail obscures meaning.
- Clutter confuses.
- Insufficient visual emphasis on key details can cause loss of design balance.
- UML diagrams must convey meaning simply and clearly.
- Class symbol attribute compartment allows limited expression.
- Relationship control external to the class symbol is more expressive.

SOLUTION

Move the attribute out of the confines of the attribute compartment by adding a class symbol for each attribute type that needs special emphasis. Then, draw composition lines from the class containing the attributes to the class symbols denoting the attribute types. From there, add roles on the aggregate side that contain the appropriate names of the attributes. The classes representing the attribute types can be positioned some distance from the primary class so that the aggregation lines can be long enough to allow room for notes and constraints to be addedto describe special information and conditions belonging to the Composite attributes.

Both primitive and true class types can be depicted in this way—with class types allowing the depiction of selected attributes and operations that can further elaborate on the function of the attribute within the primary class.

RESULTING CONTEXT

A UML class diagram with classes that have their important attributes visually emphasized.

DISCUSSION

The attribute compartment of a UML class symbol serves as a useful place to list the inventory of the class's attributes, but it is rather limited when it comes to identifying and elaborating on particular attributes. A better place for a sophisticated description of attributes is physically external to the class using UML's powerful relationship descriptors such as constraints, multiplicity (only on the non-aggregate end for composites), qualified associations, ordering information, and improved room for note and constraint attachment.

The "Notation Guide" section in the *UML Specification* specifically observes that "attributes are, in effect, composition relationships between a class and the classes of its attributes" (Rational Software Corporation 1999, 3-75). In other words, all attributes are really a particular instance of composition implemented by value. Composition also implies a constraint to single multiplicity on the aggregate side. Therefore, an attribute is actually the composition of a type with a 0 or 1 multiplicity on the source end.

Figure 4.1 is a simple class diagram, showing a class that internally lists the attributes describing a car.

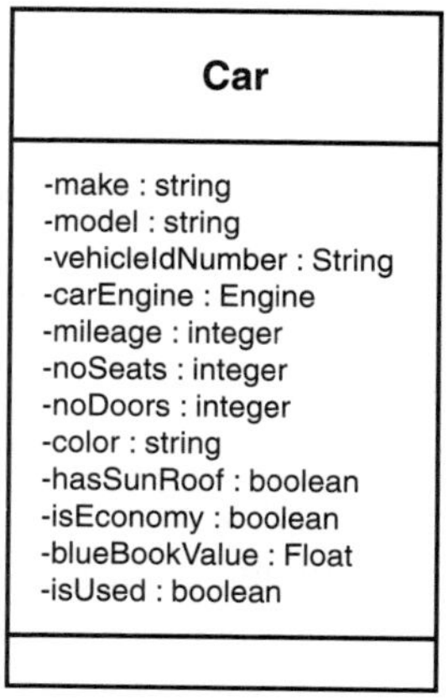

Car
-make : string -model : string -vehicleIdNumber : String -carEngine : Engine -mileage : integer -noSeats : integer -noDoors : integer -color : string -hasSunRoof : boolean -isEconomy : boolean -blueBookValue : Float -isUsed : boolean

FIGURE 4.1 *Simple class diagram, showing attributes of describing a car. All attributes are shown in the compartment, including both primitive and class.*

Applying this pattern, you can see that the resulting class diagram is more detailed and expressive (see Figure 4.2). By breaking the attributes out of the attribute compartment as compositions to class symbols of the attribute type, you can more clearly identify the attribute identified with notes and/or engaged by constraints.

Because it is the type of an attribute in the Car class, the Engine class was added to the diagram, which allows constraints to be attached that describe important conditional relationships between Engine and Car. Although having Engine and Car on the same diagram is likely to occur during initial modeling, it isn't unusual for class types to appear in attribute compartments when using classes from a class library or repository.

The two constraints shown in Figure 4.2 also demonstrate how constraints can be connected directly to attributes instead of classes.

The advantage of using this pattern is the capability to show attributes using the same notation that makes classes in a class diagram so visually compelling. An attribute shown this way gains the same range of expression that groups of collaborating classes have. This gives you improved flexibility and control over attribute definition and allows you to do the following:

- Connect UML relationships (association, generalization, and so on) to the composite
- Show details of special attribute types, such as templates and utilities
- Add ordering or sorting constraints to composite attribute
- Use qualified associations to control subset objects of the composition target
- More clearly specify target multiplicity

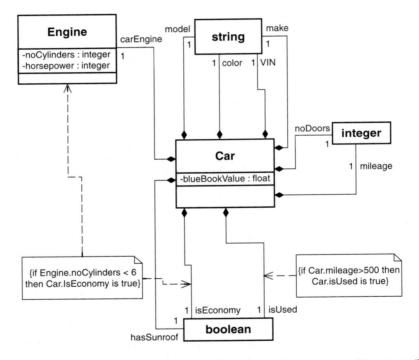

FIGURE 4.2 *Car class shown with attributes shown as compositions to attribute types.*

4.2   PROVIDING FOCUS

PROBLEM

Losing central item (class, use case) in diagram clutter.

CONTEXT

Any UML diagram containing many items.

FORCES

- A diagram must clearly communicate to its viewers.
- Oversimplified diagrams are insufficient to express sophisticated subjects.
- Clutter confuses.
- Visual emphasis can draw attention to key concepts or elements.
- Dense or repetitive diagrams reduce approachability.
- Standardized visual cues enhance readability and comprehension.

SOLUTION

Apply bold lines and fonts, or shaded areas to emphasize key details. Using colored elements is also becoming increasingly frequent. Depending on the diagram type, the target of emphasis may vary. (See Table 4.1 on next page.)

RESULTING CONTEXT

A UML diagram in which attention is appropriately drawn to the key elements of the diagram.

DISCUSSION

Visual cues that highlight important pieces of information in a standardized way help draw users' attention to important elements and emphasize central or key concepts in a diagram.

The overall readability and clarity of a UML diagram can be improved by using standard highlighting mechanisms such as bold lines and text, shaded and color areas, and spatial emphasis techniques such as key element centering (see Table 4.1).

TABLE 4.1   FORMATTING IN UML DIAGRAMS

Diagram	Bold lines	Fonts	Shading/Color	Spatial emphasis
Class	Class box, relationships	Class names, key attributes and operations, role names, stereotypes	Class box or specific compartment, packages	Put central item in middle of diagram
Sequence	Object box, key message traces (especially the entire path through key sequence)	Object names/types, operation descriptions	Object box, activation boxes	Size object boxes, depending on granularity of object
Collaboration	Object box	Object names/types, operation descriptions	Object box	Put central item in middle of diagram
State	State box, transitions	State name, actions, events, guard text	State box	
Activity	Activity box	Activity name, condition text, swimlane text	Activity box, start and end points, swimlanes	Put key activities in swim lane on leftmost side
Component	Component symbol, process symbol, dependencies, subsystem packages, interface symbols	Component name, stereotypes, interface names	Component box, process box, subsystems boxes	
Deployment	Node symbol, communication relationship	Node name, stereotypes	Node symbol	Group nodes to show areas of responsibility or common physical locations

4.3   EXPLICIT ELISION

PROBLEM

A diagram becomes too cluttered with irrelevant attributes, properties, and relationships.

CONTEXT

Any UML diagram that provides focus.

FORCES

- Clutter confuses and obfuscates.
- A UML diagram must be clean and well organized.
- A UML diagram must present a key concept of a model.
- Detail not required to describe a concept must be omitted.
- Diagrams should have a balanced tension between elements included and excluded.
- As simple as possible, but no simpler.

SOLUTION

Intentionally omit attributes, operations, relationships, classes, components, or any UML element in a diagram when the element is not central to the design idea being presented. Where possible, indicate explicitly when any list of items is not complete.

In the UML, a model element does not have to be present in a diagram that graphically expresses a view of the model. This is called *elision*. Omitted elements are said to be elided.

Elision of an element in a diagram has no impact on its status in the model itself. For example, classes can be shown without their attribute and operation compartments without implying that those attributes and operations don't exist.

However, elision by itself can make understanding UML models tricky when you can't really be sure that any given diagram is displaying the entire picture. For that reason, use explicit elision. That is, clearly state that model elements have been omitted.

For example, use an ellipsis (" . . . ") to indicate when any list of items is not complete, as in an attribute compartment where only a subset of the attributes is presented. A UML *complete* constraint can also be attached to a group of elements (such as derived classes) to indicate that the classes shown (both in the model and diagram) comprise the total elements in the list. Finally, a note can be used where the ellipsis or complete constraint are inappropriate to indicate when the elements shown are complete or partial listings.

A different aspect of explicit elision is *detail appears once*. When you model something, put the detail in only one place, and then reference it in others. For example, if you chunk your static model into several diagrams, the complete class detail appears in only one diagram and is elided in the others. Otherwise, you end up with a maintenance headache, and your diagrams lack focus.

This becomes a real challenge when you capture different types of information in different tools, such as business rules in one tool (for example, a rules engine or other tool that can check consistency) and use cases referencing them in another (for example, a text editor). In this example, you elide the business rule references in the use cases by numbering them and/or giving them descriptive names to key them into the rules engine.

RESULTING CONTEXT

A UML diagram that contains only the elements that are absolutely essential to accurately present the concept behind the view.

DISCUSSION

As a rule, keep in mind that the number of assumptions that have to be made about the presence and absence of model elements in a diagram will raise the value of the content in a UML diagram. Deciding what to include and what to exclude in a given diagram is always difficult, but the following criteria can be used:

Include:
- Model elements that aid in describing the central concept conveyed in the diagram
- Elements in lists that should always be kept together (for example, the withdraw operation in the Account class shown in Figure 4.3 should not be included or excluded in a diagram without the deposit operation)
- Relevant context information such as packages, perspective descriptions, stereotypes, constraints, and tagged values

Exclude:
- Extraneous or unimportant details that, when left out, do not reduce the information value of the diagram
- Unnecessary dependency relationships, artifact traces, implementation detail, notes, generalization branches, subtypes, and non-elided forms (for example, interface class rectangles instead of interface lollipops)

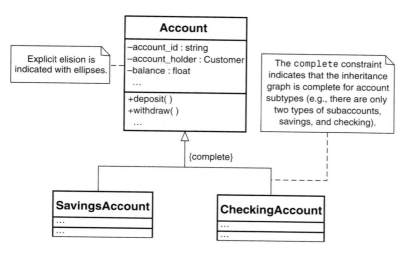

FIGURE 4.3 *Explicit elision makes the presence and absence of model elements clear to the diagram user.*

4.4   TREE ROUTING

PROBLEM

How to connect many similar UML relationships to a class in an efficient way.

CONTEXT

Modeling complex relationships of the same type in a static diagram.

FORCES

- Relationships that are related are fundamentally connected in the UML metamodel.
- Simpler, cleaner layouts create more lucid UML diagrams.
- Fewer lines are easier to distinguish visually.
- Overloaded relationship lines must make sense semantically.

SOLUTION

Roll UML relationships of the same type pointing to a class up into a single line (that is, establish a single point of contact with the target class). This is called *tree routing*. It is so named because the relationship lines branch out from the class in a central trunk line. It is especially appropriate for displaying aggregation and generalization relationships.

RESULTING CONTEXT

Controlled diagram clutter by means of space-efficient line routing.

DISCUSSION

With the exception of time-sequenced graphs, a UML diagram's layout generally has little or no semantic value. However, a lot of the communication value inherent in a UML diagram is still due to the layout skill of the modeler. This is particularly true when a large number of relationships must be drawn between the elements of a UML diagram.

Tree routing is the most efficient and cleanest-looking relationship line routing strategy that can be used in static diagrams. Not only does tree routing reduce the overall amount of diagram space and line complexity used, but it also provides a tremendous reduction in anchor space on the target class, especially in large inheritance hierarchies and complex aggregates (see Figure 4.4).

Tree routing has some basic requirements that must be met before it can be used, but they are easy to keep in mind:

- The relationships to be connected to a single trunk must be of the same type.
- Generalization and aggregation relationships form trees better than other UML relationship types, such as dependency and realization.
- Associations and aggregations must have the same multiplicity on the trunk end.

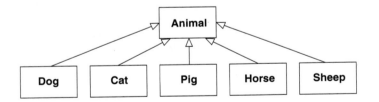

these generalization relationships can be represented
more clearly in tree form:

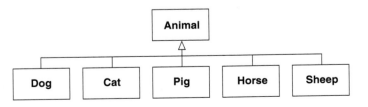

FIGURE 4.4 *The tree routing approach (bottom) often results in cleaner diagrams, especially as the number of relationships that must be connected to the class grows.*

4.5 TOMBSTONE PACKAGES

PROBLEM

The monotonous, minimally informative top-level package list, especially in models that are tool-generated; in particular, a row and column list of packages that is without any explanation of the relationships between them. Such listings (which look like rows of tombstones) often lack any explanation of (inter)dependencies, generalization, and traceability between packages, yet this is often where it's particularly needed—at the highest level of the model.

CONTEXT

At the system level (global model scope) or any package level diagram, where a non-trivial model will have the list of packages into which model elements are grouped.

FORCES

- Never waste an opportunity to specify relevant information in a model.
- Don't let tools make elision decisions.
- Always model relationships key to the diagram's purpose.
- Dense or repetitive diagrams reduce approachability.

SOLUTION

Create meaningful package diagrams that always have the relationships between them clearly stated. Be especially careful to model dependencies between packages. Layer the packages into tiers that reflect the architectural decisions made in the design of the system. This may be a three- or four-tier structure, or something altogether different, depending on the domain of the model (see Figure 4.5).

For models that separate specification and implementations, be sure to always place realization lines between the specification and the implementation. Packages can also inherit from each other. When this occurs, make sure the generalization relationship is always clearly visible in diagrams where the packages and their subpackages appear.

RESULTING CONTEXT

A diagram in which the packages are listed as well as the relationships between them, especially dependencies and generalizations. Trace relationships should be used in diagrams depicting the antecedent dependencies between packages.

DISCUSSION

Too often, especially in modeling-tool environments, automatically generated lists of packages are dumped in package class diagrams, and pages of unhelpful grids of packages are created. Typically, however, packages will have important relationships between them that should be documented. Package diagrams are important for conveying the relationships between the groups of elements in your models The savvy modeler is wise to avoid having tools draw diagrams that aren't then carefully examined and modified to suit the architecture's style, form, and usage rules.

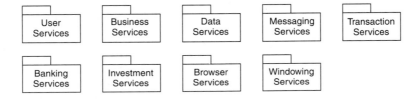

This Tombstone Package diagram can be turned into a more informative diagram by adding relevant relationships:

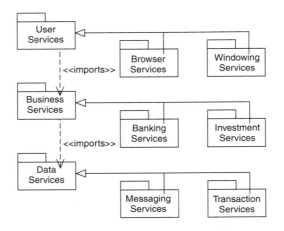

FIGURE 4.5 *These two diagrams show the vast difference between Tombstone Packages and a properly refactored package diagram.*

4.6   INHERITANCE GOES UP

PROBLEM

How to diagram the UML generalization relationship in an industry-wide, accepted way.

CONTEXT

UML use case and class diagrams that contain generalization relationships.

FORCES

- Adhering to well-known notational convention improves diagram readability.
- Limited diagram space imposes constraints on degrees of diagramming freedom.
- Standardized visual cues enhance readability and comprehension.

SOLUTION

The majority of all UML diagrams depict the generalization relationship with the more general element on top. Although exceptions can be found, the generalization arrow is expected to point toward the top of the page. So, wherever possible within the balance of forces, place the more general element above the more specific elements, and draw the generalization arrow between them. Less frequently, the generalization relationship may be seen as a horizontal line, especially when depicted as realization. Use it sparingly, however, to increase stylistic consistency. Refrain from placing the more general element under the more specific element.

RESULTING CONTEXT

A UML diagram that shows generalization with the arrow pointing above the horizontal line toward the more general element (see Figure 4.6).

DISCUSSION

- Generalization represents a relationship between the general and the more specific.
- The source of generalization is considered to have a higher level of abstraction.

Although conformity is not automatically a good thing, the upright generalization convention is one of the older ones in object-oriented modeling, and the tradition has carried through to UML in which the majority of generalization relationships are shown this way. Although the semantics of a diagram are unchanged by the application of this pattern, overall readability and usability are enhanced by its use.

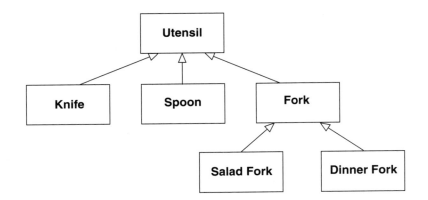

FIGURE 4.6 *The canonical diagrammatic form for the UML generalization relationship.*

4.7 ROTATED TEXT

PROBLEM

Large text labels, especially those attached to vertical and diagonal UML relationships paths, are cumbersome and waste space by sticking out horizontally.

CONTEXT

Any UML diagram element that requires a text label.

FORCES

- Limited diagram space imposes constraints on degrees of diagramming freedom.
- UML diagrams must convey meaning simply and clearly.
- Simpler, cleaner layouts create more lucid UML diagrams.
- Clutter confuses and obfuscates.
- Sideways text (especially a lot of it) is harder to read than horizontal text.

SOLUTION

Rotate text 45 or 90 degrees so that it is aligned along the relationship line or model element near which space must be conserved. Be sure to orient all vertical text labels in the diagram in the same direction. Diagonal text labels can follow the diagonal line unless they line is very steep.

RESULTING CONTEXT

A UML diagram in which the text labels are oriented in the same direction as the long side of the model element to which they are attached (see Figure 4.7).

DISCUSSION

A vertical line with a horizontal text label, especially a long one, creates a layout problem because the label will spill over in either direction, waste valuable diagram space, and appear visually ungainly. Although many modeling tools may not provide this option, rotating the text 90 degrees solves the layout problem with a slight risk of making the diagram a bit harder to read. The result, however, is simpler and cleaner than having wide text labels protruding from vertical relationship lines and model elements.

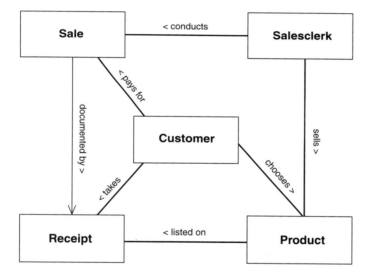

FIGURE 4.7 *Sideways text can help modelers use space far more efficiently. Note that the text label on the association between Sale and Receipt is far more compact than a horizontal label would allow.*

4.8 DUAL ASSOCIATIONS

PROBLEM

Association relationships can become visually and semantically overloaded with adornments such as multiplicity, role names, association names, reading direction arrows, association class attachments, and so on.

CONTEXT

A complex bi-directional association depicted in a UML class diagram.

FORCES

- Limited diagram space imposes constraints on degrees of diagramming freedom.
- Excessive detail obscures meaning.
- UML diagrams must convey meaning simply and clearly.
- Simpler, cleaner layouts create more lucid UML diagrams.
- Fewer lines are easier to distinguish visually.
- Overloaded relationship lines must make sense semantically.

SOLUTION

Split the association into two one-way associations. Make sure that the multiplicities match. Use the duplicate space provided by the additional association line to attach an extra reading direction text and arrow, connect an additional association class, add constraints and stereotypes, and connect the two association with a shared association class.

RESULTING CONTEXT

Two one-way association relationships in the place of a single bi-directional association (see Figure 4.8).

DISCUSSION

As long as some care is taken, two one-way associations can be equivalent to a single bi-directional association—but with twice the path and adornment space. This provides extra room for the modeler to attach necessary adornments that would not be easy or even possible when using a single association. The semantics of the two one-way associations can also express a richer set of meanings than a single relationship, such as allowing a constraint to be attached in one direction only. Although care must be exercised to ensure that the resulting associations are not confusing to the reader, the dual association is a powerful stylistic technique that can express important details that add otherwise difficult to express semantics to a model.

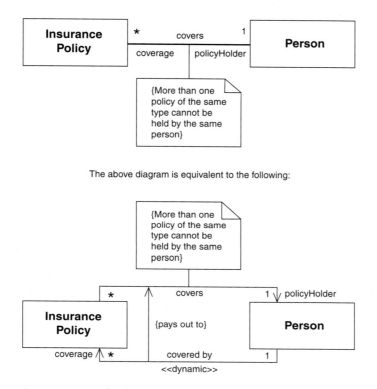

The above diagram is equivalent to the following:

FIGURE 4.8 *The diagram on the bottom shows how the Dual Association pattern can be used to supply extra adornment space and semantic control over the association between Insurance Policy and Person.*

4.9   BILLBOARD PACKAGES

PROBLEM

Providing context for use cases and classes in a UML diagram, especially as they relate to development phase, perspective, and view.

CONTEXT

UML use case and class diagrams in general.

FORCES

- Excessive detail obscures meaning.
- UML diagrams must convey meaning simply and clearly.
- Context cues orient diagram users.

SOLUTION

Physically display the use cases and classes within the packages they come from, especially when the use cases and classes are imported. Be sure to display the full package names and other context information such as package stereotypes. Always model relationships keyed to the diagram's purpose.

RESULTING CONTEXT

UML use case and class diagrams in which context is provided by the display packages that wrap external (to the native package) use cases and classes.

DISCUSSION

Packages are a management and grouping mechanism that provides a powerful way to structure models. Packages can be used to create collections of related model elements by using any criteria the modeler requires, such as development phase, abstraction, view, model type, and so on. Consequently, packages describe important context information about the model elements that they contain by virtue of the semantics that have been applied to the package (usually through stereotypes such as <<use case model>>, <<analysis>>, and so on).

One concern that Billboard Packages help with is *traceability*—showing how model elements are propagated through the various stages of development and associated models. However, traceability is allowed only between model elements in different packages; this is where Billboard Packages are effective. By placing use cases and classes within elided package icons along with their stereotype, Billboard Packages can offer important context cues to the diagram user. This helps the user understand the element's relation to the diagram and even to the rest of the model (see Figure 4.9). Note that the presence of the Inventory Control Billboard Package supplies crucial context information, such as which version of the types are being realized.

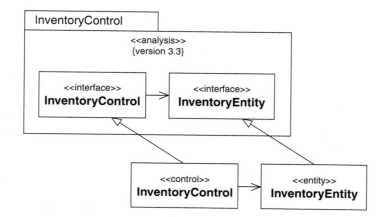

FIGURE 4.9 *This class diagram shows how control and entity class can realize interfaces defined in an analysis model kept in a separate package.*

4.10 TEXT WORKAROUNDS

PROBLEM

Many of the notations in the UML are not directly supported by all the environments in which diagrams have to be viewed. Nevertheless, for these media (such as e-mail, simple drawing tools, and HTML, to name a few) the diagrams must still be rendered in a way that is understandable without significant interpretation.

CONTEXT

Viewing UML diagrams in environments that do not directly support UML's notational constructs, including lines, rectangles, diamonds, arrows, guillemets, and so on.

FORCES

- UML diagrams must convey meaning simply and clearly.
- Simpler, cleaner layouts create more lucid UML diagrams.
- Fewer lines are easier to distinguish visually.
- Standard visual conventions are easily understood.
- Obscure conventions and unusual layout in diagrams are more difficult to understand.
- Standards, clarity, and usability are driving forces for integrating work and group collaboration.

SOLUTION

Use textual substitutions for UML model elements wherever possible (see Table 4.2). Adhere to symbols available in ASCII; and construct the boxes, lines, arrows, and other model elements using collections of ASCII characters. Use a monospace font if available, try to control the word wrapping in the hosting environment by using carriage returns, and use smaller fonts to keep as much of the diagram onscreen as possible.

TABLE 4.2 AN INFORMAL SET OF RULES FOR DISPLAYING UML MODELS IN ASCII

UML Notation	Horizontal	Vertical
Class, package, state, note, and so on	Use or (|) and hyphen (-) symbols to construct box. Use slash (/) to add depth.	N/A

	`-----------------------`
	`|                     |`
	`|      Person      |`
	`-----------------------`	

Association, composition, aggregation	Use less than and greater than (< and >) for aggregation and composition, as well as the arrow. Use pound (#) to fill in the aggregation diamond.	Use the caret (^) and capital V to draw the aggregation symbol.

	`<>-------------------->`
	`<-----------------<#>`
		`^ ^`
		`| V`
		`| |`
		`^ |`
		`# |`
		`V V`

UML Notation	Horizontal	Vertical

Generalization and realizaton	Use the hyphen, or (|), less than, and greater than to draw generalization. Insert a space between each hyphen for realization.
	
	`-------------------- | >`
	
	`< | --------------------`
		Use the hyphen, V, or (|), and caret to draw generalization. Insert a space between each hyphen for realization.
		
		`^  |`
		`-  |`
		`|  |`
		`|  |`
		`|  |`
		`|  -`
		`#  |`
		`|  V`

Dependency	Use the hyphen, less than, and greater than to draw dependency. Insert a space between each hyphen to create the dotted line.
	
	`- - - - - - - - - - - - ->`
	
	`<- - - - - - - - - - - -`
		Use the or (|), less than, and greater than to draw dependency. Insert a space between each hyphen to create the dotted line.
		
		`^  |`
		`|`
		`|`
		`|`
		`|`
		`|`
		`| V`

RESULTING CONTEXT   A usable UML diagram in an environment that does not support UML graphics directly.

4.11   SEVEN PLUS OR MINUS TWO

PROBLEM

How to make diagrams that can be grasped easily.

CONTEXT

Building diagrams that are themselves part of an overall model. In this case, you are specifically concerned with software models, but the pattern could apply to any type of potentially complex model using standardized modeling elements and syntax.

FORCES

- Models are made up of diagrams.
- Diagrams have to communicate useful views of the real world.
- A model must be comprehensive but focused.
- The real world can be complex, messy, and unfocused.
- Diagrams are not inherently limited in the number of elements they can contain.
- Human understanding of diagrams is constrained by the limits of human cognitive capabilities, such as short-term memory.

SOLUTION

Limit the number of elements in any given diagram to the magic number of seven, give or take two elements. These elements should be logically related; the diagram structure should express a sensible pattern connecting the diagram elements.

RESULTING CONTEXT

Diagrams that are easy to understand at a glance and able to be organized in a logical fashion into more complex models.

DISCUSSION

Humans have limited cognitive resources. That is, they can attend to only so many things and perform so many activities at one time. Too many elements in a diagram can be confusing and are hard to retain in short-term memory all at once. This pattern provides a simple way of ensuring that the number of elements is reasonable for most people. The related pattern called Digestible Chunks (see Chapter 5, "Patterns of Substance") explains how and why the process of decomposing a model into logical diagrams works.

Summary

By any estimation, these patterns don't represent a complete canon of style for the UML. And, being patterns, they shouldn't be considered prescriptive. Rather, they give the modeler a core of proven, broadly applicable UML diagramming techniques. The modeler can use these as a starting point for a personal modeling style, or within an organization or project as part of an overall architectural style. In a development project, style shouldn't normally be a matter of personal choice; instead it should be a project level or organizational decision. However, any standardized style should address the problems that these patterns tackle.

The architectural style for a system provides the basis for a design dialect that will be the common vocabulary for the development effort. Jacobson, Griss, and Jonsson describe architectural style as "the set of all (good) models that can be built" (1997, 51). D'Souza and Wills provide a separate package for containing the rules and "rules-of-thumb" that combine to provide an architectural style (1998).

For a more detailed discussion of some of these points, see Chapter 10, "The UML in Context."

CHAPTER 5

Patterns of Substance

Catalogue

Context

Models have a usefulness and meaning that derive from the way they are constructed, not just from the content. A modeling language must go beyond the expressive capabilities and formal rules provided by its structure and conventions. Patterns of substance are concerned with model meaning and shape—about how to be correct when using the UML in a creative way. They describe how to ensure that your UML models are valid, efficiently expressive, useful, and meaningful. They should provide information in an appropriate form, not just empty graphical rhetoric or confusing symbolic bombast.

Just as speaking correctly means more than following the rules of grammar, using the UML (or any modeling language) requires a creativity that must itself be correct. However, creativity is constrained but not usually in any ways that are obvious. Patterns provide a way of explaining how to be correctly creative.

This chapter harnesses the power of modeling idioms and heuristics to provide a starting point. Patterns of substance describe the informal and practical possibilities of representing useful information with the UML. They extend the rules rationalizing the use of the UML.

Common Forces

Modeling constructs should not get in the way of the modeling process. They should be as nearly intuitive as possible, easy to use for the modeler, and easy to understand for the reader. *But* the selection of constructs shapes the way you can know the problem and the possibilities for solutions (transparency).

The map is not the territory. But meaning happens in context and requires semantic consistency between the map and the territory (external consistency).

Symbols are expressions of model elements. Model elements are categorized by the UML into coherent semantic domains (for example, Static and Dynamic). Symbol combinations need to respect these semantic divisions. At the same time, modeling is a creative exercise, and the UML's categories and distinctions may need adjustment (internal coherence).

The language of design needs to be standard and adaptable at the same time; local dialects materialize inevitably as a result of gaps between established standards and the immediate needs of a design effort (dialectical materialism).

80 percent of the utility of a modeling language comes from 20 percent of the constructs; however, the constructs that fall within the most useful 20 percent vary from development effort to development effort (the 80/20 rule).

Discussion

The models you choose to make shape the worldview you have of the problem space and the solution. Models, like technology, are never neutral. The best models simplify a reality, but the reality they model is itself constructed and part of a worldview (situated simplicity).

5.1 STANDARD DIAGRAMS

PROBLEM

How to organize the presentation of model information to minimize overhead and maximize transparency.

CONTEXT

Building models with the UML.

FORCES

- Diagrams represent views of a model that should be semantically meaningful to the viewer; that is, both internally and externally consistent (the information represented fits both the problem and solution) and fitted to the viewpoint of the viewer).
- A literate model viewer will have expectations from experience about how common semantic domains should be represented. When looking at a diagram, an immature model user needs as much help as possible in understanding.
- Information representation, which crosses semantic categories, can be confusing and difficult to interpret.
- Only a subset of UML elements is needed in a typical project.

SOLUTION

Combine the graphical elements available in the UML into a limited and repeatable set of semantically meaningful diagram types. These types should represent categories of information that are useful to the viewer. In general, rather than inventing your own diagram types, stick with the standard diagram types that are explicitly supported by the UML (as described in Chapter 3, "UML Essentials, Elements, and Artifacts").

RESULTING CONTEXT

Shareable diagrams that rely on conventions to provide a significant amount of meaning.

DISCUSSION

In the UML, any combination of presentation elements is permitted—there are no limits to which graphical components of the UML may be combined in a diagram, and diagram meaning is mainly provided by semantics.

Diagrams organize information within a semantic domain and within a model, and so they must be internally consistent (with all elements representing the same type of information) and consistent with the scope of the semantic domain.

5.2   IMPLEMENTATION OR REPRESENTATION

PROBLEM

Modeling in a purposeful and focused way.

CONTEXT

The modeling activity in general, but especially the early stages of a project, during conceptualization and analysis.

FORCES

- The model *is* the documentation.
- If it isn't written down, it doesn't exist.
- Analysis isn't programming.
- Many aspects of models don't translate directly into a programming construct.
- A variety of audiences and views.
- A variety of purposes.
- A sketch isn't a blueprint, and neither is a specification.

SOLUTION

Distinguish between *implementation models* and *representation models* when doing modeling. In particular, distinguish between models that are meant to document your understanding of the domain (representation models) and those that are closer to blueprints—plans for the solution (implementation models). For each model that you build, determine who the audience is and what purpose it will serve.

Although it is no longer expected that the problem space and the solution space will be kept hermetically separated during development (and addressed sequentially), it is still important to avoid adding implementation details in too early or inappropriately. It is also important to stay aware that programming languages usually don't have the flexibility or the constructs needed to translate a model directly into code.

RESULTING CONTEXT

Focused models that reflect their audience and intended use.

DISCUSSION

As object-oriented approaches have matured, they have been increasingly applied to areas of systems development other than design and construction. In particular, they are being used for analysis and specification, modeling domains and business areas, organizing requirements, and describing business processes. Although many object concepts overlap between the needs of representation and implementation, some (such as modularity) may not (Parsons and Wand, 1997).

5.3   DIGESTIBLE CHUNKS

PROBLEM

How to make models that work.

CONTEXT

Building models that reflect the way people's brains and perceptive faculties work.

FORCES

- UML models must convey meaning simply and clearly.
- A model must be comprehensive but focused.
- Models are made up of one or more connected diagrams that have to be organized.
- The real world can be complex, messy, and unfocused.
- Models have to communicate useful views of the real world.
- Human understanding of diagrams and models is constrained by the limits of human cognitive capabilities, such as short-term memory.
- Human ability to organize models is constrained by the limits of human cognitive capabilities.

SOLUTION

Leverage the cognitive limitations of human perception and memory in building models. Instead of building models that include everything but the kitchen sink (and maybe even that), chunk your models into diagrams. They should be digestible bits that are individually meaningful and connected in a sensible fashion. A related pattern that is useful in figuring out how to build these digestible bits is, of course, Seven Plus or Minus Two.

RESULTING CONTEXT

Individual models that are easier to understand and manage mentally.

DISCUSSION

A variety of research over the last 20 years or so has indicated that there are definite cognitive patterns that constrain what we can understand and assimilate. These patterns seem to be there because we humans are natural pattern-building creatures, and without the limits suggested by cognitive patterns, we would be hamstrung by excessive and faulty pattern-recognition. So, rather than limits to human capability, cognitive patterns are a means to leverage the human predilection and capability for pattern making.

5.4   ATTACH THE ACTOR

PROBLEM

Clearly identifying the end-user roles to which a class or component in a system is responsible for providing services.

CONTEXT

Any portion of use-case driven model, especially implementation models (in which use case traceability is particularly lacking).

FORCES

- Use cases must be visible through all stages of development.
- All models must trace back to the original use cases.
- Models should identify the users to which they provide services (satisfy requirements).
- Role identities must be specified in models to maintain role traceability, control of scope, and appropriately partitioned architecture.
- Who is satisfied by a requirement is nearly as important as the requirement itself.
- Roles generate requirements.
- Actors hold use cases implementers accountable.

SOLUTION

Given a system element (a class, object, component, state machine, interaction, node, and so on) in a UML model, attach the actor(s) for which it will be used to satisfy the use cases the actor is involved in.

Figure 5.1 is the example of a simple graphic deployment diagram from Chapter 4,"Patterns of Style," augmented with appropriate actors. (They could be graphical icons instead of stick figures!)

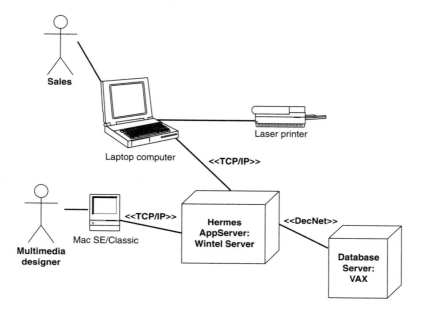

FIGURE 5.1   *Actors in deployment.*

DISCUSSION

By systematically attaching the actor to the system elements that are responsible for realizing the use case, the model will be able to directly identify the end-users to which they are accountable.

5.5 BUSINESS RULES INVARIABLY CONSTRAIN

PROBLEM

Where can a UML model hold the business rules that guide system operation? Specifically, how can rules that describe fundamental knowledge in the domain be explicitly documented?

CONTEXT

UML analysis and design models in which the modeler has significant information about the domain itself that cannot be modeled using standard UML model elements.

FORCES

- Basic UML constructs (classes, associations, and dependencies) are unable to capture business rules.
- Business rules can be formulated as declarative statements; that is, as formalized statements of what is to be done rather than as procedural algorithms.
- Complete models include business rules.

SOLUTION

Use UML constraints to describe conditions and limits between model elements that represent aspects of your application domain. For each business rule discovered during analysis and design, a declarative constraint should be attached to the model elements involved in the rule. The constraint must describe the rule in terms of a statement that is always true.

Figure 5.2 shows a typical example of how a constraint can be used to capture a business rule. The diagram shown contains a single class, Account, which represents a bank account in the problem domain. Business rules are captured during the course of the development process, perhaps as a result of the alternate flow of a use case or specification document. In this example, it says that the Overdrawn attribute in the Account class must be set to true if the balance in the account falls below zero.

The constraint that describes this business rule is shown as a UML note (rectangle with bent corner) that is attached through a dotted line to the Account class. When the system is implemented, the constraint can be realized as an invariant or other enforcement mechanism. The UML specification recommends (but does not require) that the constraint be defined in terms of the Object Constraint Language. The constraint can alternatively be defined in terms of the underlying implementation language, although is discouraged for reasons of clarity and portability.

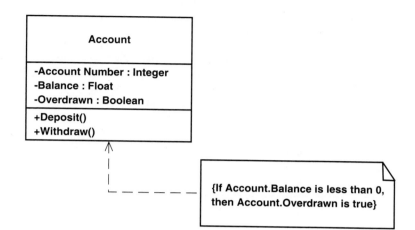

FIGURE 5.2 *Attaching business rules.*

RESULTING CONTEXT
UML analysis and design models where business rules are modeled in a consistent and accessible manner.

DISCUSSION
Constraints are relationships between modeling elements that must always be true for the duration of system operation. Because constraints describe true/false relationships, they allow a means for specifying and controlling, in a deterministic fashion, the runtime semantics of systems. Because UML constraints map right into implementation artifacts, typically programming code, they can be used to verify whether the system complies with the business rules defined during the design phase.

5.6 DYNAMIC OBJECT TYPES

PROBLEM
An object must change types by representing different but similar things at different times.

CONTEXT
Modeling any object whose role in a system changes over time.

FORCES
- Static types create rigidity and make systems brittle.
- Dynamic multiple classification is difficult to implement.
- Dynamically classifying classes reflects real-world domain roles more accurately.
- Dynamic classification works best for conceptual models.
- Static classification is ideally suited for implementation models.

SOLUTION

Enumerate the different types that the object can assume by using the generalization relationship, and then specify the overlapping constraint provided by the UML to describe that the object's type can vary during system operation. See Figure 5.3, in which an "overlapping" constraint implies that an object can change its type during its lifetime.

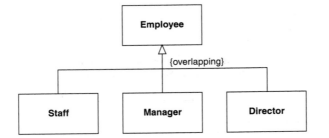

FIGURE 5.3 *An employee can change type over time.*

RESULTING CONTEXT

A description of the object that accurately reflects the different types the object can assume.

DISCUSSION

Both Fowler and Odell have made much of the dynamic classification issue, which surfaces time and again in conceptual models, but has poor support in most object-oriented programming languages (OOPLs). This disconnect has ramifications for many modelers because OOPLs have a tendency to impose their semantic limitations on the resulting implementation models.

Practically speaking, most programming languages can't support anything other than static classification: an object and its type have a one-to-one mapping. However, in reality the semantics of the domain may require that an object (such as a person object) have multiple types over time (for example, student, resident, and doctor). Therefore, semantically, although the entity stays the same over time but may have different behaviors and even different interfaces, the UML provides a mechanism for describing such behavior using a predefined constraint on the generalization relationship.

5.7 MANY-TO-MANY CLASS TRIO

PROBLEM

How to model the relationship between two classes that have a many-to-many association with each other.

CONTEXT

Modeling classes using the UML during system design.

FORCES

- Many-to-many relationships occur often in the real world.
- It can be difficult to implement many-to-many associations in some object-oriented programming languages.
- Many-to-many relationships have no direct implementation in relational database systems in which they may have to be persisted.
- Direct many-to-many associations between classes can't describe anything more meaningful than a reference to another class: associations don't have attributes or behavior.
- Occam's Razor.
- A many-to-many relationship is usually complicated enough to warrant the support of a full class to capture the semantics.

SOLUTION

Transform the many-to-many association between two classes into a trio of classes by creating an intermediary class with two one-to-many relationships (see Figure 5.4). The name of the intermediary class should describe the type of relationship being captured.

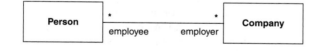

is equivalent to

FIGURE 5.4 *Modeling a many-to-many association.*

RESULTING CONTEXT

A UML model with two classes linked by an intermediary class that has a one-to-many relationship to each of the first two classes. The resulting trio of classes will match the relational model, be easier to implement, and provide a richer way to capture the details of the relationship.

DISCUSSION

Many-to-many relationships look deceptively simple to the modeler and even seem to make intuitive sense: Many people can have accounts at many banks and many Web pages can be stored on many computers. Not only does an intermediary class provide additional flexibility in representing the many-to-many relationship faithfully, but also the construct is better supported by many implementing technologies. And a complicated many-to-many relationship usually warrants the support of a full class to capture the semantics.

This is an old and hoary concern of modelers since at least the dawn of relational modeling. Fortunately, the solution that makes sense in an object-oriented environment is also the proven one that worked in the relational world. So, the proven solution provides a convenient bridge between the modeling technologies as well as pointing to an implementation approach that has demonstrated effectiveness.

The Many-To-Many Class Trio solution relies on the fact that the many-to-many relationship between two classes is logically equivalent to having an intermediary class with a one-to-many association going to each of the two primary classes. The intermediary class provides many advantages in elaborating and managing a many-to-many relationship: An intermediary object exists for each association between the two primary classes.

This allows attributes and methods to be added to the relationship, such as a date range to the Employment class in the previous example. The multiplicity can be tweaked on either side of the intermediary class to more precisely define the exact nature of the relationship. For example, the multiplicities on the left side of the Employment class in the example could be changed from many-to-one to many-to-one to reflect the fact that a person many be unemployed or have only a single job at a time. The intermediary class is often better than using an association class to solve the many-to-many problem because it permits a greater level of control over the multiplicities, and the intermediary class does not constrain the number of instances of the same association between classes like the association class does.

5.8   MODEL THE SEAMS

PROBLEM

How to identify and document the "seams" or boundaries between independent components in a system.

CONTEXT

A model of a component-based system.

FORCES

- Interface boundaries form the seams of a system.
- Well-defined interface dependencies provide insight and control over a system.
- Both interface imports and exports comprise a component's dependencies.
- Incomplete interface models reduce plugability.

SOLUTION

Identify and model the interface dependencies in the system. The classes and components that are tightly coupled when compared to other groups of classes and components are good candidates. In general, the seams between the components of a system can be found and modeled by identifying all the interfaces they expose and the interfaces they use.

For each class or component, clearly identify the interfaces it uses (imports) and the interfaces it provides to others (exports). Model the interfaces imported using the dependency relationship and the exporting of interfaces using the realization relationship. The UML interface notation (the lollipop icon) is equivalent to the dependency relationship on an interface-stereotyped class. See Figure 5.5, which shows a stock trader component with the interface that it provides and the interfaces that it is dependent on.

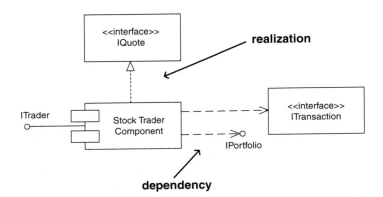

FIGURE 5.5 *Clearly identified seams.*

RESULTING CONTEXT

A component-based system model that has clearly identified "seams" around the components, using dependency and realization relationships between the interfaces. By using Model the Seams, the key aspects of component-based development are sustained, including plugable reuse, interoperability standardization, and the enforcement of independent units of configuration control.

DISCUSSION

Any non-trivial software is a maze of classes, components, and UML relationships. In a component-based development environment, the advantages of components are lost when the boundaries between components are blurred and the relationships between them imprecisely specified. By modeling the seams between the components that collaborate together to create a system, the modeler keeps the identities and semantics of the components in sharp relief. This emphasis on boundary is a reflection of a central theme in component-based development: interface/implementation separation.

The overriding goal in Model the Seams is to identify the components on both sides of an interface. By doing this, the modeler completely decouples the component, thereby providing a complete conception of how to provide support for the component (in terms of the interfaces it requires) or even to completely replace the component.

5.9 PACKAGING PARTITIONS

PROBLEM

Organizing the elements of a UML model based on a common guiding principle.

CONTEXT

The model of a distributed software system based on a multi-tiered architecture that divides the responsibilities of the system into distributed partitions.

FORCES

- Partitioning must be enforced by the model.
- Distributed systems must be clearly and crisply partitioned.
- The organization of systems is driven by their predominant architectural structure.
- Insufficient visual emphasis on key details can cause loss of design balance.
- UML diagrams must convey meaning simply and clearly.
- UML models can be organized using a variety of effective methods.

SOLUTION

One package per tier or partition; that is, organize the model elements of the distributed system by providing packages for each major partition or tier in the system. The packages are linked by defined dependency relationships between elements that communicate across the partition boundaries. For example, a common partitioning scheme for tiered systems is to isolate the presentation services (user interface tier) from the application logic (business service tier) and to keep access of information in a third tier (data service tier). Figure 5.6 shows one possible way to organize these three partitions using UML packages.

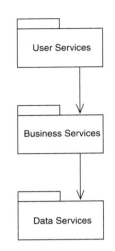

F I G U R E 5.6 *Modeling elements into partition packages.*

RESULTING CONTEXT

A UML model that reflects the logical or physical distributed structure of the system.

DISCUSSION

The notion of packages in UML is purely organizational; a package itself is not directly realized in the implementation. By using packages to enforce multi-tier architecture, however, a model enforces system partitioning by preventing elements in different partitions from intermixing in ways they shouldn't. Using partitions-as-packages to organize the elements of a distributed system encourages loose coupling, reinforcing the distributed nature of the system.

Care should be taken to organize package elements into partitions so that visibility (via dependency relationships) is carefully exposed while unnecessary implementation detail is hidden from other partitions.

Typically, each partition is constructed as a separate unit for configuration and construction purposes. Each *partition package* can vary independently, and it can be checked in and out of the model independently by each team responsible for it.

5.10   LET THE TOOLS DO THE WORK

PROBLEM

A modeler can easily be overwhelmed by the detail and prevented from focusing on the job at hand. How can this be resolved?

CONTEXT

Creating models using a software tool.

FORCES

- Tools constrain models based on what they know about the UML.
- Excessive detail obscures meaning.
- Lack of model enforcement leads to inaccurate and out-of-sync models.
- Increasing the modeler's time on essential activities is valuable.
- Creating and parameterizing automated model tasks is time-consuming and expensive.

SOLUTION

Always let the tool do as much of the UML modeling work as possible. Rely on the tool for routine and repetitive tasks. However, don't let the tool perform a particular modeling task if the results are poor or if more rework has to be done than would result by doing it by hand.

As a rule of thumb, and if your modeling tool supports it, always let the tool do the following work, as outlined in Table 5.1.

TABLE 5.1 MODELING TOOLS

Type	Description
Model enforcement	Element renaming and deleting, element search (and replace), and completeness checking. Example: Using the tool to rename a class and having it change in every diagram in which the class appears. Anti-example: Changing the name of a package and then having to visit each package, importing it and manually changing the reference.
UML enforcement	Making sure that the model adheres to the UML meta-model is the one key role of a good modeling tool. Checking that a model is expressed in proper UML is a continuous validation process performed by the modeling tool. Example: Making sure that a class doesn't inherit from itself or that the same identifier doesn't appear more than once in the same namespace.

continues

TABLE 5.1 Continued

Type	Description
Code generation	Realizing the model into executable code. Example: Converting a design model into Java by using information stored in tagged values associated with each design model element.
Reverse engineering	Converting program source code into a UML model. Example: Taking the source code for a component written in C++ and generating a UML model that reflects the structure of the component.
Configuration management	Keeping track of the changes and releases of a UML model. Example: A tool supporting configuration management allows the changes made by multiple modelers to be reconciled and merged into a single change and checked back in to the model.
Wizards	These are interactive guided tasks through which the tool assists the modeler in a standardized repetitive task by doing most of the tedious work automatically. Example: A wizard that guides the modeler through the process of making a UML class adhere to a component standard, such as COM or CORBA.
Scripting	Tasks that are repetitive but time-consuming should be codified into scripts that can perform the work automatically and quickly. Parameters can be passed to the scripts to direct the work. In general, any recurring task that occurs on a weekly basis or more frequently and takes longer than 5–10 minutes is a good candidate for scripting.
Modeling "helpers"	Automated routines that help the modeler work more quickly and accurately. They include element name auto-completion when typing, diagram auto-arrangement, hierarchical model browsers, model element drag and drop, and so on. Example: when dragging a class onto a diagram that contains another class that already has a relationship with the first, a good modeling tool will ask whether the pre-existing relationships should be shown or elided.

RESULTING CONTEXT

A modeling environment that capitalizes on the modeler's unique capabilities by reducing the amount of time spend on menial and repetitive tasks.

DISCUSSION

Creating and managing UML models involves managing a large number of factors simultaneously: checking the UML syntax, adhering to modeling rules, following internal and external modeling standards, enforcing the semantics of the model itself, and so on.

Managing the model minutiae and helping the modeler perform routine tasks is one essential role of a good tool. The amount of manual work required to manage a non-trivial model is very considerable and is in direct proportion to the size of the model. The larger a model is, the larger the web of interdependencies that will complicate manageability. By letting the modeler focus on key issues that only he can resolve, the tool can relieve its user from the cost of dealing with issues that can be taken care of by the tool itself. The tool can also perform many other tasks through scripts that would normally cut into the modeler's valuable time.

5.11 OPAQUE PACKAGES

PROBLEM

How can the modeler ensure that clients will reference elements inside a package appropriately? How is loose-coupling through well-defined interfaces best achieved? And most importantly, how can this information be communicated via UML as well as enforced in practice?

CONTEXT

A UML model consisting of services decomposed into packages.

FORCES

- Dependency reduction promotes loose coupling and increases plugability.
- Increasing package count increases the number of dependencies.
- Dependencies within packages increase with the number of elements contained.
- Gateways or facades reduce dependency by providing replace multiple dependencies with one.

SOLUTION

Make packages as opaque as possible by reducing the visibility of members of the package to private or protected. Make only essential elements public such as interfaces, facades, bridges, proxies, and so on. When displaying packages icons in diagrams, be sure to consistently display only the public elements inside them. This will uniformly communicate a clear sense of what is directly usable in the package and what is hidden implementation information. If protected or private elements must be shown, use a color/shading scheme for the package elements that shows what is visible and what isn't. Figure 5.7 shows a package containing public and private elements that use a color scheme. The shading shows which classes are not visible externally to the package. Order Processing is able to depend on the Customer package only through the Customer class.

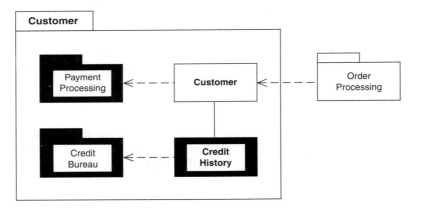

FIGURE 5.7 *An opaque package with its single publicly exported class: Customer.*

RESULTING CONTEXT

A UML model with packages whose contents are largely opaque to the result of the model. Only the elements designed to interact with the rest of the model will be designated as publicly accessible.

DISCUSSION

The indiscriminant importing of package elements creates unwanted dependencies and tight coupling. Package access control is one of the key mechanisms provided by the UML for controlling dependencies between elements. Anything made private within a package cannot be referenced outside of it, even if the package is imported.

Two key factors must be present to ensure that opaque packages are successful in controlling dependencies:

- The clear communication in the model of what is visible and what is not. This is done visually by physically placing the public elements (and only the public elements) within the package icon. This reinforces for the model user what they can legitimately expect to depend upon and what implementation details they would be wise to avoid.

- The actual enforcement of access via the modeling tool, the underlying language, or both—without a means for actually causing inappropriate dependencies to fail. There is no real penalty in the immediate sense to prevent someone from circumventing the opacity of a package and using protected or private elements. By explicitly designating the export visibility of package elements, both in the model and in an object-oriented language, the violator of the export rules will be physically prevented from breaking the dependency constraints specified by the modeler. Although most UML modeling tools provide a means for checking access violations, it is only in the visibility language constructs of object-oriented languages that the compilation of programs containing invalid dependencies will reliability be prevented.

Summary

The patterns in this chapter help you make effective use of the UML in building and managing models. Like those in Chapter 4, "Patterns of Style," they're modeling idioms, lower-level patterns that are specifically about the details of modeling. Most of them can be applied to many types of diagrams, in all kinds of modeling situations. They're general solutions to modeling problems with a specific UML flavor.

As you create your own local dialect of the UML within your organization, additional and more local idioms may become obvious. These should be documented and reviewed over time, becoming part of the vocabulary of the development process itself. Some of these patterns may even replace or refine the ones in this book.

This chapter and Chapter 4 are just a sampling of the modeling idioms that are embedded in the UML itself, or the better books written about it. Particularly good sources are *Objects, Components, and Frameworks with UML: The Catalysis Approach* by Desmond D'Souza and Alan Wills (1998); and *The Unified Modeling Language User Guide* by Ivar Jacobson, Grady Booch, and James Rumbaugh (1998a). D'Souza and Wills provide good material on documentation in general, which is worth consulting for a different look at how models should be managed. *The UML User Guide* has tips about solutions to standard modeling problems that in many cases lend themselves to being generalized as patterns.

The patterns in the following chapters are usually not idioms. They're concerned with applying the UML in constructing system models at various levels. The patterns in the last two chapters should be kept in mind when considering the use of these patterns.

CHAPTER 6

Domain Patterns

Catalogue

Context

Domains are the highest level of this pattern language. They correspond to the enterprise or business view of the problem space that used to be the starting point for analysis. However, rather than being bounded by the formal limits of an organization, domains are flexibly and practically defined.

For my purpose, they are an *area of interest* (a typical dictionary definition of *domain*) with the following:

- A shared vocabulary of business abstractions (events, concepts, and things)

- A common set of needs that can be addressed by a family of applications

Domains also provide the context and organizing structure for the models of those applications; the models that are used in guiding their design, implementation, and management.

A domain defines the context and environment for understanding the common needs that drive the development of a set of software products. It identifies the problems that are legitimate and that are solvable within the specific scope of those needs.

Domains are the starting point for serious modeling that will lead to real, substantial software. There are two types of domain that are of interest to a software developer:

- *Business domains*: Areas of interest to the business, containing *fundamental business abstractions* that are the ideas, the entities, and the events that package business services in a way that is meaningful to the business

- *Technical domain*: The infrastructure, technology vision, and technological constraints that must be respected

Common Forces

- A business domain must be a meaningful chunk of business reality to its end users.

- A domain model must be capable of being directly validated and explained by its stakeholders.

- Users know what they do, but may not know what they know.

- Too much detail can be blinding.

- Users may not understand their environment or the direction they want to pursue.

- Domains are complex abstractions to technologists.

- A common language can help members of a group define a common vision.

- A common language can help members outside a group understand the common vision.

Discussion

Most information technologists use the word *domain* to mean an *identifiable family of applications*. More astute observers prefer to include the context in their definition; for example, Jim Coplien defines domain analysis as "the study of fundamental business abstractions" (1998a). For this book, a domain is *a packaging of business features and services at some level of abstraction that is meaningful to an organization*.

Most current writers who write about the domain-modeling view see domain models as glorified information models. To some extent, this reflects the marginal status of object-orientation until the last few years. Domain engineering (the source of domain modeling) emerged during the same period as object-orientation—in response to similar needs (reuse and structure), but following a different route.

A more up-to-date version of domain modeling would incorporate considerations of behavior and interaction. Ivar Jacobson, speaking for the Three Amigos in *The Unified Software Development Process*, suggests that a domain model that only includes the classes within an area of interest "is really just a special case of (a)...business model...developing a business model is a powerful alternative" (Jacobson, Booch, and Rumbaugh 1999a, 122).

I've taken the view that domain modeling is the activity of modeling a particular aspect of a business—one that uses all of the appropriate constructs available within the UML.

A domain does not have to be contained within an organization. In particular, with the emergence of the networked organization and such trends as cooperation, partnering, and data sharing among companies, the traditional boundaries of organizational interest are dissolving. In these circumstances, a domain can include the elements from a number of organizations, such as a supply chain.

One simplistic example of a domain from automobile distribution might be *Asset Lifecycle Management*. This is a package of features and services that support the relationship between a distributor and its dealers. A distributor makes the most profit from financing and from controlling *churn*: the reselling of the car throughout its life. Dealers, not car buyers, are the distributor's real customers, and so they are both the agents and the partners in maximizing profit. Distributors work with the dealers to provide them with services and supporting systems to retain control of each car as an *asset* for as much of its life as possible. Within this business domain, a variety of applications provides focused services—for example, leasing services and systems that maximize ongoing control of a vehicle during its lifecycle.

Domain models are essential for bounding a domain so that it is useful for software planning and management. Software developers model domains to provide the basis for a family of applications. A domain model captures and situates the set of high-level requirements that are common to applications within an identified area of interest. This area of interest may be as broad as an organization (hopefully not) or as narrow as a functional area. The model can include the following:

- A definition of scope for the domain

- Information or objects at the conceptual level

- Features or use cases, including factors that lead to variation—again, high-level and business-oriented

- Operational/behavioral characteristics

To be clear, modeling at this level is sufficiently conceptual so that the only end result of our efforts is models. But because these models provide the basis for understanding and using all the other development artifacts, it is especially critical to the value of our models at all levels.

Higher-level models built to support planning and management are where the new modeling approaches are most starkly different from the traditional ones. These obvious differences most clearly illuminate the maturing of our craft, especially in the areas of why we model and what we model.

6.1 DOMAIN MODEL IS ESSENTIAL

PROBLEM
How to model the important elements of a domain.

CONTEXT
Understanding and documenting the domain context for use in building or refactoring a system or organization.

FORCES
- A domain model must be capable of being directly validated and explained by the end users.
- Users know what they do, but may not know what they know.
- Too much detail can be blinding.
- Domain information is the critical context for design decisions.
- Design decisions must be traceable to the domain.

SOLUTION
Document the components of the domain with a minimum of implementation detail. Business activities should be documented with essential business use cases. These are, in effect, scripts that describe interactions with the business or organization in which actors play essential roles. Things and services in the real world are represented as essential business objects.

RESULTING CONTEXT
The essential activities, things, and services are identified, packaged, labeled, and agreed upon. They are made available in diagrammatic form that allows for further massaging as the overall domain model is refined.

DISCUSSION
McMenamin and Palmer (1984) introduced the idea of *essential models* back in the dying days of structured analysis. In order to reduce the complexity of the information generated when analyzing the need for a new system, an essential model would contain only elements that represented the ideal system, free of any implementation considerations. Recently, the notion of essential models has been revived by writers such as Larry Constantine (who helped develop the idea in the first place). His idea of essential use cases is championed by Jacobson and others (Jacobson, Booch, and Rumbaugh 1999).

6.2 ACTORS PLAY ESSENTIAL ROLES

PROBLEM

How to identify the important interactions in a domain so that they can be modeled successfully.

CONTEXT

Understanding and documenting the domain context for use in building or refactoring a system or organization.

FORCES

- A domain model must be capable of being directly validated and explained by the end users.
- User interactions form the basis for system events.
- Domain jobs and user titles may not match responsibilities.
- Domain jobs and user titles may change.
- A domain model should not only reflect current realities.
- Too much detail can be blinding.
- Domain information is the critical context for design decisions.
- Design decisions must be traceable to the domain model.

SOLUTION

Start by examining stereotypical roles that are external to the domain—examples of types of users of the domain, rather than real users or anything else that is external to the domain that interacts with it. Each role is a candidate for being represented as an actor in your model. Establish the actors by refactoring these roles into essential roles—generic parts played by participants in the domain script, rather than job names or titles.

The intent is to establish the types of users who are interacting with the domain and the system as a starting point for listing and analyzing the interactions themselves. Avoid being too fine-grained: ATM_Customer is (normally) preferable to separate roles of Depositor, Withdrawing Customer, Balance Checker, and so on. These roles should be meaningful to your user, and they should reflect the way the business or organization actually interacts with the outside.

RESULTING CONTEXT

The main roles within the domain are identified and packaged, labeled, and agreed-upon. They are made available in diagrammatic form that allows for further massaging as the overall domain model is refined. Each role also helps to define the bounding and scope the domain. And each role provides a starting point for listing essential domain activities.

DISCUSSION

In *Software Reuse: Architecture, Process and Organization for Business Success*, Jacobson, Griss, and Jonsson (1997) use the phrase "Actors model roles" to signify how to think about actors. McMenamin and Palmer's *Essential Systems Analysis* (1984) also provides another insight into how to think of actors…that is, separated as much as possible from implementation details (for example, job titles) or technology (external systems). This pattern is eminently scalable and applies to system actors as well—anything that interacts with the system. However, the essential quality is most important in determining the actors in the domain itself.

6.3   FACTOR THE ACTOR

PROBLEM

How to model the roles that define the users and uses of the system in a useful way.

CONTEXT

Modeling the boundary and context of a product, and to a lesser extent, a domain.

FORCES

- Users can have multiple roles.
- A role can be performed by multiple users.
- Roles need to be generic but focused.
- Actors are environmental.
- Actors are contextual.
- Actor identification is iterative.

SOLUTION

Identify actors use roles iteratively. As you work through use cases, continually refine them either by moving from the specific to the abstract, or vice versa. Look at the functions and responsibilities associated with the events that trigger interactions with the domain or system by each actor. Roles that have common functions or shared responsibilities may be combined. On the other hand, significant variations between roles that are superficially the same may have to be identified as distinct actors. Variations on Customer are simple examples.

RESULTING CONTEXT   Actors with appropriate granularity that can help
                         provide a starting point for defining common
                         variations.

DISCUSSION   Actors are a critical starting point for establishing
                         the use cases that are the functional requirements
                         for products in a domain. They must be identified
                         in a disciplined fashion.

                         A domain with established boundaries and substan-
                         tial history will have clearly defined functions and
                         tacit domain experts who can kick-start the process.
                         Use them and their roles as a beginning.

                         On the other hand, if you are introducing new tech-
                         nology or processes, or involved in some form of
                         reorganization or re-engineering, you may need to
                         look at the technology or the target business model
                         for guidance in identifying abstract roles, types of
                         users, or potential job functions.

6.4   ESSENTIAL ACTIONS

PROBLEM   How to represent the activities of a domain to pro-
                         vide focus in documenting the requirements and
                         analysis model.

CONTEXT   Understanding and documenting the domain.

FORCES   • A domain model must be capable of being
                           directly validated and explained by the end users.
                         • Users know what they do, but may not know
                           what they know.
                         • Too much detail can be blinding.
                         • Unnecessary complexity can be misleading.
                         • Activities are atomic and unconnected.
                         • Processes are commonly understood packages of
                           domain actions.

SOLUTION   Document the essential actions within a domain by
                         building a set of business use cases. Focus on
                         describing the normal flow of the typical proce-
                         dures that users are familiar with. Rework these use
                         cases to reflect the real needs of the users. Use busi-
                         ness use case diagrams to help refactor the domain
                         itself; that is, to reorganize your understanding of
                         what happens in the domain, and ultimately to
                         perhaps reorganize the domain itself.

RESULTING CONTEXT   The essential activities are identified, packaged, labeled, and agreed-upon. They are made available in diagrammatic form that allows for further massaging as the overall domain model is refined.

DISCUSSION   Business use cases are simple but effective tools that can be developed by end users, frequently without any explicit guidance from technical types. After the focus on normal flow is made clear, these cases provide a convenient mechanism for unearthing the essential and the critical in discussions about the actions taking place in a domain. The diagrams provide a concise, short-form way of visually packaging the results, without excessive formalism or syntactical overhead. Again, this is ideal for supporting the joint iterative analysis of a domain with users.

6.5 ESSENTIAL VOCABULARY

PROBLEM   How to document your understanding of the domain in a way that captures the essential information and provides a common vocabulary with your users/customers.

CONTEXT   Understanding and documenting the domain.

FORCES
- Too much detail can be blinding.
- Words must work both ways.
- Many aspects of a domain may be understood tacitly and lack formal expression.
- Vocabulary-building provides insight into a domain.
- Technical language can confuse or intimidate users.
- Objects are not just for systems.

SOLUTION   Develop a domain model that consists of business use cases and a preliminary catalog of business objects.

RESULTING CONTEXT   A vocabulary of domain actions and interactions (use cases) and objects (a catalog and preliminary Business Object model) that combines graphical and high-level textual information for ease of discussion.

DISCUSSION

The essential analysis of a domain is both iterative and incremental. Broad stroke pictures that can be changed easily and quickly work best in a joint effort by the architect and users. Business use cases provide labels for activities, and business objects provide names for a basic vocabulary. Defining the use cases and objects in collaboration with the users provides a common understanding of the meaning of the elements of the vocabulary.

Designing the domain model is what Donald Schon (1983) refers to as engaging in a "reflective conversation with a situation" involving "spatial action language," a language that "combines drawing and speaking." The UML itself provides the basis for a common vocabulary for a spatial action language for business modeling. As the big picture emerges, local experiments with model elements reveal the need for new elements or the need to change the existing model.

6.6   OBJECTIFY INTERNAL ROLES

PROBLEM

How to model the roles played by people, systems, and organizations within a domain.

CONTEXT

Building a domain model and providing a context for defining product requirements.

FORCES

- An organization's interactions with the outside world can be mediated by people *or* systems.
- A domain model must be capable of being directly validated and explained by the end users.
- Internal roles interact with people or systems.
- Domain jobs and user titles may not match responsibilities.
- Domain jobs and user titles may change.
- Too much detail can be blinding.
- Domain interactions are the critical context for system design decisions.
- Design decisions must be traceable to the domain model.

SOLUTION

This is very similar to identifying essential roles as actors. Start by examining stereotypical roles, but examine those that are internal to the domain this time. Each role is a candidate for being represented as an object in your domain model. Establish the people objects by refactoring these roles into essential roles—generic parts played by participants in the domain script, rather than job names or titles. The intent is to establish the types of users who are interacting with actors and the domain's systems as a starting point for listing and analyzing the interactions themselves.

RESULTING CONTEXT
The main roles within the domain are identified and packaged, labeled, and agreed-upon as objects. Each "object" will in turn be available for further analysis as potential actors in the system-use cases that define the requirements for the product.

DISCUSSION
In modeling with the UML, only external roles can be modeled as actors. People and things within a domain that provide the domain services required by a domain actor can be modeled as objects from the perspective of the domain itself. In an essential model, both an ATM and a teller provide banking services to an actor called Bank Customer. Later on, workers as objects within the domain themselves become prime candidates for actors of the application that constitutes the product.

6.7 TOBE MODEL

PROBLEM
How to document important information about the way the domain should work.

CONTEXT
An essential model of the domain is available.

FORCES
- Product requirements need to be traceable to an idealized state of the domain.
- The idealized state of the domain should reflect the essential model.
- Domain visioning is strategic.
- Re-engineering may be necessary at the domain level.
- Visioning needs to be anchored.
- Too much detail can be blinding.

SOLUTION
Do a ToBe model *after* developing the essential domain model. The ToBe model refines the essential domain model to highlight practices that reflect a common vision of how things *should* be done. It should specifically identify potential visionary solutions to problems identified in the AsIs model. As with the AsIs model, the essential business use cases

may be extended and detailed, and the preliminary Business Object model may have visionary objects. Avoid unnecessary detailing, however, and do not include any use cases that don't add value to the analysis of either opportunities or product requirements—avoid jargon, market-speak, or philosophy. Patterns or anti-patterns can be used to compress specific and repeating elements that need additional highlighting and discussion.

RESULTING CONTEXT

A domain vision is documented that is traceable to the essential model of the domain. The product vision and requirements should be traceable to this vision. The ToBe model extends the essential model and is directly traceable to it. Red flag situations are explored in terms that are understandable to the user. Opportunities for re-engineering are highlighted. Note: the ToBe model does not need to be large if the essential model captures the critical underlying elements of the domain and if the AsIs model that highlights current problems indicates that improvement rather than re-engineering is needed.

DISCUSSION

Traditional systems analysis and business re-engineering have focused on understanding the current situation in an organization as a first step, followed by the development of an ideal vision as a replacement. Frequently, however, because of the time and resources depleted doing the AsIs model, management cuts short the modeling of the ToBe vision, reinforcing the quick solutions framed by "the way things are done" in the AsIs model. Regardless, the existence of two separate models (the AsIs and the ToBe models) creates problems for maintenance and impedes traceability.

6.8   ASIS MODEL

PROBLEM

How to document important information about the domain as it currently works.

CONTEXT

An essential model of the domain is available.

FORCES

- Problems and opportunities may need to be traceable to the current state of the domain.
- The current state of the domain should reflect the essential model.

- Focusing on "the way things are done" can impede a clear understanding of the essential aspects of a domain.
- Re-engineering may be necessary at the domain level.
- Implementation details may be problematic.

SOLUTION

Do an AsIs model after developing the essential domain model. This way, an AsIs model refines the essential domain model to highlight current practices. For example, the essential business use cases may be extended and detailed, and the preliminary Business Object model may have specific objects added that are currently in use (for example, paper documents). Avoid unnecessary detailing, however, and do not include any use cases that don't add value to the analysis of problems and opportunities. Patterns or anti-patterns can be used to compress specific and repeating elements that need additional highlighting and discussion.

RESULTING CONTEXT

Sources of current problems are modeled to extend the essential model and is directly traceable to it. Red flag situations are made visible and explained in terms that are understandable to the user. Opportunities for re-engineering are highlighted.

DISCUSSION

Traditional systems analysis and business re-engineering have focused on understanding the current situation in an organization as a first step, followed by the development of an ideal vision as a replacement. Frequently, however, the focus on modeling the current situation turns out to be both overly expensive (in time and resources) and misleading, which encourages quick solutions framed by "the way things are done." Also, the existence of two separate models (the AsIs and the ToBe models) creates problems for maintenance and impedes traceability. By starting from the essential model and adding only those refinements needed to pinpoint problems and opportunities, an AsIs model can help focus discussion around re-engineering and refactoring requirements. Note, however, that AsIs use cases are *not* requirements.

Summary

In this chapter, I've explored how the basic UML constructs of use cases, actors, and objects (or more properly, *types*) can be used in a simple fashion to capture the critical aspects of a domain. Modeling the domain properly is the first step to modeling a system successfully.

The definition of domain I've used here can form the basis for applying the idea of *domain* beyond the original narrow technical meanings of the term found in domain engineering. At the same time, it allows the developer to leverage some of the insights and techniques that domain analysis brought to the forefront: in particular, the notions of commonality and variability as a basis for thinking about reuse from the start, and the idea of treating applications as potentially part of a family.

Domain modeling using the UML is a visibly different activity from the business modeling done as part of business process improvement, avoiding the confusion and turf wars with process consultants that occasionally mar business analysis. Again, ideas from the process improvement world can be usefully appropriated in looking at domains—namely, the use of ToBe and AsIs models to help focus the understanding of what the user needs (and wants).

Although they may overlap, a business and a domain are different; it's the domain, not the business, that is of interest to the software-intensive system developer. This point is particularly critical when doing the preliminary thinking about systems that go beyond the boundaries of the business, such as support for supply chain management.

Aside from reviving the idea of domains itself and providing a new home for aspects of business modeling, domain models, as described in this chapter, emphasize the need for another well-respected idea in systems: *essential models* for analysis. Maintaining an implementation-independent perspective in understanding the problem space becomes even more important in an iterative and architecture-centric development process, which gives rise to architectural decision-making early on. Developing essential views of actors, use cases, and even business objects helps balance the scales in avoiding an architecture that is too shortsightedly based on existing circumstances.

There are a number of resources available for exploring these ideas further, as a way of enhancing your use of the UML. *Software Reuse: Architecture, Process and Organization for Business Success* (Jacobson, Griss, and Jonsson 1997) provides a good discussion of domain engineering and a critical perspective that is only slightly skewed by a bias toward a particular development process. The

Software Engineering Institute (SEI) at Carnegie-Mellon University has a number of important papers about domain engineering on its Web site (www.sei.cmu.edu). Jim Coplien's book, *Multi-Paradigm Design Using C++* (1998a), has an interesting slant on domains and is the basis for my definition.

From an IT perspective, the only current book worth reading about business modeling is D'Souza and Wills' *Objects, Components and Frameworks with the UML: The Catalysis Approach* (1998). It is especially useful because of the patterns it includes about business modeling, many of which had a role in the patterns I include here. D'Souza's patterns are the only really useful ones on business modeling in the patterns literature.

Finally, anyone interested in essential models should take a look at McMenamin and Palmer's classic *Essential Systems Analysis* (1984). Not only is it the best work on thinking essentially, but it is also invaluable for its discussion of event-based analysis—the precursor to use cases.

CHAPTER 7

Product Patterns

Catalogue

Context

Products provide the second level of structure for patterns within this language. A product is the end result of software-intensive systems development packaged as a unit, such as an application, a utility, or a workflow. Products organize the artifacts of software development for delivery and management while projects manage the work.

Back in the old days, software-development projects were long and single-minded, focused on getting an application that was as complete as possible "out the door." Maintenance was for enhancements and fixing defects. The end result was to be in service forever; not only were applications functionally monolithic, but they were seemingly born whole and lived forever.

The UML is especially designed to support an alternative approach: iterative and incremental development, combined with incremental and evolutionary deployment. But, in order to leverage the benefits associated with this newer development approach, an organizing mechanism is required. This mechanism provides an ongoing basis for managing requirements, coordinating work and reuse, controlling versions, packaging releases, and all the other management and planning activities required to support corporate IT assets.

Within a given domain, products are the complete solution to a set of requirements, including all the management needs over the life of the solution. The artifacts that comprise a product include all the models used to develop and maintain it.

Forces

- Models abstract complexity.

- Models are manageable.

- Models proxy tangibility.

- Information technology isn't tangible, but is (instead) operational.

- Information technology is tactical and strategic, as well as operational.

- Information technology is an asset, not just an expense.

- Information technology is a corporate asset.

- Assets have lives.

- Assets should be owned and managed, as well as built and supported.

- Asset management will vary, depending on the lifecycle stage the product is in.

- Ownership should be consistent and identifiable throughout the product's life.

Discussion

Product design and development has long been a well-defined discipline outside of software development. However, the idea of treating internally developed systems as products within organizations has only recently started to emerge as a way of managing corporate development. Recently, organizations such as Microsoft and object-oriented methodologists such as Brian Henderson-Sellers have recognized the need to organize development by *product* (the end result), rather than just focusing on projects (the work itself).

The Microsoft Solution Framework (MSF) is particularly interesting. MSF is Microsoft's publicly available development process—its alternative to Rational's Unified Process and Catalysis for developing component-based systems. It incorporates a number of features that can be considered UML-friendly, including an emphasis on architecture, the use of small teams for development, an iterative and incremental development cycle, and, of course, *product* as a cornerstone (details at `http://www.oteam.com/msf`).

Models are a critical element of *product* as a coherent way of packaging software-intensive systems to enhance their long-term management. They are no longer merely archival after a system is deployed; instead, they become the basis for managing and evolving a system throughout its life as a product.

I discuss *product* in more depth in Chapter 10, "The UML in Context."

7.1 MANAGABLE PRODUCT

PROBLEM   How to ensure that the end result of a development effort is manageable, appropriate, and sustainable.

CONTEXT   Planning and managing using the UML.

FORCES

- Products can be modeled from a management perspective.
- Modeling must support management as well as engineering.
- Projects have a predefined set of boundaries— both scope boundaries and time boundaries.

- The life of a piece of software is longer than any of the individual projects that create or maintain it.
- Software is an organizational asset that needs to be managed as an asset.
- The management of software development needs a broader perspective and longer timeframe than a project. Software provides solutions to business and technical problems that are ongoing and changing.
- Redundant and duplicate projects and stovepipe systems can result from project conceptualization and planning with too narrow a focus or that narrowly reflects the memory of an organization.

SOLUTION

Focus on the product being developed, not the project. Make the product model the fulcrum for development and management. Identify the requirements for the product as a whole. Model the overall solution as a product with a lifecycle of its own, from birth to death.

Start with a product definition that captures the idea of the solution without being constrained by dates and schedules. Integrate the product within a domain framework of shared services. Define how the product itself will be managed, apart from any development projects that may be required. Identify requirements and metrics with the product. Establish a set of criteria for ending the product life.

RESULTING CONTEXT

An overall framework for managing development and the results of development that aligns with the needs of customers and business management, rather than just the concerns of technical staff and the priorities of project managers.

DISCUSSION

This is one of those patterns that explains why models are important, rather than how to model.

A project focus for development emphasizes solving immediate problems and meeting a deadline. Project management has a narrow focus—solving project problems associated with providing a set of tangible end results within the timeframe and scope established by project planning.

For a software product to be managed effectively, to be planned proactively, and to provide ongoing value, it needs to be continually managed. A product-based approach allows key components of software to be managed beyond the duration of individual projects (especially requirements and quality measures), and allows for capturing experience in a more useful form.

7.2   PRODUCT STAKEHOLDERS ARE MODEL CLIENTS

PROBLEM

How to help manage a product using a product model.

CONTEXT

Identifying the roles of key players in the organized life of a product.

FORCES

- Products are part of a domain.
- Products must be planned and managed.
- Products are organized as well as engineered.
- The product organization must be defined if the product is to be planned and managed.
- Stakeholders have a role, just as users do (stakeholders are actors in the domain).
- The product has responsibilities to stakeholders.
- Stakeholders have responsibilities to the product.
- Contracts define mutual responsibilities.
- Organization is an architected abstraction.
- Models represent abstractions.
- Organizations are models.

SOLUTION

Use the UML to capture the organization model needed to make the product manageable over time. This model can be an alternative to an organizational chart or can complement it, depending on the extent to which the organization chart reflects jobs and positions, rather than roles.

The organization model should reflect roles, not jobs or positions. This is a critical aspect of defining a product, and is another type of context diagram. In particular, identify stakeholders and their roles. A stakeholder has a more general relationship to a product than the product owner(s). Some stakeholders are product owners (the people who control the money that makes ongoing development possible). Some provide other resources (for example, network bandwidth, processing time, or support staff).

A variety of product responsibilities can be identified and diagrammed for stakeholders. Typical responsibilities that should be understood up front include "advise" (keep informed) and "consent" (approve), as well as the traditional "provide resources." The range of responsibility types may be more nuanced than this, of course, but the range of responsibilities needs to be factored into types that make sense for the organizational culture and politics, as well as for the organizational architecture.

The organization model should also, of course, identify the development team roles. However, remember that the client for this model is the stakeholders—not the users and not the workers. In effect, you're creating an architectural view of the organization to provide management context.

RESULTING CONTEXT

The stakeholders can see and validate the organization architecture for the product easily, and it is presented in a fashion that is consistent with the other product management artifacts.

DISCUSSION

Ivar Jacobson addresses the larger issues of modeling an organization in *The Unified Software Development Process* (Jacobson, Booch, and Rumbaugh 1999a). The UML's business modeling profile reflects the unified process approach of modeling an organization—providing a set of extensions that facilitate using the UML in describing organizational architecture. David Taylor provides a non-UML perspective on modeling an organization as part of developing business systems (and re-engineering business) in *Business Engineering with Object Technology* (Taylor 1995).

7.3   PRODUCT EVENTS IN CONTEXT

PROBLEM

How to scope and bound the product.

CONTEXT

Planning the product and the development effort.

FORCES

- Products are part of a domain.
- Products provide services that must be clearly defined.
- A product must have a contract with its customers.
- Services must have users.
- Products must be planned and managed.

- Development work must be scoped.
- Scope and boundaries can be elusive and changeable.
- Work products must be traceable.

SOLUTION

Create a context diagram as a model of the product's interaction with the outside world. This can take the form of black-boxing the product as a package, with the system's actors attached and their interactions annotated (see Figure 7.1).

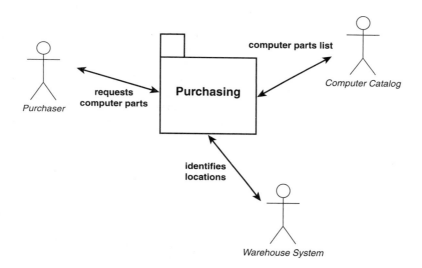

FIGURE 7.1   *A simple context diagram.*

The workers and external systems modeled in the domain model provide a starting point. Any business actors that will interact with the system are also included. In some cases, customers may interact directly with the system. In other cases, a business interaction in the domain model may be mediated by a worker object interacting with the product. Annotate the actors to document the user roles, interactions, and key business abstractions that are central to the product.

Each interaction should be explainable as an event—it should be triggered by an action on the part of the actor involved, and it should be completed by the system. Make sure that it's tangible and provides value for the actor.

Desmond D'Souza and Wills provide a comprehensive approach to modeling a system's context in their book (1998, 592). *The Catalysis Approach* extends the notion of collaborations, makes use of a variety of UML artifacts to detail the context dynamics, and uses packages and actors to define the boundaries.

RESULTING CONTEXT

Management can see the boundaries and scope of the product easily, in terms that are meaningful to them. The development team can understand the business contract that the product must meet.

DISCUSSION

Context diagrams are old and honorable tools in the arena of systems development. Although never formalized in a way agreeable to all, the need for a diagram type that establishes the environment and key interactions with the outside world (and the boundaries with that outside world) are running themes in modeling. Packages and actors, and use cases and business objects provide a UML equivalent to the data/process modeling "single bubble" that encapsulated the application inside and situated the outside world outside.

7.4   USE CASES REPRESENT REQUIREMENTS

PROBLEM

How to document product requirements in a way that is meaningful to the product user and efficient for the product developer.

CONTEXT

An evolving product within a domain, modeled by using the UML.

FORCES

- Requirements are fundamental and provide the justification for any development activity.
- Requirements need to be organized and managed.
- Product evolution needs to be robust (that is, able to incorporate change in a managed fashion).
- Product management needs to be able to organize development work.
- In an ideal world, changes should not cause rework or distort the solution provided by the product.
- Too much detail can be blinding.

SOLUTION	Document your product's business requirements in the form of use cases. If you're using a requirements management tool, map the individual detailed requirements to the use case(s) that realize them, but use the use cases as your organizing structure for planning work and increments. All requirements identified during preliminary analysis should map to one or more cases. Requirements that don't map to any use cases may be badly defined or redundant.
RESULTING CONTEXT	A coherent organized model of the business requirements that can provide a starting point for organizing work and planning product increments (the product lifecycle) in a visually graphic and textually straightforward form.
DISCUSSION	For this pattern, the important aspects of use cases to remember are that they represent an interaction with the product, and that the interaction provides added value to the user. The product requirements are made explicit by rendering the interactions pictorially and textually, and ensuring that each interaction does provide value. Use cases provide a framework for packaging and managing requirements that are meaningful to the user and beneficial to both the developer and planner.
	It is also important to remember that use cases do *not* detail the how—the underlying processes or algorithms that produce the results. They are not process models, which are specification artifacts rather than analysis artifacts.
	A properly defined use case model is a contract with the user that spells out what will be provided by the product.

7.5 BOUNDARY-CONTROL-ENTITY (BCE)

PROBLEM	How to organize the initial list of objects to facilitate further analysis, design, and implementation.
CONTEXT	Analysis has produced a preliminary set of use cases, and these have been reviewed to identify a candidate list of objects.

FORCES

- All objects are not alike.
- All objects are not equal.
- Different types of objects have characteristic behaviors and responsibilities.
- Analysis needs to be focused.
- Boundaries need to be clear.

SOLUTION

Stereotype each analysis object as either a boundary object, a control object, or an entity object to provide a logical view of the roles played by each in the domain being analyzed (see Figure 7.2). A boundary object is responsible for communication between the system and its surroundings.

According to Jacobson (1994), each *boundary object* should (ideally) be concerned only with communications and interactions with actors (including the system variety). Originally, Jacobson called them "interface objects," which is probably more expressive of their purpose, but *interface* is an overworked term. The canonical example is an ATM interface.

A *control object* performs all of the sequencing and control functions associated with a use case. In effect, it acts as a manager for a use case. Control objects, being solely responsible for the sequencing of operations and flow of control within a process (or system), should neither interact with the actor nor be concerned with managing persistence. There should be at least one control object for a use case (although they may be shared like the others).

Entity objects should be the home for any information that lasts longer than the life of a use case. Focus on the specific characteristics of each type in refining your analysis.

When appearing in diagrams of UML models, the boundary/control/entity stereotypes can be represented by using the standard angled brackets notation (<< and >>) or guillemets. The UML also provides graphical icons that can be used in place of guillemets. These are suitable when used within analysis models or where detailed information about the class that is represented isn't needed. Use the textual stereotype in the class name compartment when class details must be shown. Be careful to use the stereotypes consistently within diagrams to avoid confusion. Also, do not depart from the semantics of the boundary/control/entity stereotypes.

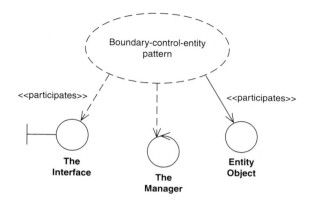

FIGURE 7.2 *Boundary-control-entity pattern as a collaboration.*

Figure 7.3 shows how the boundary-control-entity collaboration can be depicted with UML stereotypes in the classes as well as by using graphical icons. Be consistent by using one or the other.

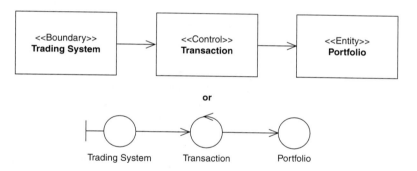

FIGURE 7.3 *Alternative UML notations for BCE.*

RESULTING CONTEXT

A more precisely defined model that establishes relationships between the objects created by development cycle iterations that can be used to explore the details of the domain. This is especially valuable for obtaining user feedback and validation, as well as to document the types of behavior the classes are intended to exhibit.

DISCUSSION

BCE stereotyping is a simple way of enriching UML models with information that may be useful to users. Also, it is closely related to the preceding use case analysis and provides an additional means of establishing traceability.

Jacobson has discussed the BCE pattern in each of his books, and applied it to both business use cases and system use cases. In *The Object Advantage* (1995), he also explains how to translate a business model expressed using the BCE pattern into the starting point for defining system interactions that support each business use case. This is refined in *Software Reuse* (Jacobson, Griss, and Jonsson 1997).

7.6   PRODUCT CHUNKS DIGEST EASILY

PROBLEM

How to scope incremental development of a product.

CONTEXT

Planning and managing a model-based product.

FORCES

- A product is incrementally developed.
- Requirements change over time.
- New requirements may be identified during the life of a product.
- Use cases define product requirements.
- Use cases drive product specification.
- Developers like a feeling of accomplishment...often.
- Users like results.
- Managers like the feeling of control.

SOLUTION

With high-level system use cases as the basis for planning, plan for short development cycles with frequent incremental releases. After each release, replan the remaining portions of the product lifecycle, including the prioritization and scope of future increments (refactor the remainder). But remember that use cases do *not* structure the product itself, only the development work—architecture structures product.

RESULTING CONTEXT

Well-formed use cases that support minimal rework in the evolution and maintenance of a product.

DISCUSSION

The UML is implicitly supportive of an incremental and iterative development style. Barry Boehm's spiral lifecycle is the closest approximation available to a development approach that combines the needs of management (control and communication) with realistic planning. Use cases provide the most reasonable approach to chunking development work so that work boundaries are meaningful to the user and incremental functionality is traceable to real requirements.

However, use cases are not architecture. Because use cases are analysis artifacts and *not* design artifacts, they provide a communication tool for working with domain management and users. They do *not* provide a way to structure the product; the product architecture does that.

7.7   PRODUCT TRACES SUPPORT ROBUSTNESS

PROBLEM

How to ensure that product changes are consistently integrated and aligned with product requirements as the product evolves.

CONTEXT

An evolving product specified, designed, and implemented with UML models.

FORCES

- Product evolution needs to be robust (that is, able to incorporate change in a managed fashion).
- Product knowledge needs to be maintained as the product evolves.
- The requirements are fundamental and provide the justification for any development activity.
- Use cases model requirements.
- In an ideal world, changes should not cause rework or distort the solution provided by the product.
- Too much detail can be blinding.

SOLUTION

Support extended traceability within the overall product model itself, using the <<traces>> stereotype of the UML to highlight connections between artifacts. Traces are used to denote connections between elements in different models (such as the analysis model and the design model); they are not allowed within a model. The connections can either result from development and refinement, such as from requirement to implementation (and vice versa), or they can result from versioning (traces between versions and version elements).

RESULTING CONTEXT

The product models specifically include key traceability information in a visually graphic form that can provide clear guidance when change requests or new requirements occur.

DISCUSSION

Jacobson emphasized robustness and traceability as key benefits of object-oriented development from early on, in the OOSE methodology that preceded Objectory. And an emphasis on traceability as a contributing factor to robustness was one of the contributions OOSE offered to the UML.

The increasing importance (and successes) of short-cycle development and incremental product evolution make robustness and traceability critical aspects of good design—and good management via models. Other parts of the UML can also contribute (for example, the "realizes" association that specifies the relationship between an interface and the class/component that actualizes it).

One of the strengths of the UML is its adaptability and breadth. A diagrammatic representation of key traces is only part of an overall traceability strategy that includes configuration management and traceability data collection during development. However, although traceability is desirable for its positive impact on product quality and manageability, the overuse of traceability via diagrams can reduce their clarity. The *UML Reference Guide* suggests using hyperlinks between model elements to identify traceability other than critical links that are needed during model development as human helpers, as reminders of changes that need to be propagated across models, for example (Jacobson, Booch, and Rumbaugh 1999b, 494).

7.8   USE CASES: WORK AS PACKAGES

PROBLEM

How to partition the development work to be done in a useful way.

CONTEXT

Managing development in an incremental process.

FORCES

- Development efforts have to provide visible and usable results for the customer.
- Incremental development requires easy integration of each increment.
- Work boundaries must have some meaning to the developer as well as the user.
- The acceptance-testing model is based on use cases.
- Granularity of work impacts ease of planning and progress tracking.
- Work products must be traceable.

SOLUTION

Define units of development work according to high-level use cases. Package use cases that will be done together. The use cases should be analyzed for risk and prioritized accordingly, depending on whether the development approach is risk-driven or risk-aversive. Map the release strategy to the use case packaging, and develop other artifacts such as manuals by use case package.

RESULTING CONTEXT

Increments that provide value to the customer, which are real chunks of functionality for the developer and have meaningful boundaries for management.

DISCUSSION

Although the UML does not, by itself, impose a development process, the notion of use cases and the strategy called use case-driven development are woven into its threads. (And besides, they make sense.)

Traceability back to requirements is via use cases, and the most sensible way to organize testing is around use cases. They provide a convenient way of organizing the work at hand for communicating with the customers and stakeholders, as well as a convenient starting point for planning. However, it is important to remember, as I've cautioned elsewhere, that as analysis artifacts, they do not drive the architecture.

7.9 TESTS NEED MODELS

PROBLEM

How to align testing with development to ensure that testing is focused, consistent, and meaningful.

CONTEXT

Supporting the life of a model-based product.

FORCES

- Object interactions are complex and may be nondeterministic for practical purposes.
- Testing should be repeatable.
- Testing needs to be planned and designed.
- Testing needs to reflect the purpose and objectives of the product.
- Users need requirements-based testing.
- Designers need architected testing.
- Developers need detailed testing.
- Managers need reassurance.
- Testing assets are expensive to create and maintain.
- Testing assets can be refactored and reused.
- Testing is expensive.
- Testing should provide closure to all, including users and stakeholders.

SOLUTION

Fabricate a test model that parallels and refactors the product model. For example, user acceptance testing should be built around the use cases validated by the users, based on scenarios developed to validate the requirements themselves.

These scenarios can also be used for usability testing and as a basis for automated stress testing.

Manage the life of the test model for a product in the same way that the other models are managed.

RESULTING CONTEXT

A basis for managing product testing throughout the product lifecycle, as well as iterations of the development lifecycle.

DISCUSSION

Testing is *not* a stage, but rather an ongoing activity. As with any aspect of an architected and model-driven process, testing needs to be based on models that are consistent with models developed for other views of the product, but differentiated according to the specific needs and perspective of the model client—in this case, the tester.

Because the underlying process for UML-based modeling is driven by use cases, and because use cases provide the basis for traceability and significant communication with the end user, the test model for a product should be derived from the use cases it includes.

This approach also provides a means of closure because the acceptance testing for each release will be based on the initial scenarios derived from the use case model, closing the loop of validation.

7.10   CONFIGURATION MANAGEMENT MODEL

PROBLEM

How to organize and control changeable models in an architected environment.

CONTEXT

Managing product models over time and, more generally, applying the UML in a consistent and uniform fashion. (Note: this is a pattern that says we use models for everything.)

FORCES

- Products need to be packaged.
- Products evolve and so need to be packaged at slices in time.
- A product is only as good as its architecture.

- An architecture is only as good as the models from which it's made.
- Product models are visible.
- Product models are management tools.
- Product components change as well as evolve.
- Development work is done in chunks.
- Work chunks need to be organized and managed.
- He who ignores history is doomed to repeat it.
- The last minute is too late.
- A chain is only as strong as its weakest link.
- The UML should be used consistently and uniformly across all domains of development.

SOLUTION

Establish a configuration-management model for the product at the start of development. From a management perspective, this is the dynamic equivalent of the product architecture.

Start by establishing the key work products that need to be managed as a whole and kept in synch. These are the core of the product and they need to be up-to-date for all product stakeholders: senior management, product management, the development team, and production.

These packages are called *configurations*, and the key work products are called *configuration items*. Using the key models from each stage of development, identify the key work products from the overall development process that will need to be managed as a whole. Model the static and dynamic relationships of these work products as a starting point for documenting the overall approach to configuration management over the development lifecycle and product lifecycle.

Define and document a configuration-management process using a UML model. This must be integrated with change management, testing, and release management (see example that follows).

RESULTING CONTEXT

A process for managing the evolution of a product that is documented consistently and that is consistent with the other documentation artifacts associated with the product.

DISCUSSION

A defined and clearly communicated model for handling the versions and configurations of a product is a core requirement for successful product management, not just project management. Various SCM tools provide variations on standard themes for how to handle configuration management, but their approaches need to be evaluated against what works in a given organization and development culture. A configuration model can be derived from a corporate model as one target that can be reused. Alternatively, a product may require a special configuration model to suit special needs.

There are an increasing number of patterns available that deal with the specifics of configuration management. A notable one is by Brad Appleton, Steve Berczuk, and others called *Streamed Lines: Branching Patterns for Parallel Software Development* at `http://www.enteract.com/~bradapp/acme/branching/branch-structs.html` (1999).

Summary

This chapter has provided a starting point for seeing how the UML can be used to help model a system from a product perspective. Identifying the context, providing support for maintenance and testing, and managing the product are all activities that need to handled with models—just as much as the actual design itself.

Many of the patterns in Chapter 6, "Domain Patterns," are also applicable at the product level, with the boundary of the area of interest shifting from the business to the system.

Designing the product is when you'll use some of the major sources of other patterns. Martin Fowler's *Analysis Patterns* (1997), the Gang of Four's *Design Patterns* (Gamma et al. 1995), and *A System of Patterns* (Buschmann et al. 1996) are the prime sources for useful patterns.

CHAPTER 8

Component Patterns

Catalogue

Context

The patterns in this chapter deal with the modeling problems connected to deploying a piece of software. These problems are different from design or construction problems—the problem domain is typically a set of *givens*, including physical elements, such as the network architecture of an organization; as well as soft elements, such as the human organizational structure. Even for a commercial software product, both the target platforms and the intent of the out-of-the-box experience need to be factored into the system model that is part of the delivered package.

Models of the physical system have a different level of abstraction and a different audience from analysis or design models. They are more closely tied to user and operational practicalities than to designed concepts. They are more direct, more like a depiction than a representation. They should provide easy-to-grasp pictures and maps; they should be blunt and straightforward; and they should be connected to the needs of users, the values of stakeholders, and the goals of management.

From a programming perspective, components are interesting because of "pluggability," "replaceability," and reuse. From a modeling perspective, components are simpler things: components are what are deployed. They are the atomic elements of executable delivery; the physical reality that is delivered to the end user on processors and devices are called *nodes* in the UML. They are also the documentation and any other support needed to make the executable solution useful and maintainable.

Discussion

The design situation that a deployment team faces is a bit of a mirror image to that of the developers. Given a product, their challenge is still to understand their users, but they do this to be better at communicating and managing the solution, not in order to see the problem as the users see it and solve the users' problems.

The deployment team uses models not in order to conceptualize and build—as a means of abstracting a complexity in order to make it amenable to translation into a solution. Instead, deployment models are practical abstractions that are meant to help manage and, if necessary, change. Even *change* has a different meaning—the intent is to minimize innovation, and maximize consistency and congruence with the original vision.

Although the problems a deployment team faces may have fewer conceptual nuances than those facing a design/development team, the impact of their solutions is no less significant.

Most development processes don't pay a lot of attention to the needs of the people who will be shepherding a system after it is made available. Many development organizations encourage production, operations, and support areas to roll their own standards for documentation, quite independently of any that exist for development. Although this made some sense in the past, given the different concerns that deployment organizations have, this is no longer warranted or even acceptable for organizations that embrace the UML as a standard modeling language. With components, deployment diagrams, and packages with their associated relationships, the UML provides the means to capture, at least, the generally useful aspects of deployment well enough to provide any generic documentation needed.

8.1 SEPARATION OF CONCERNS

PROBLEM

How to ensure that the deployed documentation is effective and useful for all stakeholders.

CONTEXT

Specification is over, and the rubber meets the road. Developers are implementing, and deployment needs models to help with planning and management after the system is turned over.

FORCES

- Implementation and deployment make operations and production environment users more visible and their needs more important.
- Users are part of the deployment environment, as well as a source of ideas for modeling and design.
- Management and operations should use the same models as the development team.
- Models should inform deployment the same way that they drive development.
- One-size-fits-all collides against complexity.
- Poor documentation contributes to architectural entropy.
- Systems outlive their creators (organizationally, at least).
- Architecture is learning, not just the concretization of ideas and the cementing of associations.
- Documentation seams require leaps of faith and understanding, just as design seams do.

SOLUTION

Understand that the stakeholders in the deployment of a system are not exactly the same as the stakeholders in the development. Ensure that their separate concerns are addressed in a fashion that is consistent with the way that development was handled.

Follow the same approach to documenting software as developing it:
- Identify your users.
- Define their needs.
- Document their interactions with it.
- Establish a common vocabulary and an architecture.
- Detail the functions and information they need.
- Identify the opportunities for reuse and recycling.
- Plan how to provide the functions and information.
- Produce and package.

The users of the documentation may have many of the same names as the users of the system, but there will be more and their needs will be different.

RESULTING CONTEXT   A deployed system with model-based and architected documentation that is user-driven.

DISCUSSION   Implementation isn't just about coding, and deployment isn't just about the physical partitioning of processes and access mechanisms. Each stakeholder has ongoing needs that a complete system must address.

The UML implicitly recognizes the importance of including consistent documentation as part of a total system package. Components are not just implementation concerns of the developers; instead, they encompass the supporting documentation and other artifacts required for making a system available. The same is true for deployment diagrams: nodes are devices, processors with processes attached, topologies that have to be established and administered—not just designs. Users need help using the system. Changes need to be managed.

So, implementation and deployment artifacts need to be documented with a long-term perspective (they can be used and maintained), not just as archival documentation. The easy way to do this is to maximize reuse and minimize "seams"—transitions in the packaging of information—between development, implementation, and deployment.

See the following pattern, "Whole Components," for some ideas on how to do this.

8.2   WHOLE COMPONENTS

PROBLEM

How to define a component to maximize its manageability and reflect the needs of all its stakeholders.

CONTEXT

Using components as model containers for long-term documentation and change management.

FORCES

- Components can contain components.
- Components are not necessarily executables.
- Operational users need to know the composition and dependencies of components.
- Components don't operate in a vacuum; they are only nearly independent.
- Components aren't built in a vacuum; they are realizations of design artifacts.

SOLUTION

Bundle all of the extras associated with an executable component (documentation, test files, source code, change history) into an overall component: a *whole component*. Document each of the extras as a component and diagram the relationships in UML-compliant fashion (typically, by using depends and realizes relationships).

RESULTING CONTEXT

UML-compliant packaging of the constituent elements and supporting artifacts that need to be managed together.

DISCUSSION

According to the *UML Specification*, "a component type represents a distributable piece of implementation of a system, including software code (source, binary, or executable), but also including business documents, and so on, in a human system" (Rational Software Corporation 1999, 3–170).

D'Souza and Wills (1998) and the Rational Unified Process both see components this way: as the executables that are delivered via implementation, and the packaging of all the additional stuff that's needed to make the implementation and deployment successful.

I call components that model the containment of all the supporting material *whole components*, which is an extension of both Geoffrey Moore's notion of whole products and the Software Engineering Institute's version of his idea. I discuss both of these in Chapter 10, "The UML in Context," but the whole product notion says that any product needs more than simply what it provides by itself in order to be successful and usable.

What else is needed depends on the product itself. Given the principles of architecture-centric and iterative development that's at the core of the UML, however, a component needs (at least) user documentation and production documentation, as well as connections to the specifying models that provide the basis for defining what it does.

These all need to be available to the stakeholders in the ongoing deployment of a component (various managers, support staff, maintenance programmers, and so on), and need to be clearly visible and accessible. A whole component provides a way of holding all of these together as a piece.

Related patterns include the following: "Icons Clarify Components" and "Components Manage Change."

8.3 ICONS CLARIFY COMPONENTS

PROBLEM

How to graphically present all the aspects and constituent parts of a component in an easy-to-grasp way.

CONTEXT

Using components as model containers for long-term documentation and change management.

FORCES

- Model elements that are different to the user need to be differentiated visually.
- Textual stereotypes are not user-friendly.
- Components can contain components.
- Components are not necessarily executables.
- Operational users need to know the composition and dependencies of components.

SOLUTION

Use standardized icons for nonexecutable components that need to be kept in synch with an executable component. These can include source code files, business documents, database tables, help files, and so on.

The icons replace the use of stereotype tags on the standard UML notation for component. The UML provides some built-in stereotypes, and *The Unified Modeling Language User Guide* (Jacobson, Booch, and Rumbaugh 1999a) recommends some icons for them:

«document»	A document
«executable»	A program that may be run on a node
«file»	A document containing source code or data
«library»	A static or dynamic library
«table»	A database table

All the relationships that are available for use with a component are, of course, available with these component types, but for the most part you'll want to show only dependencies (see Figure 8.1).

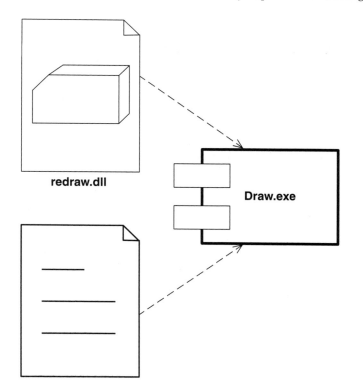

redraw.dll

Draw.exe

FIGURE 8.1 *An executable component with a help file and DLL–supporting artifacts that need to be changed as a group and, therefore, configured as a whole.*

RESULTING CONTEXT | A clear depiction of the constituent elements and supporting artifacts that need to be managed together.

DISCUSSION | The audience for the information about the system components is both the development team and the deployment team. Using iconic forms of stereotyped components helps to bridge the gap between them, providing a more accessible format that clearly distinguishes types of components visually.

8.4 PICTURES DEPICT NODES

PROBLEM | How to graphically present information about the hardware environment to maximize comprehensibility by all stakeholders in a deployment.

CONTEXT | Using deployment diagrams to support documentation of the physical architecture of a system.

FORCES |
- Model elements that are different to the user need to be differentiated visually.
- Textual stereotypes are not user-friendly.
- Nodes have types and connections.
- Operational users need to model the resources and resource dependencies of the physical architecture.

SOLUTION | Use clip art as icons for non-component elements that sit on nodes. As with component icons, these icons replace the use of stereotype tags, but in this case, they replace very localized stereotypes. Create a library of node stereotypes with icons that reflect the actual machines in use. For example:

«HPserver» | A HP UNIX resource
«PC» | A standard workstation
«router» | A hub on a WAN

Figure 8.2 shows an example of a very simple deployment diagram that uses graphic icons.

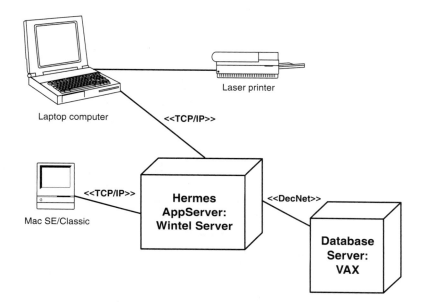

FIGURE 8.2 *Deployment diagram with clip art picture icons.*

RESULTING CONTEXT

A localized depiction of the topology of the physical architecture that can act as a map for all the stakeholders in the physical system, expressed in their visual language.

DISCUSSION

According to the *UML Specification*, "A node is a physical object that represents a processing resource...(including) computing devices but also human resources or mechanical processing resources" (Rational Software Corporation 1999, 3–168).

Because of the unique nature of each organization's infrastructure and physical environment, nodes are "probably the most stereotyped building block in the UML," according to *The Unified Modeling Language User Guide* (Jacobson, Booch, and Rumbaugh 1998a, 26–7). However, even though they're intended only for local consumption, nodes still need to be standardized as part of an organization's architectural style. Unlike components, though, they are better represented in a familiar way that is specific and local, rather than the more generic icons used for components.

8.5   SPECIFICATION BACKPLANE

PROBLEM

Documenting detailed information in a model.

CONTEXT

Making decisions about how to make information available while avoiding information overload.

FORCES

- Models combine textual information with graphical renditions of that information.
- Some information may not benefit from graphical presentation.
- The level of detail in a diagram depends on the level of abstraction that's needed when given the purpose and audience for the diagram.
- Diagrams are meant to show information that's meaningful in a context, not all the information.

SOLUTION

Leave information that is too detailed or that does not need to be highlighted in the *specification* part of the model—the text, rather than the pictures. This is different from elision: There's no need to indicate that the information is missing because it's *lookup* information rather than critical information. In some cases, such as the distributed deployment of components to nodes, it may be a lengthy list.

RESULTING CONTEXT

Clean diagrams that emphasize critical information while ensuring that model users know where to look for the details.

DISCUSSION

A *backplane* is an electronic circuit board containing circuitry and sockets for plugging in additional electronic devices on other circuit boards or cards; it is part of the motherboard in a computer. In *The Unified Modeling Language User Guide*, the term is used to describe the textual elements of a model, in the sense of a backbone that the graphics plug into (Jacobson, Booch, and Rumbaugh 1998a, 6–8).

Desmond D'Souza distinguishes between two types of textual information that are important for creating successful models: formal text and what he calls "narrative." A catalysis package has a dictionary for bridging the gap between the formal and the informal; its narrative includes "text, pictures, illustrations, anecdotes, footnotes" (D'Souza and Wills 1998, 291) and any other material needed to help human users make sense from a model.

8.6 COMPONENTS MANAGE CHANGE

PROBLEM

How to manage lifetime changes to a system model so that system changes are reflected in the model itself.

CONTEXT

Maintaining a UML-modeled system after it is deployed.

FORCES

- Iterative development is all about change (Booch 1994, 223).
- A system naturally changes over time.
- Changes that aren't architecture-driven result in system entropy.
- The architecture must be maintained when the system is maintained.
- Models are part of the system.
- Models are the only tangible expressions of architecture.
- System maintenance is performed on physical components.
- Documentation should be useful to its user, not merely archival.

SOLUTION

Tie change requests to whole components. Make them the *unit of work* for a change request. Require any analysis of a change request to include a review of changes that might be needed to any of the documents, models, and so on associated with the executable in the whole component.

RESULTING CONTEXT

The whole component provides a clear and obvious location for all the information needed to investigate a change request. Note: some of this information may be kept in the *specification backplane*.

DISCUSSION

Change requests that are received after a system is deployed are different from changes requested during the development of a system. Most notably, they reference existing executables, whether directly (for a change to an executable's functionality or performance) or indirectly (for example, a change to a help file).

In an architected system environment, the traceability of impact and the consistency of a change across all impacted artifacts are critical factors in the success of a change. However, change management has always presented management with a problem: determining the granularity of the "atomic unit of software work," as Walker Royce describes it (1999, 125). Components, especially whole components, offer an easy solution.

8.7   CONFIGURED AND RELEASED PACKAGES

PROBLEM

Establishing a model framework that will provide an easy-to-use, reliable means to organize and control revisions of artifacts. Providing support for and integration with project management, change management, and release management processes.

CONTEXT

Developing, deploying, and maintaining a system.

FORCES

- Systems evolve through multiple versions.
- Some versions are released to external users.
- Management needs to know which artifacts are in synch (that is, which artifacts constitute a whole version of a system).
- Developers (maintenance or otherwise) need to be sure they're working with the latest version of a system.
- Changes need to be synchronized.
- Architected systems use models as a means of constraining development and controlling change.

SOLUTION

Use packages as a way of bundling configurations and (by implication) releases. Each release and version should be identified in the physical architecture by means of a package, which can include all of the model elements (or references to model elements). Version numbers should be included as tagged values for each element included in the configuration.

RESULTING CONTEXT

A model that includes a disciplined approach to configuration management that encompasses both internal and external releases.

A package becomes the basis for "versioning," configuration management, reuse, and so on. All the product artifacts can be assembled in one or more appropriate packages that represent different views for different purposes. These artifacts can and should include test models, test results, business rules, relevant patterns, and anything else, including other packages.

DISCUSSION

The Unified Modeling Language Reference Guide says specifically that packages are intended to "organize large models and evolve them." It points out that every model element "must be owned by exactly one package or other model element" (Jacobson, Booch, and Rumbaugh 1999b). This ownership mechanism reinforces appropriate control in a component-based, incrementally architected environment—control that is especially important when considering the impact of reuse in doing maintenance.

Configuration management is not confined to software systems. Ideally, all electronic corporate files should be under configuration management: manuals, documentation, forms templates, document templates, management reports, and so on.

The main difference between configuration management of these non-software objects and software components such as source code, technical and user manuals, and other system-related components is that they will often not be under the control of a formal project manager because they do not often need to be promoted, and only have their versions managed.

For details about configuration management in a UML-based development environment, Walker Royce provides a good overview (1998, 174–181) which is consistent with both D'Souza and Wills (1998) and the RUP.

8.8 MODEL FOR MAINTENANCE

PROBLEM

Building models that support ongoing development and maintenance.

CONTEXT

Systems that are built and delivered incrementally, in which releases deployed after the initial Greenfield release are typically considered and labeled maintenance releases.

FORCES

- The model *is* the documentation.
- If it isn't written down, it doesn't exist (informally attributed to Bill Gates).

- Developers in post-Greenfield increments typically don't have the time or the need to understand the entire product model.
- Workers doing real maintenance need to be able to zero in on the specific elements that need to be fixed or changed.
- Uninformed or incorrect choices about what to fix in a system and how to fix it contribute to product entropy over the years.
- Eighty percent of the work and more than eighty percent of the life of a product occurs after the initial release.
- Changes need to be configured and versioned.

SOLUTION

Model from the beginning with maintenance in mind, and make a packaging of the critical model elements that are meaningful to a maintenance effort. These are typically more physical and may just be the production documentation for a release.

RESULTING CONTEXT

A consistently organized and named collection of product artifacts that supports change management, problem management, and rework.

DISCUSSION

One way to look at a package is as a "named container for a unit of development work," according to Desmond D'Souza and Alan Wills (1998, 287). D'Souza and Wills further describe a package as "its own world" and suggest that "you can know and believe only what is within it" (286).

A package becomes the basis for versioning, configuration management, reuse, and so on. All the product artifacts can be assembled in one or more appropriate packages that represent different views for different purposes. These artifacts can and should include test models, test results, business rules, relevant patterns and anything else, including other packages.

The Unified Modeling Language Reference Guide says specifically that packages are intended to "organize large models and evolve them" (Jacobson, Booch, and Rumbaugh 1999b). It points out that every model element "must be owned by exactly one package or other model element." This ownership mechanism reinforces the appropriate control in a component-based, incrementally architected environment; control that is especially important when considering the impact of reuse in doing maintenance.

Summary

The patterns in this chapter help model the logical and physical reality of a system. They can be used both for architectural and operational purposes.

Deployment and implementation typically get little attention in books about modeling with the UML. Although the UML is not intended to handle all the needs that a specialized implementation and deployment modeling tool might afford, however, it is more than adequate for the practical purposes of communicating the essentials in production documentation, as well as providing support for configuration management and release planning.

The best sources of additional information about using the UML's component and deployment artifacts are two that are specifically associated with Rational's Unified Process, Walker Royce's *Software Project Management: A Unified Process* (1999) and Phillipe Kruchten's *The Rational Unified Process: An Introduction* (1998). Royce's book is especially good at addressing the mechanics of system development, as well as managing the engineering aspects. *The Unified Modeling Language User Guide* has some especially good discussions on using the component and deployment artifacts effectively (Jacobson, Booch, and Rumbaugh 1998a).

PART III

Another Starting Point

CHAPTER 9

Patterns in Context

A very great musician came and stayed in [our] house. He made one big mistake…[he] determined to teach me music, and consequently no learning took place. Nevertheless, I did casually pick up from him a certain amount of stolen knowledge.

—Rabindrath Tagore quoted in Bandyopadhyay (Brown and Duguid 1992)

The way patterns are written and used is strikingly different from any other development artifact in the software industry:

- The social aspects of patterns are as important as their technical benefits.

- They are authoritative learning tools that don't emanate from a higher authority, and "standards" that aren't controlled or standardized.

- And, they are a "technology" that is derived from literature and architecture—not from machines.

They are different because patterns have a human side as well as a technical side. The best patterns aren't just technical and they don't exist in isolation. They have a social dimension—doing the work of development well—not just a focus on the end result. And they are embedded in a context of other patterns and life itself.

This chapter explores the human side of patterns: in particular, how software patterns connect to the way software developers work and the problems they have in working. It's meant for the reader who wants to know more about where patterns came from, intellectually and historically, as a start to becoming a well-rounded professional practitioner, rather than just a technician.

I'm going to look at the context for patterns (not just the technical roots, but the human ones) and the social, cultural, and organizational problems that patterns attempt to resolve. As part of the context, I'll talk about the history of software patterns and the patterns movement from a personal and very personalized perspective: that of the founders of the community themselves. This material is distilled from the various books, Web pages, magazine articles, and discussion-lists that document the existence and rapid growth of the patterns community. For anyone thinking of joining in, this will be useful background material that's not available in one place anywhere else. I will also look at the architectural roots of patterns in some detail.

Newcomers to patterns are frequently criticized for not doing their homework by paying their dues and reading the seminal works of Christopher Alexander, especially *The Timeless Way Of Building* (1979) and *A Pattern Language: Towns, Buildings, Construction* (Alexander, Ishikawa, and Silverstein 1977). And, for anyone who wants to use patterns in their work and understand the thinking that goes into patterns, Alexander's books are the best place to start. However, the two main books are long, and his key ideas are scattered throughout them because of the persuasive instead of didactic approach he takes to articulating those ideas.

Despite their importance to working with patterns, most of the material produced by the patterns community don't do a good job of explaining Alexander's ideas. With a few exceptions, the available explanations are typically either too brief and misleadingly simplified, or else they get caught up in the philosophical underpinnings. Alexander's ideas are not easy to simplify, and although the underlying philosophy (a combination of Taoism, Zen, and Alexander's own notions) is interesting as a philosophy, it isn't itself critical to a beginning understanding of patterns.

I try to achieve a middle path in this chapter. I present Alexander's fundamental ideas about patterns, the ones that are useful to the starting practitioner of patterns. But I avoid the more esoteric elements of Alexander's ideas, simply because they need a book by themselves—and Alexander wrote it in many volumes.

9.1 A Little Starting Context

The initial context for software patterns was object-oriented design. Software developers, particularly object-oriented ones, started getting interested in patterns ten years after Alexander's patterns books—in the late '80s—and only in a very small way at first. Software patterns emerged out of a number of needs that were becoming very evident then. Thomas Kuhn would have called the emergence of these needs *crises*: situations that challenge the existing way of doing and knowing, and so they provoke new paradigms. I'll treat them as forces, in the Alexandrian sense: conditions that need to be resolved to establish a new balance in an unbalanced situation, creating a new "wholeness."

9.1.1 Force 1: Structuring Abstraction, Abstracting Structure

The coming of patterns was driven by recognition of the need for a higher level of abstraction than objects and classes in object-oriented design. Peter Coad, a pioneer in the pattern movement, put it this way in an early article he wrote for the ACM that reflects Alexander's influence:

> Object-oriented methods tend to focus on the lowest-level building block: the class and its objects…Classes and objects correspond to Alexander's constantly repeating, lowest-level elements. Patterns of lowest-level elements and relationships between them form a building block for more effective OOA and OOD…(Coad 1992, 152)

This need reflected a force in software development that had been gaining steam since the late '70s: the trend toward structuring systems and, whenever consultants could get away with it, structuring enterprises as architectures. The increasing complexity and interdependence of business systems made the old one-at-a-time view of applications unworkable, even within the narrow confines of COBOL, JCL, and mainframe databases.

By the late '80s, objects—which started life as ways to program simulations and children's games—became both the silver bullet for structuring the complexities of interconnected systems and the first real justification for treating the idea of software architecture seriously.

However, while seemingly solving key parts of the managing-complexity problem that the first generation of commercial software tools created and couldn't solve, objects created another level of complexity that needed to be managed. Structured programs could be composed of procedures, modules, and files—chunks that made physical and logical sense—but objects were…well, objects. Although structured developers had a substantial arsenal of tools for organizing their work and their designs, object-oriented developers lacked any such facilities. So, developers asked, "How can we organize these things called objects?"

The answer: software architecture. And maybe patterns:

> Mature designers are able to see the broad patterns in the software architectures they work with…Procedures, objects, and [other] abstractions…provide the building blocks: patterns provide the overall architecture. (Coplien 1994a, 1)

Patterns also provided a convenient language that was distinct from the old language of procedures and modules (not just a step up in abstraction from objects) for this new kind of architecture:

> Patterns have given us a vocabulary to talk about structures larger than modules, procedures, or objects, structures that outstrip the vocabularies of the sound object design methods that have served us for the past decade. Many of these structures aren't new; a few people have known them for decades. Patterns bring these techniques, and a vocabulary to talk about them, to the everyday programmer. (Coplien 1997, 36)

9.1.2 Force 2: Guiding Creativity, Creative Guidance

By the late '80s, object-oriented design was maturing, and the traditional methodologies and first-generation object-oriented methodologies were not up to the task of packaging and communicating what was being learned.

A mundane need for a decent set of repeatable guidelines for object-oriented design and programming was emerging—guidelines that reflected the *interactive* quality of the technology. These were needs not being addressed by the methodologies of the day:

> The search for an appropriate methodology for object-oriented programming has seen the usual rehash of tired old ideas, but the fact is that OOP is so different that no mere force-fit of [traditional] methods will provide access to the potential inherent in OOP…these methods [do not] address the user interface design issues…[and] while E-R [for example] seems to be "object-oriented" it is not suited to the dynamic nature of objects…and encourages the use of a global perspective while designing, a sure loser in object-oriented programming…We propose a radical shift in the burden of design and implementation, using concepts adapted from the work of Christopher Alexander… (Beck and Cunningham 1987)

Patterns were seen as offering an alternative way of documenting techniques— an alternative more in synch perhaps with the world of interactive, object-based software development. By being self-contained and yet connected, they resemble objects. Patterns reflect targets implicit in object orientation, such as independence of language and platform, and adaptability to circumstances:

> The pattern form is well suited to documenting [object -oriented] design techniques. Unlike a design document, a pattern reflects something that has been used in a number of situations and thus has some generality...Patterns also express solutions in ways that allow for some variation depending on the details of a circumstance. Finally, patterns can express architectural considerations independent of language and design methodology...(Berczuk 1994)

And, by being generative (a source of creative solutions) rather than prescriptive, patterns require an interactive involvement by the pattern user:

> A generative software design pattern can be used in the same way we use a dress pattern or a boat pattern: to guide a designer to build a new dress or boat. We can weave patterns together into generative pattern languages, families of related patterns which together provide a solution set for system-building problems in a single domain. (Coplien 1997, 36)

Generative, a favorite term in the literature about software patterns, is inherited from Alexander. It suggests an indirect creativity, a way of providing the direction for a creative solution without detailing how to achieve it.

Along with a dissatisfaction with the prevailing methodologies, patterns also reflect a healthy disrespect for *Computer Assisted Software Engineering (CASE)*, the previous silver bullet that proved so disappointing and expensive. CASE ended up automating obsolete techniques and practices. In the end, automating the design process for software turned out to be as fruitless as the search for a way to "mathematicize" the design process in architecture that led Alexander to patterns.

9.1.3 Force 3: The Search for Quality and Reuse

Additional forces that supported the idea of patterns came from an emerging emphasis on software quality. In object-oriented programming, software quality combined with a focus on the possibilities of increased development productivity through reuse. Objects with patterns as an organizing principle offered the tantalizing possibility of reuse at a higher level than raw code: design artifacts, architectural elements, and, ultimately, experience:

> Patterns are forms for describing architectural constructs in a manner that emphasizes these constructs' potential for reuse. They provide a way to document and share design expertise in an application-independent fashion... (Berczuk 1994)

Patterns were also seen as a means for including the human element and a degree of evolutionary process into the arena of software quality and reuse:

> We believe the goals of software quality and productivity will be best served by the methodical cataloging of successful designs…we remain inspired by the impressive design catalog assembled by Alexander…[He] claims most good architectural ideas evolved out of uncountable genera-tions of people building structures for their own need. These ideas, passed on from generation to generation, were subject to a form of nat-ural selection…We find much encouragement in Alexander's tactic for reintroducing selection into a field of design recently taken over by [the] disinterested. (Rochat 1988)

9.1.4 Broader Cultural and Professional Forces

Any discussion of the context for understanding patterns would not be com-plete without some discussion of the intellectual and cultural currents that were flowing in the period when software patterns emerged. The feelings expressed by Rochat and Cunningham reflect a more general force that sur-faced then: a desire for what Ivan Illich, one of the key social critics of the Baby Boom decades, called "virtuous practice" in the face of "deskilling," specializa-tion, and constant change.

Ivan Illich co-authored a declaration that suggests some of the broader social context behind the patterns movement:

> Virtue is embodied practice which can only exist where custom has shaped and limited a field for its application. By virtue, we mean that shape, order and direction of action informed by tradition, bounded by place and qualified by choices made within the habitual reach of the actor. (Cayley 1992, 48)

These feelings also reflect the desire for the "demystification" of professional knowledge, which Donald Schon discusses as being embraced by many profes-sionals during the '80s. He offered the "reflective practitioner" as a model for professionals looking to open up what they do and how they do it to the out-side world and within their community—a strategy very much in keeping with the emergence of the software patterns community.

Patterns provided a convenient way for documenting the "custom" of software development in a field overrun by urgent novelty, the loss of personal control, and ever-shifting boundaries. The patterns community provided a good, old-fashioned town hall environment for sharing and demystifying technical knowledge.

9.2   The Pattern Idea

By the time Peter Coad's article appeared in 1992, which established a mind-share toehold for the idea among developers in general, the beginnings of a community had been formed.

The notion of patterns seemed to be in the air in the late '80s. The proceedings from OOPSLA86 mention *pattern* 60 times (incidentally and interestingly, a high-water mark for the term in the annals of OOPSLA for the following decade)—mostly in connection with AI, message-passing, and pattern-matching. But only one paper by Bertrand Meyer (discussing ADA versus object-oriented languages) had some tantalizing references, limited to patterns of generic parameters in ADA packages that perhaps hint at design patterns.

9.2.1   First Hints

In 1987, Tom DeMarco and Tim Lister, two well-known methodology gurus from the old school, published a book called *Peopleware: Productive Projects and Teams*. It was the first mention of patterns—but not software patterns. In studying more than 500 software projects, they found that the great majority that failed (a sizable chunk) had not failed for technological reasons. Instead, usually a project's "sociology" was at fault: its management culture, team setup, or physical space. In looking for solutions, they targeted many of the problems that have since ended up on the menu of software pattern writers. For example, they examine ways to deal with a major management failing: "a tendency to manage people as though they were components" (DeMarco and Lister 1987). And much of their discussion of the problems and solutions takes a metaphorical, essay-like form. So, they saw Alexander's ideas as a congenial base for sensible solutions to the organizational problems that were endemic to development.

In that same year, Ward Cunningham and Kent Beck started looking into applying Alexander's ideas to interface design. Kent discovered Alexander while he was an undergraduate at the University of Oregon. This wasn't too difficult because he was surrounded by Alexander there. The Oregon campus was designed by Alexander and his colleagues, using the principles that Alexander championed and ultimately published in book form as *The Oregon Experiment* (1988).

Kent Beck picked up Alexander's ideas almost by osmosis:

> Many of the students in my freshman dorm (accurate nickname "Gonads") were in the School of Architecture. Since I had been drawing goofy house plans since I was six or seven, they pointed me in the direction of Christopher Alexander. I read all of *The Timeless Way of Building* standing up in the university bookstore over the course of several months. (Beck 1994)

Awhile later, after graduating, he came across Alexander again:

> I had been working at Tektronix for a year and a half...I found a battered old copy of *Notes on the Synthesis of Form*...Alexander's excoriation of methodologists in the introduction to the second edition resonated with my biases...It seemed everything he didn't like about architects, I didn't like about software engineers. (Beck 1994)

9.2.2   The Early Years

Kent and a friend, Ward Cunningham, were developers working with Smalltalk, one of the first object-oriented languages. They were also designing user interfaces. A problem project became an opportunity to try this novel approach called patterns:

> Ward and I were consulting with a group that was having trouble designing a user interface. We decided, in Ward's VW Vanagon on the way over, to try out the pattern stuff we'd been studying. Alexander said the occupiers of a building should design it, so we had the users of the system design the interface. Ward came up with a five-pattern language that helped them take advantage of Smalltalk's strengths and avoid its weaknesses...We were amazed at the (admittedly Spartan) elegance of the interface they designed. (Beck 1994)

The first patterns?

- Window per Task

- Few Panes

- Standard Panes

- Nouns and Verbs

- Short Menus (Beck 1994)

These patterns are very simple: Window per Task determines what windows will be available and what will be done in them; Few Panes and Standard Panes divide each window into panes; Nouns and Verbs and Short Menus identify what can be done within each pane.

Unfortunately, the time wasn't quite ripe for an earthshaking revolution:

> We reported the results of this experiment at OOPSLA'87 in Orlando. We talked patterns until we were blue in the face, but without more concrete patterns nobody was signing up. (Beck 1994)

Only Grady Booch, who was even then concerned with object design methods, seemed interested at the time: he had a suggestion for a pattern language from his work with the military.

Then, between 1987 and 1993, a number of developers started to take an interest in patterns, in many cases independently. Sometimes, they met.

9.2.3   The Idea Emerges

Bruce Anderson, from IBM UK; Erich Gamma, at that point a Computer Science student in Switzerland; and Richard Helm (another IBMer) got together at EcoopOopsla90 and started talking patterns. Erich Gamma had been thinking about patterns as part of his Ph.D. He included design patterns in his thesis in 1991, and in the book that came out of it in the following year. The summer of 1991 saw Erich joining Richard Helm "on a rooftop in Zurich on a sweltering summer's day" (Coplien and Schmidt 1995, ix), and the result was the start of the first catalog of design patterns.

Later that year, there were two events at OOPSLA that provided a big nudge.

First, Peter Coad and Mark Mayfield conducted a workshop on patterns that supplied momentum. The workshop struggled with an agenda that included defining patterns, identifying a few, and figuring out their impact. One result was a long list of potential patterns—over quite a range. Another was a recognition that a lot of work was needed to make them useful—especially in the area of developing templates or standard formats. Plans were laid to repeat the workshop the following year.

Then, Bruce Anderson ran a workshop on developing an architecture handbook. This turned out to be the seminal event for the culture of patterns and *the* starting point for the patterns community. Many of the people who would later turn out to be key participants in shaping the patterns movement were there.

The WikiWikiWeb story of what happened in Bruce Anderson's workshop gives a sense of the summer camp atmosphere that helped spark the beginnings:

> [C]onflicting visions of the future were in the air. Kent Beck's vision of the future was patterns. When Bruce told the group to work in pairs to write an entry for the *Architecture Handbook*, Kent grabbed Ralph [Johnson]…They spent an hour or so writing down 8 or 9 patterns for using HotDraw [a graphics meta-tool] and then coerced Norm Kerth into acting as their test subject. They taught him the patterns, and then when it came time to present their entry to the group, they had Norm show it off by designing a dataflow diagram editor, in real-time and unrehearsed…Both Ralph and Kent thought it was a fabulous success. (Kent And Ralph At The Architecture Workshop 1997)

After the fun was over, Ralph Johnson took the patterns home with him, and soon discovered that they needed help:

> A month later, Ralph looked at the patterns and thought they looked bare and feeble. Nobody would understand them unless they were better explained. He couldn't understand why he had been so excited a month before, but trusting the memory of his enthusiasm, he fleshed out the few lines into a few pages, and started circulating them. (Kent And Ralph At The Architecture Workshop 1997)

Using his students as guinea pigs, Ralph came to the conclusion that some sort of structure was needed for the patterns to be effective for learning (Kent and Ralph had written them up as individual paragraphs). Ralph went back to the conceptual roots to come up with a format:

> I studied Alexander's pattern language again, and realized that each pattern relied on examples and that he provided explanations for his patterns in terms of underlying theories of the properties of building materials or social interaction…I integrated the examples with the pattern…[and] put enough of the theory of design in the first pattern to define the main vocabulary and put the rest as far down in the patterns as possible…The patterns are the only documentation for a version of HotDraw that has been distributed since early 1992, and users say they are satisfied with it…Writing the patterns was not hard once I figured out the format. (Johnson 1995)

Meanwhile, on a parallel track, Jim Coplien from AT&T had produced a collection of *idioms* (language-specific C++ patterns) that were making their way around AT&T as early as 1989. In 1991, they were published as a book, *Advanced C++ Programming Styles and Idioms* (Coplien 1991). (Jim and Ralph have since become the bookends of the pattern community, each acting as conscience and goad when the community seems to lose touch with the original spirit and intentions.) By 1992, Jim had been exposed to Alexander as well.

IBM itself became interested: Bruce Anderson, by now godfather of patterns workshops and still an IBMer, held a workshop that IBM sponsored at its Thornwood education center in May 1993, with many from the inchoate patterns community in attendance.

9.2.4 The Beginnings of PLoP

August 1993 saw a number of the original Architecture Handbook workshop participants, and others such as Jim Coplien, holed up at a mountain retreat in Colorado initiated by Kent Beck and Grady Booch. Their mandate: "evaluating patterns as an answer to the question, What comes after objects?" (Coplien 1994a).

They decided to start a formal group to sponsor further work on patterns, including what was to become the Pattern Languages of Program conference series (PLoP). They called their group the *Hillside Generative Patterns Group*, after spending a "breathless" session on a hillside working with Alexander's patterns directly and thinking about a design for an office for the group. They used the term *generative* originally to indicate that they wanted patterns that worked like Christopher Alexander's—as creative tools for planning and building, rather than simply those that "captured observations" (Cunningham and Beck 1997).

Planning for the first PLoP started in April 1994. The group was joined by Richard Gabriel, then a professor of computer science at Stanford who had started looking into Alexander's ideas seriously in 1992. He was also a struggling poet and fit the culture of the group well:

> We wanted something really wacky and unusual...[Dick Gabriel] exhorted us all to go into PLoP with confidence and act as though we knew what we were doing. On August 4, about 80 people came together at the Allerton Park estate near Monticello, Illinois, to do just that. Things went well, with even the weather cooperating. Ward Cunningham and Ralph Johnson were program and conference chair, respectively. Kent, who had just welcomed a new addition to his family, couldn't make it...The PLoP proceedings came out in May, 1995, as "Pattern Languages of Program Design." (Cunningham and Beck 1997)

Jim Coplien regarded the PLoP conference as a "watershed event" (Coplien and Schmidt 1995, ix–x). Some of the other attendees were a little less overwhelmed with the proposed new addition to the programmers' and designers' family of tools. Robert Martin, like Coplien a C++ guru, commented:

> I arrived at PLoP with high hopes of a very dynamic and information packed conference…a pragmatic conference…In many ways, this is just what I got. The majority of the papers presented were well done and worth reading…[but] there were several things that bothered me…I wanted to hear people discuss their own successes and failures with certain patterns…Instead, there seemed to be a lot of folks at the conference who felt that "patterns" was the "way," the "solution," the long sought "magic bullet"…Excitement was high, but in many cases substance was low…there was a tendency to talk about patterns in general; as if there was some spiritual significance in the word "pattern"… (Martin 1994)

9.2.5 The Gang of Four and After

While PLoP was being born, Erich Gamma, Ralph Johnson, Richard Helm, and John Vlissides had gotten together to continue the work Erich and Richard started on the rooftop in Zurich in 1991. After a flurry of emails, and a context that included "…four countries, three…marriages and the birth of two [unrelated] offspring" (Gamma et al. 1995, 429), the result was to be *the* book on object-oriented patterns and one of the key works on object-oriented design. Called *Design Patterns: Elements of Reusable Object-Oriented Software* (1995), it was finally published in 1994, just in time for OOPSLA94. It was a runaway success from the start:

> It sold 750 copies at the conference—more than seven times the highest number of any technical book Addison-Wesley had ever sold at a conference. The book is still doing very well. In fact, *Journal of Object-Oriented Programming* (JOOP) named it (in their September 1995 issue) both the best object-oriented book of 1995, and the best object-oriented book of all time. (Cunningham and Beck 1997)

Robert Martin's reaction highlights the significance of the book:

> For some of us, the patterns in Gamma's book are not new ideas. We have been using techniques like them for years. What is new, however, is the notion of giving them names and standard forms and putting them in a catalog. Giving these patterns names and standard forms allows us to reason about them, and to use them as formal components in our designs. Cataloging them makes them accessible to those of us who have not stumbled across the techniques on our own. (Martin 1994)

The cataloguers came to be known as the Gang of Four, named after the anti-Mao faction in the Chinese Communist Party in the '70s, and the book and its patterns are frequently cited as Gang of Four patterns.

Other works started appearing. In 1995, Peter Coad resurfaced with his book *Object Models: Strategies, Patterns, and Applications* (Coad 1996), which broke ranks with the emphasis on following Alexander. He suggested instead that software patterns be treated as templates and examples without any extraneous philosophical baggage—an ongoing debate.

The proceedings from PLoP1 were published in book form in 1995, edited by Jim Coplien and Doug Schmidt (Coplien 1994a). PLoP2 and PLoP3 carried on this "tradition" with PLoP3's collection co-edited by a now convinced Robert Martin (1994). *Pattern-Oriented Software Architecture: A System of Patterns* (also called "the POSA book") (Buschmann et al. 1996) has already been mentioned. Since then, books such as *Analysis Patterns* (1997) by Martin Fowler have extended the scope of the genre, and *AntiPatterns: Refactoring Software, Architectures, and Projects in Crisis* (1998) by William J. Brown, Raphael C. Malveau, William H. Brown, Hays W. McCormick III, and Thomas J. Mowbray have opened up different ways to use the pattern notion.

9.3 Patterns as Literature

Aside from their technological roots, software patterns emerged out of another movement in the late '80s: literate programming and the notion that documentation and even programs *could be* and *should be* written as literature. The concept of literate programming originated with Donald Knuth, and influenced Kent Beck noticeably, from practical considerations:

> Traditionally, the programmer's role has been to understand a problem and encode that knowledge in a program a computer can execute. The problem with this approach is that focusing on the computer as the consumer of programs leads to programs that are difficult for other programmers to understand....A literate program is a literary entity, written to be read from beginning to end, and taking on the character of a book or essay. Literate programming expands the role of the programmer to include the responsibility for organizing a program in such a way that a reader is led naturally to an understanding of the decisions that shaped the code. (Beck and Cunningham 1987)

In order to produce literate programs, an appropriate programming language was necessary. None of the familiar ones were suitable. In some ways, patterns could be seen as an available model or even as an alternative.

Christopher Alexander's patterns are self-conscious literature. He uses an essay-like form for structuring patterns and, in particular, for describing the problems they solve. The simplicity and practicality of these essays, almost stark in their directness, gives his patterns a special power. The quality of his writing—again simple, straightforward, and direct—gives his patterns a resonance. The best of his patterns provoke strong emotional reactions and urge a creative response in their readers.

For example, a pattern called Dancing in the Street talks about the physical conditions that will encourage people to do just that—dance in the streets. He notes that dancing in the street is an "image of supreme joy" in the music and theater of most cultures, and mentions "Balinese dancers who fall into a trance whirling around in the street." But, he laments, it has mainly disappeared in our culture. He suggests that there may be opportunities to reintroduce dancing in the street and says:

> [T]he right setting can actualize it and give it roots. The essentials are straightforward: a platform for the musicians, perhaps with a cover; hard surface for dancing, all around the bandstand; places to sit and lean for people who want to watch and rest; provision for some drink and refreshment (some Mexican bandstands have a beautiful way of building tiny stalls into the base of the bandstand, so that people are drawn through the dancers and up to the music for a fruit drink or a beer... (Alexander, Ishikawa, and Silverstein 1977, 321)

Ideally, it was felt that software patterns should do the same. And, just as Alexander's more human way of building captured the attention of software developers, literature (including Alexander) offered the promise of a more human way of communicating—similar to *Koans, Metaphors, and Parables* (Coram 1997).

The patterns community has attempted to meet this ideal by treating software patterns as a body of literature, and by treating pattern-writing as a creative exercise to be nurtured the way creative writing is nurtured: through workshops, open publication and discussion, and communal review. This attitude carries through to a respect for the work of individual authors:

> As you examine the contents of [PLoP1] carefully you will observe a rich diversity of pattern forms....We made every effort to preserve the authors' original forms. We avoided tampering with individual expression as much as possible: We made no attempt to enforce a uniform writing style. Although the book lacks the voice of a single author, we wouldn't have it any other way. We hope you join us in celebrating this diversity in the formative stage of a new body of literature. (Coplien and Schmidt 1995, ix–x)

Along with the literary bent came a focus on reflection, introspection, and experience as a source of knowledge, as opposed to what is perceived as a current obsession with the new:

> [The founders of PLoP] had come to realize that the advance of their discipline was limited by a bias in its literature…a product of the traditions of scientific publication…to favor the new, the recent invention or discovery, over the ordinary, no matter how useful. The founders' interest in the ordinary may have come…from their observations that projects fail despite the latest technology for lack of ordinary solutions. [They all] agreed to focus their attention on the dissemination of solutions. (Johnson and Cunningham 1995, ix-x)

However, although the idea of patterns-as-literature is well served by the practices of the patterns community, the results rarely live up to the ideals. Software developers being software developers and not writers (usually), they are typically more comfortable with the concrete and defined than the elusive and allusive. And so, the opposite side of the coin is apparent in any review of the patterns literature: an abundance of templates and recipes, and very few essays that create the *aha reaction*, as it's called.

For those pattern writers who have the necessary skills and needs to complement literary ambitions, the results verge on real literature: Jim Coplien and Dick Gabriel come to mind. The following "Simply Understood Code" is an example from Dick Gabriel:

> Simply Understood Code
>
> …at the lowest levels of a program are chunks of code. These are the places that need to be understood to confidently make changes to a program, and ultimately understanding a program thoroughly requires understanding these chunks.
>
> * * *
>
> In many pieces of code the problem of disorientation is acute. People have no idea what each component of the code is for and they experience considerable mental stress as a result.
>
> Suppose you are writing a chunk of code that is not so complex that it requires extensive documentation or else it is not central enough that the bother of writing such documentation is worth the effort, especially if the code is clear enough on its own. How should you approach writing this code?

People need to stare at code in order to understand it well enough to feel secure making changes to it. Spending time switching from window to window or scrolling up and down to see all the relevant portions of a code fragment takes attention away from understanding the code and gaining confidence to modify it.

People can more readily understand things that they can read in their natural text reading order; for Western culture this is generally left to right, top to bottom.

If code cannot be confidently understood, it will be accidentally broken.

Therefore, arrange the important parts of the code so it fits on one page. Make that code understandable to a person reading it from top to bottom. Do not require the code to be repeatedly scanned in order to understand how data is used and how control moves about.

* * *

This pattern can be achieved by using the following patterns:

- LocalVariablesDefinedAndUsedOnOnePage, which tries to keep local variables on one page.
- AssignVariablesOnce, which tries to minimize code scanning by having variables changed just once.
- LocalVariablesReassignedAboveTheirUses, which tries to make a variable's value apparent before its value is used while scanning from top to bottom.
- MakeLoopsApparent, which helps people understand parts of a program that are non-linear while retaining the ability to scan them linearly.
- Use FunctionsForLoops, which packages complex loop structure involving several state variables into chunks, each of which can be easily understood. (Coplien 1997)

For the template-oriented (and "practical") pattern writers, whose skills and needs are decidedly technical, the focus on creating a literature can result in what some have called "tedious" verbiage. But both factions have their place in the patterns community.

9.4   Types of Software Patterns

There are as many software pattern formats as there are definitions for patterns, and there are almost as many schools of thought within the patterns community that delineate various flavors of acceptability. The clearest distinction is between generative and non-generative patterns. Conveniently, each type is associated with a particular format for structuring the resulting patterns.

As I've already mentioned, generativity can be seen as a capacity for facilitating a creative resolution to a problem. Generativity is indirect, not coming from the pattern directly but from the creative opportunities that it suggests and makes possible.

Generative patterns are concerned with the *act* of building. They are meant to embody the Alexandrian ideals, although no one has seriously created a pattern language that matches the scope and ambition of Alexander's.

In generative patterns, the discussion of the problem is most important because it provides the basis for understanding and reworking the solution. The Patron pattern from Jim Coplien (which I will discuss in detail in the section 9.4.1, "CoplienForm"), is an example of a generative pattern. In it, the discussion of the problem includes the forces and the rationale, as well as the simple problem statement itself. It's left to the reader to figure out the best way to realize the role of a patron for their development project. I call these patterns *CoplienForm*, after their originator.

On the other hand, a non-generative pattern is instructive, the solution is what's important, and the problem statement is meant to be observational and practical rather than suggestive.

Non-generative patterns are meant to be descriptive and useable as individual statements of best practice—ultimately as templates. They are concerned with the *artifacts* of building—using patterns to demonstrate and explain recurring good solutions to normal design problems.

These are frequently called Gamma, or Gang of Four, patterns—I'll call them *GammaForm* patterns. They originated in the book *Design Patterns* (Gamma 1995), and examples pop up frequently in object-oriented magazines. They're more closely aligned in intent with another definition that Alexander provides:

> The pattern is, in short, at the same time a thing, which happens in the world, and the rule which tells us how to create that thing, and when we must create it. It is both a process and a thing; both a description of a thing which is alive, and a description of the process which will generate that thing. (Alexander 1979, 247)

Between these two formats, there's a difference in focus that makes them useful to different audiences and different tasks. The resulting differences in style and usage mean that they both have to be understood by a pattern user wanting to make the most of the patterns that are out there.

But no matter. The purposes are different; the approaches are different. A user of software patterns benefits from the flexibility of different formats and rationales, and from being able to pick and choose patterns to use/reuse without having to worry about the documentation being inappropriately formatted. This is one area in software development in which the lack of a standard is a blessing.

9.4.1 CoplienForm

Here's a breakdown of Coplien's format, by section:

- *Name*—Jim suggests that the name for a pattern should be chosen with as much care as the name for a firstborn child. Although GammaForm names tend to be iconic and "hard" (for example, Façade and Adapter), CoplienForm patterns tend to have names that suggest roles or relationships and that describe the solution (for example, Patron or Architect Also Implements).

- *Problem*—The question to be resolved: What task is this pattern helping to make possible? What question is it answering?

- *Context*—This is how you help the pattern practitioner determine the applicability of a pattern. There are two things to consider:
  - What larger-scale contextual information is necessary? (For example, language/technical architecture/business domain/infrastructure concerns.)

  - What are the critical success factors to this pattern that will make it work or not in a given situation?

  Given the absence of a pattern language to provide a context, these two considerations are paramount. Examples can be useful here. Coplien also suggests that if there are any patterns that were expected to have been employed already, they can be mentioned here.

- *Forces*—Oddly enough, a pattern should be both obvious and mind-bending. It should identify the elements that need to be addressed to make it more than a one-off solution or a cliche. At the same time, it should avoid the temptation to be clever at the risk of being impenetrable. The forces in a pattern are where all of this becomes clear. A good pattern can succinctly describe why a solution isn't immediate or straightforward. Or, as Coplien puts it, "What makes this a hard problem? Capture that in a force." Forces also describe the elements that may (preferably should) be in conflict.

- *Solution*—As in real life, solutions are balancing acts. All the forces must be resolved and harmonized. The overall solution must fit the context.

- *Sketch*—Not necessarily a UML diagram or similar object-oriented graphic, this can be a hand-drawn image that represents the forces involved in a symbolic fashion. Coplien suggests that a rough, hand-drawn graphic is actually better because it can be suggestive rather than misleadingly technical.

- *Resulting context*—How has the context changed as a result of the solution?

- *Rationale*—Discuss why the problem exists, what lead to the solution as described, and the motivation behind the pattern. Examples and extended commentary can also be included here.

Here's an example, taken from Coplien's organizational pattern language in PLoP1 (Coplien 1994b):

PATRON

PROBLEM	Giving a project continuity.
CONTEXT	A development organization in which roles are being defined. *Patron* works only if *Developer Controls Process*.
FORCES	<ul><li>Centralized control can be a drag.</li><li>Anarchy can be a worse drag.</li><li>Most societies need a king/parent figure.</li><li>An organization needs a single ultimate decision-maker. The time to make a decision should be less than the time it takes to implement it.</li></ul>
SOLUTION	Give the project access to a visible high-level manager who will champion the cause of the project. The patron can be the final arbiter for project decisions, which provide a driving force for the organization to make decisions quickly. The patron is accountable for removing project-level barriers that hinder progress, and is responsible for the organization's "morale" (sense of well being).

RESULTING CONTEXT

Having a patron gives the organization a sense of being and a focus for later process and organizational changes.

Other roles can be defined in terms of the patron's role.

The manager role is not to be a totally centralized control, but rather to be a champion. That is, the scope of the manager's influence is largely outside those developing the product itself, but includes those whose cooperation is necessary for the success of the product (support organizations, funders, test organizations, and so on). This role also serves as a patron or sponsor; the person is often a corporate visionary.

DESIGN RATIONALE

- I have observed this in Phillippe Kahn in *QPW*; Sethi, et al. in C++ *efforts in AT&T*; for a manager in a high-productivity Network Systems project; and in another multi-location AT&T project.
- This relates to the pattern *Firewalls*.
- Block talks about the importance of influencing forces over which the project has no direct control
- The term "pattern" comes from Middle English *patron* (and the more ancient French *patron*), which still means both "patron" and "pattern." In the sixteenth century, patron, with a shifted accent, evidently began to be pronounced "patrn;" and it was spelled as "patarne," "paterne," and "pattern." By 1700, the original form ceased to be used of things, and *patron/ pattern* became differentiated in form and sense. "The original proposed to imitation; the archetype; that which is to be copied; an exemplar (J.); an example or model deserving imitation; an example or model of a particular excellence…"—from a dictionary of medieval terms.
- Putting the developer in charge of the process implies that management (see *Firewalls*) titles become associated with support roles. This works only in a culture in which the manager *decides* to be the servant of the developer (an insight from Norm Kerth).

9.4.2 GammaForm

GammaForm patterns are motivated by a concern for good object-oriented design. They describe ways that objects can collaborate and communicate to produce a standard solution, and are not regarded as generative. Instead, they are deliberately observational and descriptive. To the extent that individual patterns are connected, the connections are relationships…indirect rather than necessary. Alexander's works are an inspiration, but no more.

In *Design Patterns* (Gamma et al. 1995), the differences are made clear:

- There are no classic examples of software design to draw from, and certainly none that are publicly visible. So, reflection and introspection about your own work and the work of designers you respect becomes an additional source of patterns, as well as established best practices, rules of thumb, and general heuristics.

- GammaForm patterns are organized as a catalog, not a language. There is no organic order to their relationships or use. Each pattern can stand alone. The context is not a connection to a higher level, and certainly not to a broader social context. Interestingly enough, one inspiration for taking a catalog approach is the writings of Donald Knuth, who provided Kent Beck (among others) with the inspiration for taking a literate approach to patterns.

- GammaForm problems are focused on the solution, not the problem. In fact, the solution descriptions are lengthy and provide the bulk of the value of GammaForm patterns.

Some of the other differences cited in *Design Patterns* seem to reflect a misunderstanding of Alexander, or at least the kind of misinterpretation that a technologist can make when dealing with the allusive language of the architect or poet. For example, Alexander's Pattern Language is seen as deterministic and prescriptive.

An easy way to see the connection between architectural patterns and GammaForm patterns is to think of objects as building components. Forces are things such as requirements, constraints, and elements of the underlying technical environment that shapes any solution. Then, in the same way that Alexander's patterns describe ways to combine walls, windows, pathways, and eating areas that generate real living spaces, so GammaForm patterns can show time-proven ways to combine objects and classes to create real working, living software.

The format that Gamma and others used in *Design Patterns* shows the differences with Alexander in form and spirit very clearly:

- *Pattern name and classification*—As with CoplienForm, the name is critical. GammaForm patterns use a name that is almost iconic and captures the essence of solution in as few words as possible. For example, Façade is a pattern about using a "unified interface."

- *Intent*—The rationale, motive, and specific problem that the pattern addresses.

- *Also known as*—The pattern may have other names it goes by in the development neighborhood. What are they?

- *Motivation*—This section is a (badly named) textual version of Alexander's picture. A motivation is a "scenario that illustrates the design problem," which provides a practical description of how the pattern solves the problem.

- *Applicability*—A mixture of context and forces. Describes situations in which the pattern is appropriate and guidelines for evaluating its fit.

- *Structure*—A "graphical representation of the classes in the pattern." In the *Design Patterns* book, this is an OMT class diagram or an interaction diagram from Booch (Gamma et al. 1995). Now, we use UML notation. In effect, a sketch.

- *Participants*—Part of the solution: classes and their responsibilities.

- *Collaborations*—Another part of the solution: how the classes work together to carry out the solution.

- *Consequences*—Yet another part of the solution, this time including a discussion of tradeoffs and results.

- *Implementation*—An extension of the instruction aspect of a solution; issues to think about when applying the pattern.

- *Sample code*—An extension of Implementation, consisting of real-life code examples.

- *Known uses*—Real-world validation where the pattern has been used in existing systems.

- *Related patterns*—Identifies other patterns similar to this one or that this one can be used with.

As you can see, there are many overlaps with CoplienForm patterns. Perhaps the main difference is that GammaForm patterns are specifically didactic, closer to spelled-out versions of Kuhn's exemplars with the solutions added. To the extent that they are concerned with personal and social transformation, it is in an indirect and professional way. For example, *Design Patterns* talks about the *Aha experience*:

> Once you understand the design patterns and have had an "Aha!" experience with them, you won't ever think about object-oriented design in the same way. You'll have insights that make your designs more flexible, modular, reusable, and understandable. (Gamma et al. 1995, xi)

Unfortunately, GammaForm patterns are typically too long to make it easy to provide an example here. *Design Patterns* is the best place to go for a detailed introduction.

9.5 The Roots: Alexander on Patterns and Pattern Languages

For Alexander, patterns, like people, are not isolated, separate, and distinct. Their value comes from their connectedness. What is important to establish first are the connections that any one pattern has. Then, within a pattern, establish its value and generativity by showing how it connects and combines the elements of the solution in a way that provides opportunities for creative use. Finally, patterns are woven into an interconnected web—a pattern language that the user can traverse in an endless variety of ways, depending on the needs of the particular situation.

The form of Alexandrian patterns is anecdotal and essay-like. Each starts with a picture, which is meant to represent an archetypal example. This is followed by a description of the context as an introduction. The description is intended to provide the first level of connectedness for the pattern by explaining how it helps to complete larger patterns—that is, by identifying other patterns in the pattern language at a different higher scale that can work with the pattern at hand.

Two versions of the problem statement follow:

- The first Alexander dubs the *headline*: a short statement of the essence of the problem in bold type.

- The second version is an extended discussion that includes examples, indications of how it can be "manifested" and validated, and anything else that helps the reader situate the problem.

Finally, separated from the rest of the pattern by a highly visible "Therefore:" comes the solution: simple, terse, straightforward text and a sketch illustrating the solution to finish the pattern. Both the words and the pictures are necessary. They constitute what Donald Schon describes as "the language of designing:"

> Drawing and talking are parallel ways of designing, and together make up what I call the language of designing. The verbal and non-verbal dimensions are closely connected. (Schon 1983, 41)

Because Alexander is an architect, his solutions are concerned with the built environment. His patterns are too long to quote in one piece, but a summary of a typical pattern provides at least some of the flavor of both their organization and their impact.

In one example, Alexander talks about the forces that have to be considered while solving the problem of building entrances. The general context is that a building is connected to public space. The context within the language is defined by other patterns dealing with Main Gates and Half-hidden Gardens.

The forces involved include the need for a "feeling of arrival," specifically, a psychological need to signal the possibility of more intimate behavior than the "street behavior" common to a public space. Coming in from the outside usually means bringing this psychological balloon of street behavior along, however.

Then, for a house (for example), there's also a need to feel that entering means entering a private domain. But the outside world is visibly public, so how is the change from public to private going to be made apparent and reinforced? (Both of these "forces" work in reverse as well; "leaving" is as much a part of the picture as arriving.)

Finally, there are technological forces to consider: at home (again as an example), most people these days arrive and leave via a car. But where and how a car is parked may be determined by convenience and add forces that are related to the convenience of the entrance with respect to the car's parking spot.

There are really three interrelated patterns here. Alexander's three solutions: create a visible and identifiable main entrance; have a varied, graduated and obvious transition area; and treat the connection to the car as a special form of transitional space. He calls these patterns Main Entrance, Entrance Transition, and Car Connection. His solutions are a great deal more detailed than my summary statement, and the descriptions of context and forces include examples and are not at all cut-and-dried. But all follow the same meta-pattern, regardless of level or topic. In software terms, his patterns are scaleable, as well as reusable and architected.

Of course, Alexander has a large number of patterns that are more bricks-and-mortar than this one. All of them emphasize what might be called social geometry, however: the relationship between how you organize what you build on the grid of the social dimensions that are the underlying needs to be met.

In the same way that words combined into phrases make speech possible as a creative act, patterns in combination are the basis for creative design and building. As in spoken language, a tacit structuring of the patterns as language elements in the pattern language—and the possibility of dynamically arranging and rearranging them—is what gives both patterns and the pattern language a generative and creative aspect.

For the patterns practitioner, the interconnectedness of the patterns makes possible results, which are themselves also connected and more than the simple sum of their parts. Alexander describes this as "compression": Putting *A* together with *B* results in a whole that is richer and healthier and better than the individual parts in isolation, and it is denser in "meaning"—more than simple synergy. A quality emerges from the combination that is inexplicable solely in terms of the individual elements.

Alexander's pattern language is structured by scale. But his scale combines the physical and the social; it is not just about "numbers of houses." It is also about the events and interactions—the life—that take place in those houses, a life that both derives from and shapes the way they are arranged and built. So, his patterns include social context and comment in discussing the driving forces behind each solution.

For example, at the highest level, patterns about the size of regions and the physical interweaving of city and country are leavened by a pattern called Lace Of Country Streets, which includes the observation that "the suburb is an obsolete and contradictory form of human settlement" (Alexander, Ishikawa, and Silverstein 1977, 244). Another example is Scattered Workplaces, which talks about the need to avoid dead spaces where only work is accommodated: "Prohibit large concentrations of work, without family life around them."

9.6 A Note on This Language

The pattern language in this book is subject to the same criticisms that I've leveled at the body of software patterns in general. The patterns here don't rise to the level of literature, and the pattern language itself lacks the obvious connectedness of Alexander.

Ideally, patterns about modeling should be able to incorporate social dimensions and cognitive dimensions where these are useful. At the same time, they need to be pithy and practical. In order to achieve these goals, I used a framework that will prove serviceable for evolving this language over time, and a language structure that fits the subject matter, rather than following Alexander directly or copying any existing software patterns approach.

The connectedness of the language is built into the recursiveness of its levels and the commonality of its idioms. It is explicitly expressed in a discussion of common forces that precedes the body of each chapter, and brief notes on related patterns and other material that end each chapter.

I broke the language into levels and idioms. The levels (Domain, Product, and Component) reflect the implicit architecture of what is being built: models of modern software-intensive systems. The levels themselves are recursive: for example, patterns at the Domain level can also be applied at the Product level, and to some extent at the Component level. The levels are conceptually convenient, but not watertight. The idioms apply across all levels.

Alexander connected his patterns between levels and within levels via references in the context section. With a smaller number of patterns, I drew out common forces for each level that are inherited in whole or in part across many of the patterns in that level. The connectedness between levels has been left, for the moment, to the discussion that begins a chapter.

Alexander connected his patterns to life and the world outside architecture through non-architectural quotes and ideas embedded in his patterns. I did this a little, but I relied, for the most part, on using the introductory chapters and this end section as the location for those connections.

So, to some extent, my solutions to shaping a language are compromises that may disappear with more patterns. However, they also represent first thoughts on how a language like this one should ideally be shaped.

9.7 The Importance of Patterns

I started this chapter by differentiating patterns from other artifacts of software development, emphasizing their social, learning, and non-technical qualities. I detailed the history of patterns in order to provide them with a human and social face, and to provide the reader with an understanding of how something as different as patterns can emerge naturally as collective learning in response to critical professional needs. I explored the two significant alternative forms for patterns in order to underline the flexibility of the pattern idea. The two formats are not competitive, but complementary. However, to be useful, they require the user's understanding of the reasons behind differences that are anything but cosmetic. Finally, I included some significant detail on Alexander, essential background for anyone who wants to really understand patterns.

What remains is to explain why patterns are important, beyond the importance of any one pattern or set of patterns, and where they're going.

To me, their importance stems from the way they support the unchanging nature of work and learning in software design, within emerging forms of social practice. In particular, they reinforce the non-technical aspects of the practice of software design—the parts that make systems work differently from engineering and more than the boys-with-toys mania that seems to be the focus of so many technologists in information technology.

The collaboration, constant churn of ideas, shifting boundaries, and human social problems that have been the bedrock of systems development as a practice since the start resist easy formalization or ongoing efforts to make working with computers into a science. Patterns, with their lack of standards, social nature, and collaborative purposes and origins, help maintain a connection with the human side of what we, as developers, do.

In this, they exemplify and enhance the social practice of development. The quote on "stolen knowledge" that starts this chapter is from a piece by John Seeley Brown and Paul Duguid of The Institute for Learning Research, an offshoot of Xerox's famous PARC research lab (1992). They explain that the Tagore "stole" knowledge by watching and listening to the musician playing outside his classes, for his own and others' entertainment: "[o]nly then, and not in dismembered didactic exercises, was Tagore able to see and understand the social practice of musicianship." That is, the way making music is about a shared doing and a social context that connects the musicians and their ever-shifting audience.

Both as the basis for an informal set of practical processes, within a development effort and between practitioners, and as a vehicle for the results, patterns have turned out to be a means of enabling "stolen knowledge."

Patterns have also turned out to be sublime collaborative technology:

> …a truly collaborative technology is one which allows participants to transform a shared experience that is lacking clear possibilities for action into an experience that can be routinely and meaningfully handled by their community…Collaborative technology…allows the community to reconstruct a shared experience continually so as to produce greater meaning and greater potential for successful future action. (Roschelle 1995)

One way to look at patterns that throws light on their almost paradoxical quality is from the perspective of *situated learning* and *communities of practice*, two recent ideas that are related—and ones that echo parts of Kuhn's writings on scientific paradigms.

The Institute for Learning Research started using the term *situated learning* at about the same time that the patterns community was forming. A formal definition from one of its papers describes the connection between situated learning and communities of practice:

> Situated learning…[holds that) enquiries into learning and cognition must take serious account of social interaction and physical activity. A unifying concept emerging from situated learning research is "communities of practice"—the idea that learning is constituted through the sharing of purposeful, patterned activity…This idea stresses "practice" and "community" equally. Knowledge is seen as practical capability for doing and making…a community of practice arises through the coordinated use of technologies (broadly defined to include language) to arrive at mutually intelligible resolutions to shared problematic experience. (Roschelle 1995)

Fortune magazine described communities of practice less formally:

> Groups that learn, communities of practice, have special characteristics. They emerge of their own accord: [a number of] people find themselves drawn to one another by a force that's both social and professional. They collaborate directly, use one another as sounding boards, teach each other… (Managing: Ideas and Solutions/The Leading Edge 1996)

Communities of practice have typically been defined by theorists as occurring *within* well-bounded organizations. And, indeed, one of the significant social and cultural benefits that patterns can bring to an organization is to provide the vernacular that facilitates the emergence of so-called *local communities of practice*. However, as the history of the pattern community sketched in this chapter suggests, a broad-based community of practice can emerge that crosses organizational boundaries and, in a networked world, reworks the ratio of social interaction and physical activity.

A broad-based community of practice provides a foundation for a common culture focused on learning and sharing, without being prescriptive and dependent on explicit rules. The reason for this, to paraphrase Thomas Kuhn, is that paradigms precede and have priority over rules—explicit rules are not necessary after a shared paradigm is established. A shared paradigm makes possible normal intellectual activity within a community of practice. As Donald Schon puts it, an individual practitioner builds up "a repertoire of examples, images, understandings and actions"(1983) that combine art and technique, and permit problems to be dealt with creatively and uniquely. This repertoire is the practitioner's conceptual toolkit.

A community of practice such as the patterns community finds ways to share these toolkits via a common vocabulary that includes not only words, but also actions and images.

The PLoP and OOPSLA workshops; and the various books, Web pages, magazine articles, and discussion lists that have resulted all document the existence of a patterns community. It is informal, self-defined, and ever-changing. Although ephemeral in these respects, it is very important to the core of patterns enthusiasts who shape the direction of patterns and provide the intellectual ferment necessary to generate new ideas.

In the case of patterns, the Alexandrian paradigm made it possible for a general community of thinkers and doers to emerge, as well as making possible the general body of ideas they produced. And, in promoting a form of community of practice, the paradigm (using Kuhn's meaning) established an example for the best way to do and use patterns.

9.8   Where Is It All Going?

Peter Coad's 1992 *Communications of the ACM* article ended on a note that is still very appropriate today, by identifying work that still needs to be done to make patterns truly useful:

> This article is only a very small beginning of the work to be done on investigating, finding, and applying object-oriented patterns. Additional investigation is needed on pattern discovery and usage. Given a large number of OOA and OOD results, can one apply a systematic approach to discovering and cataloging patterns? Is there a hierarchy of patterns— How does one look at examples and derive guidelines for best usage? What strategies can be used for connecting one pattern to another? When does the occurrence of one pattern imply the need for another companion pattern? (152-159)

And Jim Coplien insists that patterns are going to be about something more than object-oriented design, perhaps as a critical element for avoiding the potential rigidities inherent in a modularized, component approach to systems:

> [Objects] happened to be the predominate worldview when patterns took root. I believe patterns took root in the face of complexity. Objects may have aided the rise of patterns just because they're so antithetical to patterns, and underscore the need for something like patterns. Alexander himself underscored the danger of building from pre-manufactured parts. Patterns offer a broader view of software, helping us think about software at the system level, the architectural level. I think there's a strong future there. But it will be a folk development that will blossom of its own accord, and best be left to its own maturation without too much conscious direction or tampering. (Coplien 1997)

Ironically, the future of patterns may be shaped by the very trends abjured by the patterns community. Currently, the shifting sands of software development fashion favor components over objects. The baton of the silver bullet has been passed on, from essentially handcrafted objects to a form of industrial development that is off-the-shelf. The coming of e-commerce, the Internet, other networks, and the millennium have ramped up the issue of complexity-management. So, although patterns may now be seen as the putative salvation of objects, perhaps soon they will be saving "componentware" development from itself.

Regardless of what else they help happen, patterns have become established as a part of the future of software development. Their real benefit may be realized some time in the future when they help to mature a noticeably immature craft:

> Alexander's pattern language contains over 250 patterns, organized from high level to low level. The goal in documenting patterns that exist in software architectures is to arrive at a similar system, but this will take time. (Berczuk 1994)

CHAPTER 10

The UML in Context

There is no right or wrong model, merely one that
is more useful for the job at hand.

—*Martin Fowler, Analysis Patterns (1997, 2)*

Chapter 2, "The Unified Modeling Language," explored the roots of the UML within the traditions of software development. Chapter 3, "UML Essentials, Elements, and Artifacts," described (briefly) the elements and artifacts of the language. And, of course, the patterns in Part II have given a glimpse of how to use the UML for modeling. This chapter will situate the UML in the practice of modeling and discuss the basic ideas behind the UML—but as a modeling language, not just a development tool. In particular, I will explore some of the ideas that are important in making the UML different from previous modeling faculties, such as its emphasis on abstractions and architecture, and its flexibility. I intend to leave the reader with the basis for forming a critical appreciation of the UML, which will help to come to terms with how to use it now and how to respond to the changes that will inevitably reshape it as it matures.

10.1 Why Make System Models?

As is the case with so many terms in software development, a certain ambiguity has shaded the connections between modeling, design, and building in the practice of developing systems.

In many methodologies, there is a *design phase* that is distinct from the analysis and implementation phases (for example). Partly as a result of the rigidities of mainframe development, for many the practice of design has become synonymous with the activities that are part of the design phase—even after the demise of mainframe culture. The Gang of Four design patterns book (Gamma et al. 1995) is a reflection of this labeling; the book focuses on patterns that fit neatly into that middle world between identifying requirements and implementing the results in code.

The old notion (frequently preached, seldom practiced) of getting the requirements 100 percent complete and verifiably correct before design has, of course, been replaced by more practical approaches that emphasize iterative analysis, design, and development, and the gradual evolution of requirements. In particular, increasingly sophisticated approaches to modeling have made it possible for developers to treat requirements and analysis activities as elements of the design process and to use a broader palette of design techniques in their work.

Meanwhile, at the other end of the development process, building code is a separate activity, although one that is driven in a sensible organization by models. It should also be noted that the resurrection of modeling has brought with it renewed respectability for prototyping. In some ways, the building of prototypes is now an element of the design process that needs to be performed differently from coding as well. But coding in the traditional sense remains a personal skill with, frequently, an idiosyncratic quality. It is constrained by standards but, it is usually executed in solitude.

In contrast, modeling is a critical design skill with communal qualities, constrained more by the need to communicate and describe effectively than by prescriptive standards. Design itself has become an ongoing and collaborative process that permeates virtually all of the activities in modern software development. Even planning and management are shaped by the iterative, incremental, architected approach to development that both reflects and encourages the re-emergence of modeling. As a result, modeling is becoming a community effort that helps ensure that what is developed is what was intended and agreed upon, not just a compromise between the designer's vision and the technical constraints.

So, one answer to the question of "Why make systems models?" is that they are the keys to a collaborative design process that is becoming the core of software development today. One implication of all of this is that the practice of design must now be considered separately from the process of development—the usual context for looking at systems design and software modeling. In fact, the practice of design needs to be understood by anyone engaged in systems development.

10.1.1   What Use Is a Model?

Another answer to the question of "Why make system models?" comes from the end result: the models themselves. Models are useful ways to manage the complexity of software development by means of a technique called *abstraction*. In short, a model represents edited details of a system reality from an aggregation of specific perspectives.

Because business modeling is one of the valid uses of the UML, and a business is a *system* from a systems perspective, models are abstractions of a system that can include a business in the UML.

Models are the products of the (small *d*) design process: interpretations, representations, and specifications of two simplified and connected realities (one descriptive and one prescriptive). There are two realities involved. The real world, including the context of the system and the things that it interacts with in the outside world, need to be modeled—just as much as the end result. Models are containers for knowledge about both the why and how of the system.

In effect, the system reality being modeled connects the problem space being described (requirements, analysis, and functional specification) with the solution space being prescribed (design, construction, testing, and deployment). Unlike any other technology in the history of humanity, software development goes to great pains to connect an interpretive conceptualization of the problem space being addressed to a prescriptive solution. Models mediate this connection.

This is the obvious role of models: the end products of system design, the realization of the idea of the system. Even here, though, there's a nuance to consider. The style and shape of a model is a reflection of cultural, social, and political forces at work in the development process and in the development and client organizations. A model is not only a standardized representation, even in the most prim development shop. And UML models, in particular, are situated culturally and socially in the organizations and processes that they both reflect and shape.

More narrowly, even within the confines of the technical aspects of a system, the architectural style of a system is not just a product of the architectural constraints and choices that are made, but also a reflection of the modeling constructs consciously selected by the architect. As Ivar Jacobson, Martin Griss, and Patrick Jonsson explain in *Software Reuse: Architecture, Process and Organization for Business Success*, "[W]e can think of the architectural style as the set of all (good) models that can be built" using these constructs (1997, 51).

The UML specifically caters to the idea of modeling as an active medium for design, shaping both the process and the results. Stereotypes and other extension capabilities provide for graphical customization. The acceptance of incompleteness and inconsistency as givens for some models and diagrams sometimes encourages the use of models as gestures in an ongoing dance with users and stakeholders. The notion of models being *view-driven* reinforces the shaping force of interpretation. The inclusion of flexible packaging constructs provides for variations in the structure of models for purposes that aren't just technical and implementation-bound.

10.2   Every Picture Tells a Story: The UML as a Modeling Language

A good place to start with the UML is to think about the difference between a programming language and a modeling language.

Unlike a programming language, which derives its effectiveness from syntax (the orderly and correct arrangement of its elements), a *modeling language* relies on its semantics, the meaning implicit in each element, and the way elements connect conceptually to achieve a useful end result.

A program is just so many pieces of text; every piece of text has a functional meaning defined by rules of usage. The syntax is critical: a word used in the wrong place is meaningless, or (worse) an error. The semantics is only local—source code can call an apple an orange and still execute properly, as long as the intent is to uniquely name an object and the naming is consistent. The name has nothing to do with the underlying operations. Naming and labeling are quite separate.

Because a program does something, like a machine, only the instructions have to be correct. However, there's no room for clever interpretation. Any cleverness is left to the program creator, by means of algorithmic and organizational compression rather than clever abstraction. But because a programming language is prescriptive and we don't expect prescriptions to be interpreted, even logical compression itself is regarded as bad style in programming because it forces maintenance programmers to interpret and puzzle out meaning that should be explicit, even obvious.

Models are different—less focused on the machine. One way to look at a model is as a structured collection of collaborating symbols—an architecture of abstractions. The syntax is important, but because a model exists to communicate, not do, interpretation is the key.

A model has no life on its own; it lives only through the meaning that its human interpreters provide collectively: in a model, unlike a program, calling an apple an orange will confuse or perhaps be taken as poetic. In presenting models, graphical syntax is important but not critical—the location of symbols or the shape of their connections is as much a result of style or convenience as anything else.

This distinction goes to the heart of the purpose of modeling and is critical to achieving a level of comfort with the UML.

UML models are not formal specifications by themselves; they are analysis, design, and management tools. Trying to equate them with blueprints muddies the metaphorical waters for modeling practitioners in an effort to tie modeling to one ultimate end product—constructed software systems. Blueprints are working drawings; they are, hopefully, rigorous specifications for constructing a physical reality in an unambiguous fashion. Their purpose is translation, not interpretation and communication, so syntax is more important than semantics. The real architectural analogy is to architectural drawings as a whole, not just to blueprints. J.A. Zachmann made this point in his seminal paper on architectural frameworks for information systems back in 1987. Zachman emphasized that each standard architectural representation used in the design and construction of a building "differs from the others in essence, not merely in level of detail" (1999, 460). He made those differences an important part of his explanation of system architecture.

The difference isn't just in content and level of detail; it's also in purpose and the way the act of drawing (or modeling, in the case of software systems) impacts the process. In *Why Architects Draw*, Edward Robbins talks about the different types of drawings an architect produces, ranging from those that are very personal and conceptual to working drawings, "conventionalized representations… produced at the end of the design process" for the builders and lawyers. "[W]ith the exception of the working drawings, how one chooses to draw suggests a whole series of complex viewpoints" that are selectively rendered in different kinds of drawings (1994, 27). The art and the usefulness are in the selection as well as in the result; the act of drawing shapes is the end result beyond the content of the drawings. Only working drawings are conventional and, therefore, not situated in the particular culture and context of the design.

The *UML Specification* says something similar: "The choice of what models and diagrams one creates has a profound influence upon how a problem is attacked and how a corresponding solution is shaped" (Rational Software Corporation 1999, 1–3). Interestingly enough, the UML as a collective product recognizes a distinction that individual interpreters usually don't. It goes on to identify other considerations that echo the way drawings are used in architecture:

- Every complex system is best approached through a small set of nearly independent views of a model. No single view is sufficient.

- Every model may be expressed at different levels of fidelity.

There are other similarities between architectural drawings and system models; in particular, both are used as the basis for the planning of work and, more importantly, for conceptual experimentation. "Models give us the opportunity to fail under controlled conditions" (Booch 1994, 22).

There *are* dissimilarities. Unlike the free-form conceptual compositions of architectural drawing, in a model every element has some meaning; the UML does impose rules about what can and can't appear in presenting a model element in a diagram. But still, like a drawing, each diagram and model is meant to be taken as a whole, with the context playing a primary role in telling the story. The context for a model is the view it realizes. In the UML, each model is a reflection of the user and the uses of the model. It represents the system from a particular viewpoint.

Every picture tells a story, as one rock-and-roll song suggests. Sometimes, the story is meant to be creative and informal, sometimes it is formal, sometimes it is about organizing work. Regardless, with the UML, it is always a story with a point of view.

10.3   The *UML Specification* and Metamodel

System models, like fashion models, depend on "body language" to convey the ineffable, but they rely on standard postures and gestures to get the point across. Semantics define the standard postures and gestures for a modeling language (and notational style is the graphic equivalent of body language).

The UML formalizes the semantics of modeling in its *Specification* document. The language is based on a model itself, a metamodel, that is consistent with the object-oriented paradigm that gave it birth. The metamodel defines the connection between a system and its representation in UML models, and the architecture of the language.

The metamodel defines modeling language architecture in a way that reflects standard object-oriented constructs; for example, a modeling language is an instance of the metamodel. Recursively, a model then "define(s) a language that describes an information domain" (Rational Software Organization 1999, 2–5). In effect, each set of models of a system is a dialect of the modeling language, in which the basic rules are set by the language, but the actual realization is a product of the forces at work within the development environment.

The *UML Specification* fleshes out the metamodel, and comprises a very detailed understanding of models and their essential elements, one that is important to understand to be able to get the most benefit out of using the UML as a language.

In the UML, a system is packaged into one or more models, each reflecting a perspective on the system in a way that is useful for users rather than fitting some prescribed theoretical framework. In turn, models are made up of model elements. And, as mentioned earlier, models represent either the external reality of aspects of the real world or the internal reality of a constructed reality—a software system.

UML models are *not* diagrams and pictures. Although models and model elements *represent* the system they refer to, they are distinct from the graphical presentation used to communicate their meaning symbolically. The following is from the *UML Specification*:

> *model*
>
> An abstraction of a physical system, with a certain purpose.
>
> See: physical system.
>
> *physical system*
>
> 1. The subject of a model.
>
> 2. A collection of connected physical units, which can include software, hardware, and people that are organized to accomplish a specific purpose. A physical system can be described by one or more models, possibly from different viewpoints. (Rational Software Corporation 1999)

The original Greek meaning of symbol (*symballein*) was "to bring or throw or put together" (Illich 1996, 31)—a collectively understood token or mark. Symbol took on the notion of *sign*, with the implications of some real connection to an external reality, much later.

The ancient Greeks got all hung up about whether art should be *matching* (copying the real world) or *making* (inventing one). Modeling faces a similar controversy: should we use objects to denote abstractions in the domain, or does this imply an implementation that is premature? The schizophrenic etymology of symbol is partly at fault.

UML diagrams combine symbols as tokens with symbols as signs, but in a way that magically reverses the history of symbols. The real world is presented through tokens of a collective understanding, attempts to match things out there; the constructed, imagined world is embodied in signs. As modelers, we can know the real world only as shadows, but we know our constructions in an intimate and unique way because we make them. The trick is to juggle the two when we build models to communicate and express our understanding, something that the UML makes uniquely possible.

The graphical presentation of a model is defined by the notation standards of the UML. The UML mandates notational standards to ensure semantic consistency in the use of models to represent and communicate. The *UML Specification* describes the UML notation as "[a] human-readable notation for representing OA&D models...an elegant graphic syntax for consistently expressing the UML's rich semantics...an essential part of OA&D modeling and the UML" (Rational Software Corporation 1999, xi).

Various presentation elements are used to communicate the meaning of a model. Each model element has one or more alternative presentation elements that the modeler can use in depicting views of the model. Presentation elements are packaged by means of diagrams, which are themselves a type of model element.

A *diagram* is a specific instance of model information. Diagrams provide succinct views of aspects of the model that are practical and meaningful for a particular purpose. Each presents a subset of information about a particular model at a point in time.

The model itself provides the overall view that defines the landscape from the perspective of the viewer. Within a model, each diagram shows information useful for a purpose, but (usually) not all the information available. The UML allows the suppression or omission of many diagram elements to facilitate visual clarity or to emphasize a specific aspect of a model. So, a particular UML diagram may or may not show all there is to see about the model elements being presented.

Because the graphical syntax of the UML is so flexible and limited in its con-straining effect, the UML rules governing syntactical correctness are not expres-sions of some theoretical perspective, but are practical and sensible instead. In fact, rather than talking about *correctness*, the UML talks about "well-formedness," a soft-edged concept that allows for precise rules applied with discrimination.

For example, vendors are "expected to apply some discretion about how strictly the well-formed rules are enforced. Tools should be able to report on well-formedness violations, but not necessarily force all models to be well formed. Incomplete models are common during certain phases of the develop-ment lifecycle, so they should be permitted" (Rational Software Corporation 1999, xvi). At any rate, well-formedness is a matter of semantics rather than syntax, and the *UML Specification* seems especially muddled about what well-formedness is, although each ModelElement does come with a set of rules.

10.4   What Do We Model?

Although the *UML Specification* talks about modeling "software-intensive systems" (Rational Software Corporation 1999, 1–7), it leaves that idea largely undefined. A better way to look at systems modeling is in terms of the three elements that go into making a software product and that form, in a loose way, the real system behind any application, as illustrated in Figure 10.1.

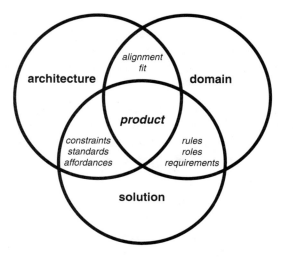

FIGURE 10.1   *The elements of a system product.*

Typically, modeling is not just about the end product itself. Instead, designers model the architecture, the domain and the solution, in the process of arriving at a model of the product. Each of these can be looked at and modeled in a recursive fashion. And increasingly, with component-based and iterative development, and the focus on reuse at every level, modeling will build on previously developed models by means of refinement and refactoring instead of being an exercise in reinventing the wheel.

10.4.1 Architecture

As an abstraction, an architecture provides a high-level view of the system or portions of the system. It highlights the most important elements and key features of a system and provides a framework for the details. It is not the design (or as Jacobson, Griss, and Jonsson [1997] maintain, the design is not just the architecture). Rather, it is the embodiment of the strategic decisions around organization and structure for a given technical or business solution.

For a system, architecture is recursive: a system embodies an architecture and also reflects exogenous architectures of different types, such as the enterprise architecture and the network architecture. In fact, architecture provides a "context for the systematic integration of IT into business and a conceptual framework for thinking about the business itself" (Wladawsky-Berger 1999, 449) that facilitates strategic alignment and functional fit.

At the level of an application, an architecture is a structured representation of the pieces of a system and the connections between them. It may include dynamic elements (explanations of behavior) as well as static elements (explanations of organization). It is not the system design; as Philippe Kruchten writes: "Architecture is what remains when you cannot take away any more things and still understand the system" (1998, 78).

It is multi-leveled and loosely recursive. For example, the architecture of an application is constrained by the technical architecture of its target environment and shaped by the enterprise architecture it services. In turn, the technical architecture may be made up of a network architecture, a service architecture, a workstation architecture…and more.

An application may be a packaging of components. Each component might have an architecture itself if coarse-grained, or it may adhere to an architectural framework that provides the key standards for its development and use. In most cases, this architecture will be standardized; Enterprise JavaBeans is an example. Component purchases will more than likely need to be managed through contracts that specify architecture as well as services and interfaces because only the architecture can provide a measure of the complexity of a component, and therefore a handle on the risk.

The multiple uses of the term *architecture* in systems actually cover three similar but different ideas: architecture itself, framework, and topology. The UML metamodel I described briefly is a good (although abstract) example of an *architecture* model. A *framework* is narrower in scope, typically covering a specific domain or even an application: a financial suite architecture would be one example. Finally, a *topology* is more like a map; a network architecture showing the deployment of LANs and routers would be an example.

Even though the distinction that I drew between the three types is not part of the standard vocabulary of systems, it suggests using different types of models for each architecture type:

- A conventional layered, static model for an architecture.

- A package of collaborations for a framework.

- A deployment diagram for a topology.

And, in fact, this seems to be an emerging pattern.

The idea of architecture requires more discussion, not the least because the UML has made architecture an active ingredient in modeling to such an extent. Therefore, I'll return to it in detail a little later.

10.4.2 Domains

A domain is an *area of interest* (the typical dictionary definition of *domain*) with the following:

- A vocabulary of business abstractions (events, concepts, things) that can be shared across applications

- A common set of needs and, perhaps, opportunities

A domain provides the immediate context for software development, and defines the scope of the area of interest and focus of attention for a solution.

This is my definition, synthesized from the multiple variations being used. The idea of domains, like the idea of systems' best practices that I discussed earlier, is in the eye of the beholder. For a software developer with a reuse perspective, a domain may be a *family of applications* or a *product line*—that is, a collection of products. For someone doing business re-engineering, it may be the overall enterprise or a functional area.

Domain engineering and analysis are recent additions to the development toolset, and so there's still a lot of terminological churn around *domain*. Beneath the hubbub, they added a key area (beyond those of scope, context, and vocabulary) that needs to be modeled in the face of an emerging emphasis on reuse: commonality/variability.

Visability
Perspective

Domain models define boundaries and scope for engineering, design, and management. They provide the common vocabulary that brings together the development team and the user community. They are created with or by *domain experts* (the stakeholders formerly known as *subject matter experts*). They are analyzed for elements of commonality that can be factored out to provide a basis for high-level reuse. Within a domain, chunks of significant variations provide the basis for distinguishing individual products.

A domain can and should be modeled in a fashion that is equally as recursive as an architecture. The enterprise as a whole, or even an interpolation of enterprises, may need to be modeled to provide the context and vocabulary for the problem space. The result, an enterprise model, is used to align a high-level technology architecture with the strategic direction of the business.

For example, shared systems that support multiple *co-opetive* organizations by providing shared services and a common infrastructure need to be modeled across organization boundaries. Supply chain and extranet-based systems may need to be modeled similarly, without regard to the fading "Berlin Walls" of organizational boundaries.

Of course, there are multiple even overlapping domains within an organization that can be viewed and modeled, depending on the focus of the analysis and the business needs to be served. A functional perspective may serve the operational aspects of the organization. A workflow perspective may serve the customer-driven aspects of an organization.

Chapter 6, "Domain Patterns," provides a picture of the essential elements of domain modeling based on the previous discussion. However, some development approaches extend the notion of domain. Jim Coplien talks about concepts such as problem domains and solution domains in his latest writings. The Shlaer-Mellor methodology breaks a system down into multiple interacting domains, including an application domain (the area of interest to the end user) and a variety of technical domains, covering the technology and infrastructure aspects of the system.

10.4.3 Products

A product is both narrow and extensive. On the one hand, it is what is delivered to the customer one slice at a time. On the other, it is what is managed by the producing organization, through its life. Ultimately, a product is what is planned, managed, and delivered to the end user as a unit.

Products have a life and a lifecycle that is separate from the development lifecycle, especially now with iterative design and incremental delivery. They are birthed, introduced, evolved, matured, and theoretically have a sunset. Whether internal to an organization or sold on the open market, they need to managed and modeled beyond the boundaries of a single development project, and provide the context for specifying and designing each development spurt. The product "owns" the design artifacts, including the requirements.

10.4.4 Solutions

In some ways, the great technological achievement of the nineteenth century was the discovery of systems. The focus of technology innovators shifted from the individual tool or invention—the machine—to the whole environment that was needed to make a piece of technology practical, useful, and profitable. Both Edison and Ford were examples of whole system thinking: for example, the electrical lamp required the provision of generating stations, distribution facilities, and a marketing infrastructure. A product was not enough.

In the schema you're exploring, a *solution* is the total package—what Geoffrey Moore, the technology marketing guru, called a "whole product" in his influential book *Crossing the Chasm* (1991, 110–135). It's the idea of the product extended to include varying perceptions of the product and an enlarged understanding of what is needed to make a product successful. Although Moore's book is about marketing new technology, rather than developing it, many of the points he raises need to be part of the design process to help shape the models that are produced. They provide an additional aspect of product context, beyond what's identified from investigating the domain.

Essentially, in discussing the idea of a product, Moore says he is leveraging the work of Theodore Levitt (1984). According to Moore, Levitt suggested that there's a gap between the marketing promise made to the customer and what the customer gets.

This is familiar territory to software developers, for whom managing user expectations is a skill as critical as marketing, and for whom communications among the players in a development effort is never perfect. Anyone who's been in software development for any length of time has seen the cartoon that shows a swing built by IT as understood from the perspective of the roles of analyst, designer, programmer and user. What the user wanted, a board hanging from a tree branch by two ropes, ends up as a tire suspended across the trunk of a tree. The tree is held up on poles, with a hole in the trunk to accommodate the swing.

Levitt identifies four perspectives for a product, which, as I interpret them for software development, include the following:

- The generic product—what the user gets.

- The expected product—what the user thought he or she was getting—the minimum configuration needed to satisfy the user.

- The augmented product—the product fleshed out in a way that will meet the maximum expectations of the user.

- The potential product—the product's room for growth as supporting products become available and enhancements are made.

Each is a slice of the product in time as envisioned by the designer.

Moore uses a PC as an example. The generic PC is the basic box. The expected product includes a keyboard, monitor, and mouse. The augmented product includes a printer, some software, training, and real support. The potential PC could include blue-sky add-ons such as voice recognition and an integrated development environment. (Since *Crossing The Chasm* was published in 1991, its influence has become obvious in the way that PCs are marketed today.)

These perspectives are worth incorporating into the design and planning process for software, and some might be useful to model as part of an incremental development lifecycle. For example, one corollary consideration Moore presents is that the different *types* of product may be useful at different stages in the life of a product; with early adopters, for example, being more forgiving and adaptable when presented with a product that is generic.

Moore offers his own vision of the whole product that is more directly and obviously applicable to thinking about a solution. It provides the basis for that outside-the-box thinking that needs to be a part of the modeling exercise. His version has two components rather than the four product types: the product as delivered and the supporting services and features that need to be provided to make the purchase and use successful. So, his whole product diagram includes items such as testing, installation, training, and documentation. These are all aspects of a successful development effort that need to be considered early on, rather than at the end, and need to be evolved as the development effort proceeds as well as over the life of the product.

These insights can be applied usefully within an organization as well. The Software Engineering Institute, source of the Capability Maturity Model, is currently working on a process for facilitating the adoption of new technology that interprets Moore's ideas.

Neither Levitt's nor Moore's version of whole product thinking in defining a solution is supported directly or even required by the UML. Despite an understanding that products evolve, both when being designed and after, there's not much in the UML to support a product lifecycle or whole product thinking. Both fall into the category of items that need to be documented and made part of the model packaging as text and non-standard diagrams that supplement the UML diagrams.

Perhaps this is a good thing. As Desmond D'Souza and Alan Wills write, the emphasis should be "on small fragments of models interleaved with explanatory prose" (1998, 708) by using narrative text to communicate the informal elements rather than glossy diagrams in a picture book. In a sense, this approach consists of applying the whole product idea to UML models themselves.

10.5   Abstraction and Architecture Made Simple

Abstraction and *architecture* are the two key concepts that the UML enshrines, in a way that previous generations of modeling tools and methodologies didn't. So far, I used the terms without detailed explanation, relying on a general sense of what they mean to carry the day. However, despite the often self-proclaimed desire of a large part of the systems community to embrace formality and rigor, these terms in particular suffer from "definitional diarrhea" in common use. So, because they are both so important within the UML, it's worth taking some time to ground them.

10.5.1   Abstraction

For the UML, abstraction is the key conceptual connection with object-oriented programming. Modeling is about making, manipulating, and managing abstractions. Objects *are* abstractions—ones that cross the threshold between modeling and programming.

Abstractions are to modeling and object-orientation what algorithms are to structured programming: the meat of the matter. As Booch puts it: "[D]eciding on the right set of abstractions for a given domain is the central problem in object-orientation" (1994, 42). His comment applies to modeling using the UML just as easily.

Models manage complexity by means of abstraction. A modeling language provides a variety of means for abstracting, often in ways that parallel abstraction in object-oriented programming languages.

For the most part, the UML documentation invokes only a basic explanation of abstraction: abstraction as a filtering of reality, an elimination of unnecessary details, and the creation of simplified views.

This could be seen as the fundamental abstraction for programming, which is probably why it has became a touchstone definition for abstraction itself within the UML. The UML as a modeling language has a different scope from programming languages, as part of a broader set of purposes. Therefore, many of the abstractions used in modeling are not programmatic. In the UML, abstractions frequently reflect the abstractions of object-oriented programming, but often they don't. For example, *association* (basically, a loose link between classes) and *aggregation* (a loose collection of classes) can be approximated with varying precision by a programmer, depending on whether the target language is Smalltalk, Java, or C++. Other abstractions, such as role or use case, don't have any directly corresponding programming abstractions.

The UML implicitly supports a broad understanding of the process of abstracting:

- *Models themselves abstract by packaging.* Packaging is typically a management abstraction, whether the management in question is for communication or conceptualization (or both), or simply to organize models. Management is easier with packages, as long as the packaging is understood to be driven by exogenous considerations, and may not have any essential connection to what is being modeled.

  The UML provides *packages* (details in Chapter 3) as a construct for a model organization that resembles programmatic modularization in intent. That is, it facilitates the grouping of logically connected elements while minimizing connections between individual elements of different groups, following the principles of coupling and cohesion. Desmond D'Souza and Alan Wills wisely suggest that documentation should be structured around package structure (1998, 709).

  Models and diagrams are also packaging abstractions, and in some ways, the UML's approach to patterns can also be seen as a way of performing conceptual packaging.

- *Model and presentation elements abstract by filtering.* Unnecessary details about things and their connections are hidden from sight, and what is left as necessary depends on the diagram's perspective or view. This is the meaning that the UML documentation relies on for abstraction in general, and is what is intended when elision is mentioned. The UML actively supports the idea of leaving out unnecessary information from a diagram and having multiple expressions of the same model elements that show different pieces of the puzzle.

- *Model and presentation elements (such as symbols and forms) also provide operational abstractions.* This is the term Desmond D'Souza uses for black-box abstraction, derived from Booch. It is used, for instance, when testing against a specification. In modeling, operational abstractions are placeholders that have implied *effects* (modeling features, services, and behaviors) that can be associated with the instance that is being represented. For example, because a box symbolizes *class* or *type*, a box called Customer in a class diagram can be assumed to exhibit the syntactic and semantic behavior of a class in the model that contains the diagram.

Note

D'Souza and Booch sprinkle their main books with good material on abstraction—D'Souza with more of a design flavor (1998) and Booch with more of a programming flavor (1994).

The *UML Specification* also enshrines abstraction idiomatically as a model element in the metamodel, by means of constructs that are not so clearly programmatic. In other words, it supports abstraction explicitly as well as implicitly.

The explicit version of abstraction in the UML is focused on modeling needs— inevitably because it is part of a specification. In particular, it gives the modeler the means to organize the model components in ways that are more sophisticated than the simple hierarchical structures of Chinese boxes that preceded the UML.

An abstraction is a dependency relationship between two model elements or sets of model elements. According to the *UML Specification*, the abstracting takes place between a *supplier* element and a *client* element, but this implies a hierarchy, which is not necessarily the case. There *does* have to be an overt relationship between the two—they have to "represent the same concept at different levels of abstraction or from different viewpoints" (Rational Software

Corporation 1999, 2–19). Being good object-oriented citizens, the supplier-client relationship can be one to many in either direction, or even many-to-many. It can be unidirectional or bi–directional.

Abstraction is presented graphically as stereotyped versions of the dependency relationship. I've already mentioned the abstraction stereotypes (as of UML 1.3): derivation, realization, refinement, and trace (see Chapter 3).

10.5.2   Architecture

The *UML Specification* clearly focuses on architecture. It identifies architectural models as first-class citizens in the modeling world, along with the familiar static models, behavioral models, and usage models (Rational Software Corporation 1999, xi). It is *architecture-centric*.

Although static models and behavioral models can be interpreted easily from software history, and usage models are obviously a nod in the direction of use cases, the idea of architectural models never gets defined; it is neither historical nor intuitive as an idea.

Nor is it possible to rely on the field of architecture itself for a conceptual leg-up because the field of architecture doesn't really have an equivalent to what systems call *architecture*. To some extent, the systems notion of architecture as talked about here has echoes in plans at various levels (regional, urban, community). As used, it also suggests high-level blueprints, although these are working drawings and not conceptual ones, which is quite a mix.

The first application of the term *architecture* came in the '50s. IBM's Gerritt Blaauw, one of the early giants who worked with Howard Aiken on the Harvard Mark III system and later was part of the System/360 effort, used the term to describe the logical structure of a modular mainframe computer system, including both the hardware and software. Then, as now, it was a way to manage complexity when a simple hierarchy was insufficient.

By the late '80s, the idea was being applied more generally, as the need to do real planning when developing potentially distributed IT resources became evident. Over time, the same needs that drove the original invention of system architecture for describing expensive and complicated mainframes (and then the enterprises that used them) began to be applied to applications themselves. The seminal paper in this transition was "A Framework for Information Systems Architecture" by John A. Zachman (1999). (I introduced him in Section 10.2, "Every Picture Tells a Story: The UML as a Modeling Language.") He attempted to use the way architects work and the models they create as the basis for structuring the various views of a system.

Zachman's idea of the working practices of an architect were simplistically biased toward the software engineer's ideal development process of the time, and so provide a basis-in-analogy that is misleading if seen as an explanation of the practice of design (1999). His version of the way an architect works is eerily reminiscent of the infamous waterfall methodology that is now merely a remnant of mainframe wishful thinking. And he compounded the error by validating his understanding against a typical manufacturing product development cycle of the time, also (now) outdated.

But the framework he proposed is solid, and still forms the basis for most of the thinking on the subject of architecture within IT. It is the most comprehensive approach that has been proposed.

The *UML Specification* echoes Zachman in many ways, however indirectly. Two ideas that Zachman introduced are critical to using the UML, and critical to its development:

- Building a complex engineering product requires a set of architectural representations that reflect the perspectives of the participants.

- A product can be described in a variety of ways, reflecting the purposes of the description as well as the perspectives of the participants.

Zachman's original version of an architecture proposed a matrix of models, with one dimension being *role* (Owner, Designer, Builder) or *goal* (Ballpark, Product). The other dimension originally consisted of the answers to three questions: what, how, and where? The first two are familiar to any analyst or designer; the last is usually asked by Operations if not brought up as part of the scope.

Each cell in the matrix was home for a unique model type. The "what" models focused on requirements, the "how" models on implementation, and the "where" on deployment. Any set of models that was complete could explain the strategic decisions in these areas that comprised a solution. The product that resulted was in the details, of course—just like the devil.

Although Zachman's framework continues to be a considerable influence (for example, in the OMG's attempts to define a Business Objects Framework), it is scarcely mentioned in any of the literature on the UML. There are (probably) good reasons for this:

- Zachman's framework (1999) is pre-object, and so his model types reflect a structured view of development and deliverables; they have not been updated.

- Zachman went on to add columns to his matrix to cover "who," "when," and "why"—elements that complicate what is supposed to be a way of managing complexity. The resulting thirty-six-cell matrix adds to the complexity rather than resolving it.

- Zachman and his supporters felt that his framework could also be applied at the enterprise level, and most of the follow-up efforts have been directed at enterprise modeling. This has turned out to be a blind alley. An enterprise model typically requires years to create (after which it is out-of-date) and an attention span from senior management that simply is not available. It also adds complexity.

However, at the system level, Zachman's original framework is still the best way to conceptualize all the elements of a system strategically, including how they interact (1999).

Of course, there *is* a role for *enterprise architecture*. But, like any enterprise at the turn of the millennium, it has to be agile and flexible. At the enterprise level, architecture should simply model an organization's technology portfolio and the configuration of its components. As an alternative to a complicated matrix, an enterprise architecture organizes the enterprise's strategic chunks into layers and levels, providing an easy set of packaged abstractions and their relationships.

There are object-oriented frameworks contending to be successors to Zachman's.

The International Standards Organization (ISO) has a "Reference-Model for Open Distributed Processing," which has been noted approvingly by working groups of the Object Management Group at various times (one example is the Business Object Component Architecture Proposal). A UML working paper says that, although the UML "stems from an earlier generation of object analysis and design methods (Booch, OMT, OOSE)…it is possible to achieve a large measure of compatibility with the ODP modeling language by using the UML extension mechanisms where there are no direct correspondences" (MCI Systemhouse Corporation 1997, 37). The ODP architecture framework covers the range of possible viewpoints from the enterprise domain down to deployment, using object concepts that reflect the work of Desmond D'Souza and Fusion more than the Three Amigos. The viewpoints are abstract, however; they do not reflect the concerns of specific stakeholders as Zachman's does.

Another contender is the Four+one framework from Phillippe Kruchten (1998), which is so named because it consists of four technical viewpoints plus a user viewpoint. This has become the official framework for Rational Software and, by extension, the Three Amigos. In effect, it provides a way of structuring both the work and the strategic information about an application. Unfortunately, in doing so, it doesn't separate the "what" and "how" concerns within a viewpoint, and it only really addresses the engineering aspects of a system. In *The Unified Modeling Language User Guide*, Jacobson, Booch, and Rumbaugh (1998a) make it clear that an architecture would combine portions of the models from each view, rather than simply being the set of all the views. It is basically a framework fitted to a method—useful as a way of organizing deliverables in the context of a development workflow, rather than a real architecture.

Pattern Oriented Software Architecture: A System of Patterns, the so-called POSA book (Buschmann et al. 1996), provides the best discussion of software architecture from an object-oriented viewpoint, including lucid pattern-based descriptions of major architectural frameworks such as Model-View-Controller.

10.6   Perspectives: A Generic Modeling Framework

Models need organizing. But if your toolset doesn't provide a usable organizing approach, and if the architecture-focused ways of organizing seem inappropriate, you'll need to improvise a basic framework of model types. The core set of UML diagrams can be used in a variety of models at various stages of a development process, so, by themselves, they don't provide enough organizing structure. Development methods often don't go beyond identifying the existence of analysis and design models, and suggesting that the code itself is the implementation model. However, *Syntropy*, a pre-UML object-oriented process, discusses categories of models (*perspectives*) that provide an informal idea of how to organize your models. The following are the Syntropy perspectives:

- *Essential perspective*: This perspective models the ideas and relationships that appear in the domain. The result is a conceptual model that is free of implementation language details. Types and collaborations in the model reflect domain concepts directly, although there often is no direct mapping. The purpose of the conceptual model is to accurately represent the domain in its own terms: to capture its essential structure, relationships, and processes.

- *Specification perspective*: The focus in this perspective is on software, but particularly on the interfaces of the software rather than the implementation. A specification model has an emphasis on *who* provides *what* services to *whom* without explaining the mechanics of how it is done. Classes in this perspective represent types (abstracted interfaces) rather than programmed classes.

- *Implementation perspective*: All the implementation details are exposed here and the specifics of system behavior are described in detail.

Martin Fowler, Kendall Scott, and Ivar Jacobson mention this approach approvingly in *UML Distilled: Applying the Standard Object Modeling Language* because it facilitates some critical distinctions about the way object, class, and type should be used (1997). Significantly, it helps avoid getting trapped in discussions about whether an object is an implementation abstraction, and so is out of place in analysis and possibly specification. Fowler's book has a good detailed description of the impact of these perspectives, which is outside the scope of this discussion, but worth consulting for anyone concerned with producing models that are clear and practical.

CHAPTER **11**

Putting It All Together: Reflecting on the Work of Design

...when you build a thing, you cannot merely build that thing in isolation,
but must also repair the world around it, so that the larger world at that one
place becomes more coherent, and more whole, and the thing that you make
takes its place in the web of nature, as you make it.

—*Christopher Alexander (Alexander, Ishikawa, and Silverstein 1977, xiii)*

Normally, long before the end, a book on the UML describes a development process to be used by the reader as a mental framework for embedding the work products of modeling. Because the UML is independent of process, a framework *has* to be provided, and that framework is invariably interpreted as the work of development.

A predefined process is tempting as a framework; as a canned solution, it obviates elaborate discussions of the context and forces within that context that constitute the real reasons for using the UML. And a process provides an easy means of embedding the UML in the work-to-be-done, via stereotypical examples that function as Kuhn's exemplars for the budding UML user.

In this book, I've taken a different approach, showing how modeling itself, as a skill and an activity, provides a context for using the UML. I've also relied on patterns to provide a starting point for looking at how modeling should be done, both generally and idiomatically.

However, there's an additional purpose that a process provides for a software book, which is still missing here: A process ties everything together—the theory, the artifacts, the techniques—and weaves a whole out of the parts, even if the process is only an indirect contributor to the book's contents. In this chapter, I will provide this missing ingredient. I'll take a different approach by pulling together rather than tying together the various elements of the book. And, rather than the work of development, I'll focus on the work of design. In particular, I'll be using the ideas on the practice of design that Donald Schon of M.I.T first published twenty years ago—ideas that are just now getting serious attention in the systems development world. With Schon's help, I'll attempt to show a different way of seeing how the UML and patterns fit into the work-to-be-done of design.

11.1   The Work of Design

I avoided grounding the UML in any one specific process for two reasons:

- This provided me with an opportunity to take the UML's process-independence (and mutt-like quality) seriously. I was able to focus on the ideas that are the UML itself, rather than the way they are used. And, I've been able to use examples from both Rational's Unified Process and Desmond D'Souza and Alan Wills' *Objects, Components and Frameworks with the UML: The Catalysis Approach* (1998) to process polar opposites in many ways in which process-specific differences are significant.

- I felt that focusing on one process, however good, would continue the unstated, perhaps unconscious, focus on development-as-programming that has permeated the UML literature (but *not* the UML itself, interestingly).

The latter reason was the more important reason of the two for me personally.

I went through my own personal paradigm shift some time ago, but as a modeler, not as a programmer. As part of a previous generation of developers, I'd seen the emergence of modeling as a distinctive skill within the framework of structured methods—the old paradigm.

As a modeler, objects became interesting to me because of intransigent problems I continually ran into when doing traditional modeling. The abstractions produced as artifacts were unrelated to the world of the user, and they were difficult to use in establishing their needs and validating the results. Once defined, the process of translation into programmer-readable format was frequently a tortured one with many magic moments of smoke and mirrors mediating the translation. The models we produced, although useful to management, were less useful to their real supposed beneficiaries.

Objects presented a way out of this dilemma, and object-oriented analysis and design became the achievement that, in Kuhn's terms, redefined the work I did.

The UML and patterns, taken together, are for me the final linchpins in this personal paradigm shift. They are not silver bullets. They *do* provide the tools to do design differently, in a way that is fully congruent with all of the other significant achievements over the last ten years. Combined, they add up to a paradigm shift for system development in general, and for system design in particular.

11.1.1 What Is Design?

The forces that need to be balanced in looking at the work of system design will be familiar from earlier parts of this book:

- The initial situation is one of uncertainty and complexity, in which the problem(s) to be addressed may be expressed poorly or incompletely, may not even be right, or may not be the right one(s).

- Context and situation are important parts of the problem to be solved, not just information to be archived.

- Vision, and not just current problems, is a motivator and shaper of the end result.

- Although problem solutions in software are typically technical, the problems are typically business problems.

- Feedback is as important as feedforward (that is, conceptualization) in the "artistic performance" of design, but the levels and types of abstractions required for each may be significantly different.

- Prototyping and modeling are both activities in design; they are taught as techniques but need to be applied as skills. Models can be seen as documentation and specification; prototypes can be seen as simulations and experiments. But a designer can experiment with models and specify with prototypes.

- Representation is *not* presentation. The way the world and the system are represented in a model and the way that model is presented reflect different needs. "The map is not the territory," as Sessue Hayakawa used to preach.

These forces have appeared in various guises already as forces in the patterns. They are also obvious elements in the thinking behind the UML, and in the thinking behind processes such as RUP and Catalysis (D'Souza and Wills 1998). However, most discussions of software design bury them or treat them as being tacitly understood—shared knowledge, and so not in need of explicit attention.

Generally, what constitutes *design* in the context of systems development is as fuzzy as most of the other ideas we development professionals seem to profess. For example, Ivar Jacobson, Grady Booch, and James Rumbaugh can maintain that *design isn't just architecture* (1998a), while Jim Coplien can take the position that *design is making architecture* (1998a). I already mentioned the widely held tacit notion that design is only a stage in the standard development lifecycle between analysis and construction. Even the Rational Unified Process only avoids this view by reinventing it: for RUP, design is that part of an iteration that falls between requirements analysis and implementation.

There's also the view of design as tied to a specific role. Designers design, architects architect, analysts analyze, and programmers develop. Each role applies known techniques specific to that role and recurring problems that are well-formulated for that role.

Much of this approach came from IBM's early attempts to bureaucratize the development process via programming teams and IBM's view of architecture. Of course, the real picture has always been somewhat smudged, and it was when IBM helped formulate it. Analysts encroach on the design turf at the beginning of development, and programmers are known to indulge in design fixes at the end.

There *is* a need to distinguish design from engineering. Design is emphatically *not* engineering, although it complements engineering, and many engineers do design as well as engineering.

Narrowly viewed, engineering is like the normal science that Kuhn describes—problem-solving in a well-defined conceptual framework. Design is broader and messier than that.

David Kelly, CEO of IDEO and a design consultant at Stanford, puts it this way: "(t)he designer has a dream that goes beyond what exists, rather than fixing what exists...design defines what it ought to be...engineering does it" (Winograd et al. 1996, 152–157). Although admitting that clear distinctions between engineering and design only caricature either, Kelly adds that engineering "is not supposed to be messy...you try to assume away the messiness...that only works when you are solving a well-formulated problem.... Designers try to understand the mess (instead)" (1996, 153).

Engineers may rightfully protest that this narrow view of engineering represents only a limited portion of the things engineers do. Engineering as a practice embodies many ways of knowing and doing that we find in design. Even Kelley admits that, in his experience, "[G]ood engineers are really designer-engineers...designers in every sense of the word" (Winograd et al. 1996, 153). But design is still not engineering, however much the two complement each other and are practiced together.

In systems, design permeates any development process, and constitutes a practice—a repertoire of ways of knowing and doing—engaged in by systems professionals, rather than being a technical role or set of activities. As Jim Coplien puts it, in this reality "we can't separate design from architecture and implementation" (1998a, 40). And, as modeling becomes a key element of managing and operating the software products that development produces, in some ways design also becomes part of management and operations, and things get smudged even more.

11.1.2 Beyond Patterns and Paradigms

What do designers do, then, that's different from engineering? And how do they do it?

An alternative to the engineering view of things is provided by Donald Schon in his books on the *reflective practitioner*. Schon emphasizes the ongoing role of professional reflection and the importance of practical knowledge in ensuring the effectiveness of professional practice.

He uses the term *professional practitioner* as a general description of a professional engaged in providing a service for a client (who may be called something else, such as *patient* or *student*). He leverages both meanings that are usually associated with the word *practice*. His notion of practice combines the performance of a range of services and the preparation for performing them. Ultimately, for Schon, a professional practitioner is "a specialist who encounters certain types of situations over and over again" (1983, 60).

In Schon's view, rather than simply applying technical expertise to well-formed problems, a professional is continually being confronted with surprises that require "reflection-in-action" about both the knowledge that is being brought to bear and the actions being taken. He balances theoretical knowledge with a repertoire of practical knowledge, some of which may be tacit and not easily articulated. Improvisation that is acquired from practice is at least as important a component of performing well as any lessons learned in graduate school.

Design is a special case of reflective practice, but it is more than that.

In a way that parallels Coplien's understanding of the role of design in systems development, Schon sees design as permeating all aspects of professional practice. When Schon discusses the role of reflective practice in engineering and the sciences, for example, he implicitly echoes Kelley's comments that "(g)ood engineers are really designer-engineers" (1983). However, it's clear that although design can be an element in the practice of those professions, it isn't essential to them. (But reflective practice might be seen to be essential in engineering and the sciences in a different way—in the creation of new paradigms when surprise anomalies need to be accounted for.)

Schon's model for the design process is what he calls a "reflective conversation with the situation" (1983, 40). In a nutshell, it *could* be described as an iterative, incremental, architecture-centric, user-driven, but informal process.

The best summary of Schon's idea about design is by Schon himself:

> A designer makes things. Sometimes he makes the final product; more often, he makes a representation, plan, program, or image of an artifact to be constructed by others. He works in particular situations, uses particular materials, and employs a distinctive medium and language. Typically, his making process is complex. There are more variables—kinds of possible moves, norms, and interrelationships of these—than can be represented in a finite model. Because of this complexity, the designer's moves tend, happily or unhappily, to produce consequences other than those intended. When this happens, the designer may take account of the unintended changes be has made in the situation by forming new appreciations and understandings and by making new moves. He shapes the situation, in accordance with his initial appreciation of it, the situation "talks back," and he responds to the situation's back-talk.

> In a good process of design, this conversation with the situation is reflective. In answer to the situation's back-talk, the designer reflects-in-action on the construction of the problem, the strategies of action, or the model of the phenomena, which have been implicit in his moves. (1983, 79)

11.2   Elements of Reflective Design

Schon embeds design into what he calls an epistemology of practice, "reflection-in-action." For simplicity, I'll use the term *reflective design* to cover an extended view of design that folds the key aspects of reflection-in-action into his discussion of the details of design.

For the details of design, I'll rely on Schon's description and analysis of an architectural design session between a teacher and a student, his example for introducing those details. He uses the session as a starting point because "architecture is the oldest recognized design profession, and, as such, functions as prototype for design in other professions" (1983, 77).

Not all of Schon's discussion of design in architecture maps easily to systems design. But his analysis of the design process provides an important starting point for examining otherwise unstated aspects of design as a personal process, to use Watts Humphrey's term—process from a personal perspective rather than an organizational one.

The practice of design should be as important in shaping a modeling language and its application as the technical goals that it is meant to support. As a working tool for modeling, the UML needs to be consistent with the working practices of designers. Also, given the fast and loose way that writers on the UML talk about architecture, his example also provides a fascinating example and explanation of real architectural thinking. It can provide a valuable antidote to the representations of architectural practice that are out there.

Schon (1983) identifies a number of elements in reflective design that combine to define professional practice:

- Problem setting

- A language of design

- A language about designing

- Performing

- Closure

I'll use these categories to explore the way Schon's elements of design combine to form a practice, and how the UML and patterns can support reflective design.

These categories are my own and may be considered somewhat restricting and limited by anyone who's really familiar with Schon's work. Schon's fluid, almost anecdotal style masks a subtle architecture in his writing that makes simple summarization difficult. His writing is better approached as music to be played, where a not-always-obvious shaping comes from a gradual appreciation of phrasing that often has to be coaxed out of the material.

As categories, they're useful because of some obvious parallels with the formal processes that most developers will be familiar with. However, they should be seen as interconnected and in some ways overlapping, rather than as separate activities. Certainly, in Schon's writing about design, they appear and reappear in recursive and iterative fashion, to be applied improvisationally as surprises pop up.

11.2.1 Problem Setting

A designer is initially presented with problematic situations rather than problems—situations that are "puzzling, troubling and uncertain" (Schon 1983, 40). The first step in reflective design, then, is to make sense of the situation, to construct its reality, and provide a framework for understanding and interacting with it. This sense-making is *not* technical. Problem setting "is *not* itself a technical problem" (40). Means and ends are "framed interdependently" (165).

Schon adds:

> When we set the problem, we select the things we will treat as the "things" of the situation, we set the boundaries of our attention to it, and we impose...coherence...we name the things to which we will attend and frame the context in which we will attend to them. (1983, 40)

But problem setting is not merely the establishment of a context. It is an active framing of the situation that at least implies some elements of the design that will result. In framing the situation, the designer brings to the "framing experiment" the practitioner's repertoire—of experience and knowledge—models to start from.

This description should resonate immediately with UML modelers and patterns users.

- The question of architectural style is dealt with early in any process using the UML. This can be considered part of the framing because, to repeat what the *UML Specification* says: "(t)he choice of what models and diagrams one creates has a profound influence upon how a problem is attacked and how a corresponding solution is shaped" (Rational Software Corporation 1999, 1–3).

- The identification of business objects and/or types; the establishment of context via actors, events, and interactions; and the focusing of attention via use cases are all aspects of problem-setting when modeling with the UML.

- The clear separation of analysis from design, coupled with a lengthy postponement of implementation concerns, is being replaced by iterative, recursive cycles of analysis and design, interleaved with an early focus on architecture.

In using patterns, problem-setting is explicit. You start by creating your own small pattern language from all the patterns available. According to Alexander, Ishikawa, and Murray, "the character of what you build will be given to it by the language of patterns you use" (1977, xxxvii). A pattern language is local; it starts when you begin to build or design.

Each pattern is a miniature frame, containing elements that help with the mapping to a situation. In particular, there should be a mapping of the forces in the selected patterns to forces in the situation, in an effort to establish congruence between patterns and the situation. Successful mappings help "frame the context," and so help create a basis for conceptual coherence in setting the problem appropriately and fittingly.

11.2.2   A Language of Design

The "conversation with the situation" that Schon refers to is, of course, not meant to be taken literally. He's describing the back-and-forth, give-and-take interaction between the situation and the designer. The dialogue between the two takes many forms, but always involves more than just drawing. Think of the whiteboard as a medium for interaction.

In the same way that models are both text and graphics, a language of design involves "drawing and talking…[as] parallel ways of designing" (Schon 1983, 80) that is local to a situation—not generic—like pattern languages. The emphasis is on *a* language of design, not *the* language of design.

In some ways, a language of design bridges the gap between a generic modeling language such as the UML and a generative pattern language. The verbal and nonverbal interact, especially in the performance of collaborative design activities. Nonverbal information is reinforced, enhanced, extended, and clarified by informal verbal information. In successful projects, verbal and nonverbal shorthand eventually emerges in the form of a dialect. Models become repositories for dialects, parts of which may be more private, whereas other parts may be public in varying degrees. Some of the information may be formalized and recorded; some of it will be temporary and improvisational.

In using the UML, this back-and-forth interplay among model, modelers, and clients is critical. Rather than simply being archival documentation, models are used to facilitate this interplay. Tactics such as the elision of unnecessary detail, local and temporary stereotypes, and the use of notes can play useful roles in the process. Scenario-building and exercises such as CRC cards can be powerful tools in the emergence of a language of design for a project.

Unlike traditional architectural drawings, UML models are deliberately both text and graphics. Furthermore, the UML explicitly encourages the use of hyperlinks as a way of building connections and facilitating conceptual navigation. Thus, the UML provides tools that can augment a language of design in a variety of ways. Some of this can be formalized, but only after the fact. For example, Catalysis provides a construct—a stereotype of package called *dialect*, which supports such formalization (D'Souza and Wills 1998).

Patterns, of course, can supply much of the rich vocabulary that can be the base for a language of design. Public patterns can be reused; variations can be introduced that reflect local conditions more closely; private patterns that are local to the design dialect can be created.

The process of creating patterns is itself an aspect of a language of design. Workshops, study groups, and other activities that have evolved as sound ways to surface and evolve patterns can be part of the development of a language of design.

11.2.3   A Language about Designing

Schon carefully distinguishes "a language of design" from "a language about designing—a *metalanguage*" (1983, 81). This too needs to be a part of practice. Professional practice isn't just about the personal responses of practitioners to local situations; rather, it too has a larger context, which is the context of the practice itself. Ideas about the nature of competency are interwoven into the interactions that take place, and provide some of the framework for communicating the results. Professional standards, exemplars that provide guidance, and heuristics all need to be available as part of the design conversation.

Again, both the UML and patterns provide different ways of addressing this need. The UML explicitly responds, via the metamodel and Specification. Patterns can be found that exemplify both "a language of design" and "a language about designing." And finally, mentoring and pattern-writing are ways to include a language about designing into every designer's practices.

11.2.4   Performance

Problem setting and naming-and-framing lead to a set of performed responses to the situation. Schon uses words such as *move*, *stance*, and *sketch* to indicate the performative utterances and actions that a designer engages in.

He leverages the ambiguities of the word *performance* the same way he leverages similar ambiguities in the word *practice*. For him, performance is both successfully creating an end product and the artistic doing of it. The reflective designer is engaged in a dance with the client that must also produce tangible results.

Having a problem framework as a starting point and a domain language as a beginning point to design is still just being at the starting line. The designer has to "perform" design—to act in collaborations, draw, write, and, ultimately, architect a whole that is greater than the parts.

The following sections discuss the essential elements of design performance as Schon portrays them.

Moves

A *move* is a design action that produces potential problem-solutions in miniature with consequences that need to be appreciated and implications that need to be understood. Moves are the increments of design that, like models, "give us the opportunity to fail under controlled conditions" (Booch 1994, 22). The important thing is to be able to see the changing whole, as well as the parts: "[e]ach move is a local experiment that contributes to the global experiment of reframing the problem" (Schon 1983, 94).

The process is like a chess game that redefines its rules as the game proceeds. This is where "back-talk" comes in. The situation may "resist" the move; that is, the move may not contribute to the quality of the overall solution. The evaluation of a move may reveal unexpected consequences—some useful and some not.

The language of design provides the vehicle for communicating and assessing these moves. Schon suggests that a designer use categories to organize both her moves and her responses. He calls these categories *design domains*; each domain corresponds to an area of concern and an aspect of the repertoire of experiences and knowledge that a professional brings to the situation. A domain organizes the questions that need to be asked: What will the costs be? What name should I give this design element? What form should it take? Is it like anything else I know about or that I've done?

Consequences

Each move results in changes to the situation that need to be expressed. They also need to be explained and assessed, both as intentions and by examining unintended consequences, by using the language of design within the design domains at hand. Past experience and intuition both come into play in examining how a design change or addition might have consequences.

Schon uses the term *appreciation* to describe the designer's act of considering the possible effects of a move. This term captures the intuitive and aesthetic aspects of the designer's reflective performance in a way that *assessment* or *evaluation* doesn't. Appreciation includes a sense of fit and quality, as well as a consideration of the effects at the global scale—not just an identification of the local impacts from a technical perspective.

So, the designer has to be able to see the whole, feel the qualities present in the whole, and work in terms of the ongoing evolution of the whole—not just be buried in the parts.

Implications

Having considered the intended and unintended consequences of a design experiment, the designer has a decision to make about committing to the results. The designer has a variety of options: accepting the move, reframing the problem, or adopting a new stance in considering the consequences (revisiting the appreciation).

Whereas the process in considering the consequences was one of appreciation, the process at work in considering the implications is more one of testing. When a decision is being made, the implications of the decision have to be worked out and evaluated in the context of the implications of past moves: "(T)here is a literal logic of design, a pattern of 'if...then' propositions that relates the cumulative sequence of prior moves to the choices now confronting the designer" (Schon 1983, 99).

The set of implications built up over the course of design moves creates its own complexity—the complexity of all the decisions and their implications through the life of a design. Schon describes this complexity as the "web of moves" in which "systems of implications" become "disciplines" for the design process (1983, 131).

Any decision establishes what might be called a new conceptual baseline that will be used in considering future moves. These baselines are, of course, not cast in stone. The designer doesn't have to honor the implications of previous moves. They're there to facilitate consistency, coherence, and fit, and to help manage the complexity of the "web of moves."

If a new move has been appreciated as sufficiently special in some way, then it can violate the logic of the design. It establishes a new logic, perhaps, or creates a new discipline to impose on the process. If the move is not sufficiently special, then reframing the problem or revisiting the appreciation may be needed:

- Reframing the problem permits a designer to review the problem setting and attempt to fit the situation into a new way of understanding the problem. Reframing may take the form of reflection-on-action or reflection-on-practice—two additional types of professional reflection that I won't deal with in detail. Essentially, *reflection-on-action* takes place outside of the ongoing design process, whereas *reflection-on-practice* might include questioning the nature of the design practice itself.

- Revisiting the appreciation provides an opportunity to reconsider the consequences of the move, perhaps by looking at the prioritization of the design domains used in making the appreciation of the move.

11.2.5   Closure

Reframing the problem or revisiting the appreciation may lead to reiterating the process of moves—consequences—implications, or the designer may move on. A degree of closure occurs. What Schon calls the *stance* of the designer toward the design changes; the designer commits to certain aspects, their implications become more fixed, and there's a shift in the attention paid to specific design domains, typically toward those domains concerned with building and away from conceptualizing. At the same time, however, because of the interactive and exploratory nature of the process, new questions may have been raised and new opportunities identified.

Closure is never final; it is useful and subject to the results of further design iterations. Closed problems may need to be reviewed and reworked down the road. But there is an implicit understanding that design decisions have been made, and it is time to move forward.

11.2.6   Reflective Design and Systems Modeling

The design process I've summarized doesn't have any obvious connections to the main artifacts of the UML. However, it is implicit in working with the UML properly. It can be seen "in action" in many of the books about system design that have case studies illustrating how the work of design is actually carried out—both pre-UML and when using the UML.

Two good examples of moves—consequences—implications from before the UML are David Taylor's *Business Engineering With Objects* (1995), and Nancy Wilkinson's *Using CRC Cards: An Informal Approach to Object-Oriented Development* (1995). The best example that deals specifically with using the UML is *Applying Use Cases: A Practical Guide*, by Geri Schneider and Jason P. Winters (1998). The "moves" described in the latter book about establishing an initial architecture of subsystems is an especially good description of architectural performance as reflective design.

11.3   To Be Continued...

...to make an end is to make a beginning

The end is where we start from. And every phrase

And sentence that is right...is an end and a beginning...

...history is a pattern

Of timeless moments...

...the end of all our exploring

Will be to arrive where we started

And know the place for the first time

Through the unknown, remembered gate (Eliot 1966, 58-59)

My overview of Schon's ideas on reflective design is necessarily just a brief sample. His books on reflective practice contain much more that could be useful to anyone doing systems design. I believe that all good designers follow the approach Schon discusses, but tacitly. Like Alexander, Ishikawa, and Murray, Schon surfaces ways of doing that are timeless and perhaps universal. The UML and patterns are expressions of a similar need to leverage experience and connect with proven ways of knowing and doing.

This is the end of my book, but a book like this is never complete. The UML is still a work-in-progress, and patterns are always changing. There are many other valuable patterns, articles, Web pages, and books that can be connected. Much of the material that is here can be improved, detailed, and refined. Therefore, until UML 2.0 comes out and a real stable UML base is available, I'll be maintaining a Web site (www.umlpatterns.com) that will be the home for new patterns, better examples, and extended links.

References

Alexander, Christopher. 1979. *Timeless Way of Building*. New York, NY: Oxford University Press.

———. 1988. *The Oregon Experiment*. New York, NY: Oxford University Press.

Alexander, Christopher, Sara Ishikawa, and Murray Silverstein. 1977. *A Pattern Language: Towns, Buildings, Construction*. New York, NY: Oxford University Press.

Appleton, Brad, Steve Berczuk, et. al [online]. 1999. *Streamed Lines: Branching Patterns for Parallel Software Development*. Available from Internet: www.enteract.com/~bradapp/acme/branching/

Beck, Kent [online]. 1994. *Portland Pattern Repository*. Available from Internet: http://www.c2.com/ppr/about/author/kent.html

Beck, Kent, and Ward Cunningham [online]. 1987. *Expanding the Role of Tools in a Literate Programming Environment*. Presented at CASE '87. Boston, MA: Available from Internet: http://c2.com/doc/case87.html

Berard, Edward V. [online]. 1998. Be Careful with Use Cases. Available from Internet: www.toa.com

Berczuk, Steve. [online]. 1994. Finding Solutions through Pattern Languages. *Computer* 27, no. 12 (December): Available from Internet: http://crit.org/http://world.std.com/~berczuk/pubs/Dec94ieee.html

Booch, Grady. 1994. *Object-Oriented Analysis and Design with Applications.* Reading, MA: Addison Wesley.

Booch, Grady, Doug Bryan, and Charles G. Petersen. 1993. *Software Engineering with Ada.* Reading, MA: Addison Wesley.

Booch, Grady, and Jim Rumbaugh. [CD-ROM]. 1996. Comments in panel on *Methodology Standards: Help or Hindrance?* Presented at OOPSLA94. Reported in *OOPSLA CD-ROM Compendium* 1986-1996.

Brown, John Seely, and Paul Dunguid [online]. 1992. *Stolen Knowledge.* Educational Technology Publications. Available from Internet: http://www.parc.xerox.com/ops/members/brown/papers/stolenknow.html

Brown, William J., Raphael C. Malveau, William H. Brown, Hays W. McCormick III, and Thomas J. Mowbray. 1998. *AntiPatterns: Refactoring Software, Architectures, and Projects in Crisis.* New York, NY: John Wiley and Sons.

Buschmann, Frank, Regine Meunier, Hans Rohnert, Peter Sommerlad, and Michael Stal. 1996. *Pattern-Oriented Software Architecture: A System of Patterns.* Chichester, UK: John Wiley and Sons.

Cayley, David. 1992. *Ivan Illich in Conversation.* Concord: House of Anansi Press, 48.

Coad, Peter. 1992. Object-Oriented Patterns. *Communications of the ACM* 35, no. 9 (September): 152-159.

———. 1996. *Object Models: Strategies, Patterns, and Applications.* Upper Saddle River, NJ: Yourdon Press.

Coplien, James O. 1991. *Advanced C++ Programming Styles and Idioms.* Reading, MA: Addison Wesley.

———. 1994a. *Progress on Patterns: Highlights of PLoP/94.* Proceedings of Object Expo Europe. London: UK. (September 26-30).

———. [online]. 1994b. *PatronRole.* Available from Internet: http://www.bell-labs.com/cgi-user/OrgPatterns/OrgPatterns?PatronRole

Coplien, James O., and Douglas Schmidt (ed). 1995. *Pattern Languages of Program Design.* Reading, MA: Addison Wesley.

Coplien, James O [online]. 1997. Idioms and Patterns as Architectural Literature. *IEEE Software Special Issue on Objects, Patterns, and Architectures.* 14.1 (January): 36-42. Available from Internet: http://www.computer.org/software/so1997/s1toc.htm

————. 1998a. *Multi-Paradigm Design for C++*. Reading, MA: Addison Wesley.

————. [online]. 1998b. Online Interview. *Object Magazine*. (January) Available from Internet: www.sigs.com

Coram, Todd [online]. 1997. Koans Metaphors and Parables. *Portland Pattern Repository*. Portland, OR: Cunningham and Cunningham, Inc. November 19, 1997. Available from Internet:
http://c2.com/cgi/wiki?KoansMetaphorsAndParables

Cunningham, Ward and Kent Beck [online]. 1997. History of Patterns. *Portland Pattern Repository*. Portland, OR: Cunningham and Cunningham, Inc. August 27, 1999. Available from Internet:
http://www.c2.com/cgi/wiki?HistoryOfPatterns

DeMarco, Tom, and Timothy Lister. 1987. *Peopleware: Productive Projects and Teams*. New York, NY: Dorset House.

D'Souza, Desmond, and Alan Wills. 1998. *Objects, Components and Frameworks with UML: The Catalysis Approach*. Reading, MA: Addison Wesley.

Eldredge, Niles. 1999. *The Pattern of Evolution*. New York, NY: W.H. Freeman and Company.

Eliot, T.S. 1996. "Little Gidding." *Four Quartets*. London: Faber and Faber, 58-59.

Fichman, Robert G., and Chris F. Kemerer. 1993. Adoption of Software Engineering Innovations: The Case of Object Orientation. *Sloan Management Review* 34, no. 2: 7–22.

Foote, Brian. 1997. Hybrid Vigor and Footprints in the Snow. In *Pattern Languages of Program Design 3*, eds. Robert Martin, Dirk Riehle, Frank Buschmann, and John Vlissides, ix–xiii. Reading, MA: Addison Wesley.

Fowler, Martin. 1997. *Analysis Patterns*. Reading, MA: Addison Wesley.

Fowler, Martin, Kendall Scott, and Ivar Jacobson. 1997. *UML Distilled: Applying the Standard Object Modeling Language*. Reading, MA: Addison Wesley.

Gamma, Erich, Richard Helm, Ralph Johnson, John Vlissides, and Grady Booch. 1995. *Design Patterns: Elements of Reusable Object-Oriented Software*. Reading, MA: Addison Wesley.

Illich, Ivan. 1996. *In the Vineyard of the Text: A Commentary to Hugh's Didascalicon*. Chicago: University of Chicago Press.

Jacobson, Ivar. 1994. *Object-Oriented Software Engineering: A Use Case Driven Approach*. Reading, MA: Addison Wesley.

————. 1995. The Use Case Construct in Object-Oriented Engineering. In *Scenario Based Design*, ed. John M. Carroll, 309–336. New York: John Wiley and Sons.

————. 1998. The Methods War Is Over. *Object Magazine.* (April): 72.

Jacobson, Ivar, Grady Booch, and James Rumbaugh. 1998a. *The Unified Modeling Language User Guide.* Reading, MA: Addison Wesley.

————. 1998b. *The Unified Modeling Language Reference Manual.* Reading, MA: Addison Wesley.

————. 1999a. *The Unified Software Development Process.* Reading, MA: Addison Wesley.

————. 1999b. *The Unified Modeling Language Reference Guide.* Reading, MA: Addison Wesley.

Jacobson, Ivar, Maria Ericsson, and Agneta Jacobson. 1995. *The Object Advantage: Business Process Reengineering with Object Technology.* Reading, MA: Addison Wesley.

Jacobson, Ivar, Martin Griss, and Patrick Jonsson. 1997. *Software Reuse: Architecture, Process and Organization for Business Success.* Reading, MA: Addison-Wesley.

Johnson, Ralph E. [online]. 1995. *Documenting Frameworks using Patterns.* Available from Internet: ftp://st.cs.uiuc.edu/pub/patterns/papers/documenting-frameworks.ps

Johnson, R., and W. Cunningham. 1995. *PloP1Intro.* Reading, MA: Addison Wesley. ix-x.

Kent And Ralph At The Architecture Workshop [online]. 1997. *Portland Pattern Repository.* November 6, 1997. Available from Internet: www.c2.com/cgi/wiki?KentAndRalphAtTheArchitectureWorkshop

Kruchten, Phillipe. 1998. *The Rational Unified Process: An Introduction.* Reading, MA: Addison Wesley.

Kuhn, Thomas S. 1970. *The Structure of Scientific Revolutions* (Second Edition). Chicago: University of Chicago Press.

Levitt, Theodore. 1984. *The Marketing Imagination.* New York, NY: Free Press.

Malone, Thomas W., and John F. Rockart. 1991. Computers, Networks and the Organization. *Scientific American* 256, no. 3 (July): 92–99, 128–136.

Managing: Ideas and Solutions/The Leading Edge [online]. 1996. *Fortune* 134, no. 3: 173+. Available from Internet:
`http://pathfinder.com/@@7yDPYQcAHl0KKQ03/fortune/magazine/1996/`
`960805/edg.html]`

Martin, Robert [online]. 1994. PLoP, PLoP—Fizz, Fizz. *C++ Report*. OOD Column. Available from Internet: `http://www.objectmentor.com/`
`publications/PLoP.pdf`

MCI Systemhouse Corporation [online]. 1997. Relationship of the Unified Modeling Language to the Object Models of the Object Management Group. Available from Internet: `http://enterprise.shl.com/uml-odp/uml-odp.pdf`

McMenamin, Steven, and John Palmer. 1984. *Essential Systems Analysis*. Englewood Cliffs, New Jersey: Yourdon Press.

Moore, Geoffrey. 1991. *Crossing the Chasm*. New York, NY: Harper Collins.

Nonaka, I., and H. Takeuchi. 1995. *The Knowledge Creating Company*. New York, NY: Oxford University Press.

Object Management Group [online]. 1999. *UML Specification, Version 1.3 Beta R7*. (June) Available from Internet: `www.omg.org`

Parsons, Jeffery, and Yair Wand. 1997. Using Objects for Systems Analysis. *Communications of the ACM* 40, no. 12 (December): 104–110.

Rational Software Corporation [online]. 1995. *UML FAQ*. Available from Internet: `www.rational.com`

———— [online]. 1999. *UML Specification, Version 1.3*. (July). Available from Internet: `www.rational.com`

Robbins, Edward. 1994. *Why Architects Draw*. Cambridge, MA: MIT Press.

Rochat, C. [CD-ROM]. 1988. *The Vision of the Pattern Language of Programs*. Submitted to OOPSLA88.

Rochelle, Jeremy [online]. 1995. *What Should Collaborative Technology Be? A Perspective from Dewey and Situated Learning*. Institute for Research on Learning. Available from Internet: `http://www.cica.indiana.edu/cscl95/`
`outlook/39_roschelle.html`

Royce, Walker. 1999. *Software Project Management: A Unified Process*. Reading, MA: Addison Wesley.

Rumbaugh, James, Michael Blaha, William Premerlani, Frederick Eddy, and William Lorensen. 1991. *Object-Oriented Modeling and Design*. Upper Saddle River, NJ: Prentice Hall.

Schneider, Geri, and Jason P. Winters. 1988. *Applying Use Cases*. Reading, MA: Addison Wesley.

Schon, Donald. 1983. *The Reflective Practitioner*. New York, NY: Basic Books.

Shlaer, Sally, and Stephen Mellor [online]. 1999. Project Techology, Inc.—Shlaer-Mellor Method. Available from Internet: www.projtech.com

Taylor, David. 1995. *Business Engineering with Object Technology*. New York, NY: John Wiley and Sons.

Wilkinson, Nancy M. 1995. *Using CRC Cards: An Informal Approach to Object-Oriented Development*. Upper Saddle River, NJ: Prentice Hall.

Winograd, Terry, John Bennett, Laura De Young, and Peter S. Gordon (eds). 1996. *Bringing Design To Software*. Reading, MA: Addison Wesley.

Wladawsky-Berger, I. 1999. Turning Points in Information Technology. *IBM Systems Journal* 38, no. 2 & 3: 449.

Zachman, John. 1999. A Framework for Information Systems Architecture. *IBM Systems Journal* 38, no. 2 & 3: 460.

Zuboff, Shoshanna. 1998. *In the Age of the Smart Machine*. New York, NY: Basic Books.

Index

P

Advanced Information
Cutting-Edge Technologies

Books from MTP Offer Advice and Experience

Technology Series

The *Technology Series* is a comprehensive and authoritative set of guides to the most important computing standards of today. Each title in this series is aimed at bringing computing professionals closer to the scientists and engineers behind the technological implementations that will change tomorrow's innovations in computing. These titles are written and reviewed by those responsible for creating the technology and writing the standards.

Network Architecture and Development Series

The *Network Architecture and Development Series* is a complete set of guides that provide computing professionals with the unique insight of leading experts in today's networking technologies. Each volume explores a technology or set of technologies that is needed to build and maintain the optimal network environment for any particular organization or situation.

Circle Series

The *Circle Series* is aimed toward the growing community of advanced, technical-level networkers who must work with operating systems such as Linux, UNIX, Windows NT, and Windows 2000 as an architect, developer, or administrator. Each title focuses on a single component or tool used within the framework of the related technologies. These books provide network designers and programmers with detailed, proven solutions to their problems.

Windows NT

Windows NT Automated Deployent and Customization
by Richard Puckett
1st Edition
$32.00
ISBN: 1-57870-045-0

Time-saving advice that helps you install, update, and configure software on each of your clients without having to visit each client. Control all clients remotely for tasks such as security and legal software use. Includes reference material on native NT tools, registry edits, and third-party tools.

Windows NT Shell Scripting
by Tim Hill
1st Edition
$32.00
ISBN: 1-57870-047-7

A complete reference for Windows NT scripting, this book guides you through a high-level introduction to the shell language itself and the shell commands that are useful for controlling or managing different components of a network.

Windows NT and UNIX Integration
by Gene Henriksen
1st Edition
$32.00
ISBN: 1-57870-048-5

This book provides you with an all-in-one guide to integrating NT and UNIX in the same network. It begins with the fundamentals of both NT and UNIX and follows with discussions of file sharing, proven solutions to the problems related to printing in an integrated environment, and more.

Windows NT Device Driver Deployment
by Peter Viscarola and
W. Anthony Mason
1st Edition
$50.00
ISBN: 1-57870-058-2

This title begins with an introduction to the general Windows NT operating system concepts relevant to drivers. Then, it progresses to more detailed information about the operating system, such as interrupt management, synchronization issues, the I/O Subsystem, standard kernel mode drivers, and more.

Windows NT Heterogeneous Networking
by Steven B. Thomas
1st Edition
$40.00
ISBN: 1-57870-064-7

A complete reference for internetworking all major systems with Windows NT, both at the OS and protocol levels, you'll find information on how to successfully develop an enterprise model as well as coverage of how to optimize hardware, domain controllers, and enterprise service traffic.

Windows NT Thin Client Solutions
by Todd W. Mathers and
Shawn P. Genoway
1st Edition
$35.00
ISBN: 1-57870-065-5

Explore the cost-saving features of Windows Based Terminal Server that allows applications to be run on a server as well as the software based on Citrix's core Independent Computing Architecture (ICA) protocol, which provides enterprise capability.

Windows NT Win32 Perl Programming: The Standard Extensions
by Dave Roth
1st Edition
$40.00
ISBN: 1-57870-067-1

See numerous proven examples and practical uses of Perl in solving everyday Win32 problems. This is the only book available with comprehensive coverage of Win32 extensions where most of the Perl functionality resides in Windows settings.

Windows NT Domain Architecture
by Gregg Branham
1st Edition
$39.95
ISBN: 1-57870-112-0

As Windows NT continues to be deployed more and more in the enterprise, the domain architecture for the network becomes more critical as the complexity increases. This book contains the in-depth expertise that is necessary to truly plan a complex enterprise domain.

Windows 2000 Server: Planning and Migration
by Sean Deuby
1st Edition
$40.00
ISBN: 1-57870-023-X

Windows 2000 Server: Planning and Migration can quickly save the NT professional thousands of dollars and hundreds of hours. This title includes authoritative information on key features of Windows 2000 and offers recommendations on how to best position your NT network for Windows 2000.

Windows 2000 Quality of Service
by David Iseminger
1st Edition
$45.00
ISBN: 1-57870-115-5

As the traffic on networks continues to increase, the strain on network infrastructure and available resources has also grown. *Windows 2000 Quality of Service* teaches network engineers and administrators how to define traffic control patterns and utilize bandwidth in their networks.

Windows NT Applications: Measuring and Optimizing Performance
by Paul Hinsberg
1st Edition
$40.00
ISBN: 1-57870-176-7

This book offers developers crucial insight into the underlying structure of Windows NT as well as the methodology and tools for measuring, and ultimately optimizing, code performance.

Windows 2000 and Mainframe Integration
by William Zack
1st Edition
$40.00
ISBN: 1-57870-200-3

Windows 2000 and Mainframe Integration provides mainframe computing professionals with the practical know-how to build and integrate Windows 2000 technologies into their current environment.

Windows Script Host
by Tim Hill
1st Edition
$35.00
ISBN: 1-57870-139-2

Windows Script Host is one of the first books published about this powerful tool. The text focuses on system scripting and the VBScript language, using objects, server scriptlets, and ready to use script solutions.

Programming

Handbook of Programming Languages, Volume I
Edited by Peter Salus
1st Edition
$49.99
ISBN: 1-57870-008-6

This is the most comprehensive source on the principal object-oriented languages. It covers languages from Smalltalk to Java with explanations of the languages' histories, descriptions of their syntax and semantics, how-to information and tips, and pointers to potential traps.

Handbook of Programming Languages, Volume II
Edited by Peter Salus
1st Edition
$49.99
ISBN: 1-57870-009-4

The four most important imperative languages are covered in this title: Fortran, C, Turbo Pascal, and Icon. Evaluate them to find the best imperative language for your purpose at hand, and learn how these languages are related to each other historically and syntactically.

Handbook of Programming Languages, Volume III
Edited by Peter Salus
1st Edition
$49.99
ISBN: 1-57870-010-8

Beginning with Jon Bentley's discussion of little languages, this book continues to discuss languages "specialized to a particular problem domain"—such as Perl, sed, awk, SQL, Tcl/Tk, Python, and more.

Handbook of Programming Languages, Volume IV
Edited by Peter Salus
1st Edition
$49.99
ISBN: 1-57870-011-6

This book begins with the functional programming group, descended from John McCarthy's LISP of the late 1960s, and moves on to discuss its offspring: Emacs Lisp, Scheme, Guile, and CLOS.

Smart Card Developer's Kit
by Scott B. Guthery and Timothy M. Jurgensen
1st Edition
$79.99
ISBN: 1-57870-027-2

This is all the practical information a computing professional needs to write programs that use and run on smart cards. Smart card communications and commands, SDKs, terminal-side and card-side APIs, security, financial applications, and e-commerce are all covered in this title.

DCE/RPC over SMB
by Luke Kenneth Casson Leighton
1st Edition
$45.00
ISBN: 1-57870-150-3

Security people, system and network administrators, and the folks writing tools for them all need to be familiar with the packets flowing across their networks. Authored by a key member of the SAMBA team, this book describes how Microsoft has taken DCE/RPC and implemented it over SMB and TCP/IP.

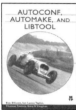

Autoconf, Automake, and Libtool
by Ben Elliston, et al.
1st Edition, Spring 2000
$34.99
ISBN: 1-57870-190-2

This book is the first of its kind, authored by Open Source community luminaries and current maintainers of the tools, it teaches developers how to boost their productivity and the portability of their applications using GNU autoconf, GNU automake, and GNU libtool.

Delphi COM Programming
by Eric Harmon
1st Edition
$45.00
ISBN: 1-57870-221-6

Delphi COM Programming is for all Delphi 4 and 5 programmers. After providing readers with an understanding of the COM framework, it offers a practical exploration of COM to enable Delphi developers to program component-based applications. Typical real-world scenarios, such as Windows Shell programming, automating Microsoft Agent, and creating and using ActiveX controls, are explored. Discussions of each topic are illustrated with detailed examples.

glibc: A Comprehensive Reference to GNU/Linux libC
by Jeff Garzik
1st Edition, Spring 2000
$40.00
ISBN: 1-57870-202-X

glibc: A Comprehensive Reference to GNU/Linux libC comprises over 1,800 functions. This complete reference work encompasses a single-volume version that gives quick coverage to each function. It includes an easily-searched index to provide added value. The book content consists of an index of functions by category (networking, threading, string, and so on) and an alphabetical function listing.

Networking

LDAP: Programming Directory Enabled Applications
by Timothy A. Howes Ph.D. and Mark C. Smith
$44.99
ISBN: 1-57870-000-0

This overview of the LDAP standard discusses its creation and history with the Internet Engineering Task Force as well as the original RFC standard. LDAP also covers compliance trends, implementation, data packet handling in C++, client/server responsibilities, and more.

ASDL/VSDL Principles
by Dr. Dennis J. Rushmayer
1st Edition
$44.99
ISBN: 1-57870-015-9

ASDL/VSDL Principles provides the communications and networking engineer with the practical explanations, technical detail, and in-depth insight needed to fully implement ASDL and VSDL. Coverage includes the fundamentals of the transmission theory and crosstalk in the outside plant, including the details of modeling and simulating the expected performance of ADSL and VSDL under different operating conditions.

DSL

by Dr. Walter Y. Chen
1st Edition
$54.99
ISBN: 1-57870-017-5

DSL is ideal for computing professionals who are looking for information on new high-speed communications technologies and information on the dynamics of ADSL communications in order to create compliant applications. Get calculation examples for all signal environments, coverage of ADSL, and a multitude of other xDSL technologies.

Gigabit Ethernet Networking

by David G. Cunningham Ph.D. and William G. Lane Ph.D.
1st Edition
$50.00
ISBN: 1-57870-062-0

Gigabit Ethernet is the next step for speed on the majority of installed networks. Explore how this technology will allow high-bandwidth applications such as the integration of telephone and data services, real-time applications, thin client apps such as Windows NT Terminal Server, and corporate teleconferencing.

Supporting Service Level Agreements on IP Networks

by Dinesh Verma
1st Edition
$50.00
ISBN: 1-57870-146-5

An essential resource for network engineers and architects, *Supporting Service Level Agreements on IP Networks* will help you build a core network capable of supporting a range of service. You'll also learn to create SLA solutions using off-the-shelf components in both best-effort and DiffServ/IntServ networks. See how to verify the performance of your SLA—as either a customer, or network services provider—and use SLAs to support IPv6 networks.

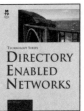

Directory Enabled Networks

by John Strassner
1st Edition
$50.00
ISBN: 1-57870-140-6

Directory Enabled Networks (DEN) is a completely new paradigm for leveraging the network. Although networks are currently able to provide Class of Service and Quality of Service, these services currently have high associated cost of ownership. If these services can be centrally controlled and provisioned by simpler means, they can support existing applications as well as new network-aware applications that require dynamic, yet guaranteed, levels of service while reducing the Total Cost of Ownership.

Understanding Public-Key Infrastructure

by Carlisle Adams and Steve Lloyd
1st Edition
$50.00
ISBN: 1-57870-166-X

This book is a tutorial on, and a guide to the deployment of, Public-Key Infrastructures (PKIs). It covers a broad range of material related to PKIs, including certification, operational considerations, and standardization efforts as well as deployment issues and considerations. Emphasis is placed on explaining the interrelated fields within the topic area to assist those who will be responsible for making deployment decisions and architecting a PKI within an organization.

Intrusion Detection

by Rebecca Gurley Bace
1st Edition
$50.00
ISBN: 1-57870-185-6

Intrusion detection is a critical new area of technology within network security. This comprehensive guide to the field of intrusion detection covers the foundations of intrusion detection and system audit. *Intrusion Detection* provides a wealth of information, ranging from design considerations to how to evaluate and choose the optimal commercial intrusion detection products for a particular networking environment.

Designing Addressing Architectures for Routing and Switching

by Howard C. Berkowitz
1st Edition
$45.00
ISBN: 1-57870-059-0

One of the greatest challenges for a network design professional is making the users, servers, files, printers, and other resources visible on their network. This title equips the network engineer or architect with a systematic methodology for planning the wide area and local area network "streets" on which users and servers live.

Understanding and Deploying LDAP Directory Services

by Timothy A. Howes Ph.D., Mark C. Smith Ph.D., and Gordon S. Good
1st Edition
$50.00
ISBN: 1-57870-070-1

This comprehensive tutorial provides the reader with a thorough treatment of LDAP directory services. Minimal knowledge of general networking and administration is assumed, making the material accessible to intermediate and advanced readers. The text is full of practical implementation advice and real-world deployment examples to help the reader choose the path that makes sense for the specific organization.

Switched, Fast, and Gigabit Ethernet, Third Edition

by Robert Breyer and Sean Riley
3rd Edition
$50.00
ISBN: 1-57870-073-6

Switched, Fast, and Gigabit Ethernet, Third Edition is the one and only solution needed to understand and fully implement this entire range of Ethernet innovations. Acting as both an overview of current technologies and hardware requirements as well as a hands-on, comprehensive tutorial for deploying and managing switched, fast, and gigabit ethernet networks, this guide covers the most prominent present and future challenges network administrators face.

Wireless LANs: Implementing Interoperable Networks

by Jim Geier
1st Edition
$40.00
ISBN: 1-57870-081-7

Wireless LANs covers how and why to migrate from proprietary solutions to the 802.11 standard, and it explains how to realize significant cost savings through wireless LAN implementation for data collection systems.

Wide Area High Speed Networks

by Dr. Sidnie Feit
1st Edition
$50.00
ISBN: 1-57870-114-7

Networking is in a transitional phase between long-standing, conventional wide area services and new technologies and services. This book presents current and emerging wide area technologies and services, makes them understandable, and puts them into perspective so that their merits and disadvantages are clear.

The DHCP Handbook
by Ralph Droms
and Ted Lemon
1st Edition
$55.00
ISBN: 1-57870-137-6

The DHCP Handbook is an authoritative overview and expert guide to the setup and management of a DHCP server. This title discusses how DHCP was developed and its interaction with other protocols. Also, learn how DHCP operates, its use in different environments, and the interaction between DHCP servers and clients. Network hardware, inter-server communication, security, SNMP, and IP mobility are also discussed. Included in the book are several appendices that provide a rich resource for networking professionals working with DHCP.

Designing Routing and Switching Architectures for Enterprise Networks
by Howard C. Berkowitz
1st Edition
$55.00
ISBN: 1-57870-060-4

This title provides a fundamental understanding of how switches and routers operate, enabling the reader to effectively use them to build networks. The book walks the network designer through all aspects of requirements, analysis, and deployment strategies; strengthens reader's professional abilities; and helps them develop skills necessary to advance in their profession.

Software Architecture and Engineering

Designing Flexible Object-Oriented Systems with UML
by Charles Richter
1st Edition
$40.00
ISBN: 1-57870-098-1

Designing Flexible Object-Oriented Systems with UML details the UML, which is a notation system for designing object-oriented programs. The book follows the same sequence that a development project might employ, starting with requirements of the problem using UML use case diagrams and activity diagrams. The reader is shown ways to improve the design as the author moves through the transformation of the initial diagrams into class diagrams and interaction diagrams. The author continues offering tips and strategies for improving the design and ultimately incorporating concurrency, distribution, and persistence into the design example.

Constructing Superior Software
Paul C. Clements, et al.
1st Edition
$40.00
ISBN: 1-57870-147-3

This title presents a set of fundamental engineering strategies for achieving a successful software solution with practical advice to ensure that the development project is moving in the right direction. Software designers and development managers can improve the development speed and quality of their software, and they can improve the processes used in development.

M T P New Riders How to Contact Us

Visit Our Web Site

www.newriders.com

On our Web site, you'll find information about our other books, authors, tables of contents, indexes, and book errata. You can also place orders for books through our Web site.

Email Us

Contact us at this address:

nrfeedback@newriders.com

- If you have comments or questions about this book
- To report errors that you have found in this book
- If you have a book proposal to submit or are interested in writing for New Riders/MTP
- If you would like to have an author kit sent to you
- If you are an expert in a computer topic or technology and are interested in being a technical editor who reviews manuscripts for technical accuracy

nrmedia@newriders.com

- For instructors from educational institutions who want to preview New Riders/MTP books for classroom use. Email should include your name, title, school, department, address, phone number, office days/hours, text in use, and enrollment in the body of your text along with your request for desk/examination copies and/or additional information.
- For members of the press who want to review copies of New Riders/MTP books. Email should include your name and the publication or Web site you work for.

Write to Us

New Riders/MTP
201 W. 103rd St.
Indianapolis, IN 46290-1097 USA

Call Us

Toll-free (800) 571-5840 + 9 + 4511
If outside U.S. (317) 581-3500. Ask for New Riders/MTP.

Fax Us

(317) 581-4663

M T P   We Want to Know What You Think

To better serve you, we would like your opinion on the content and quality of this book. Please complete this card, and mail it to us or fax it to 317-581-4663.

Name _____

Address _____

City _____ State _____ Zip _____

Phone _____

Email Address _____

Occupation _____

Operating system(s) that you use _____

What influenced your purchase of this book?

- ❏ Recommendation
- ❏ Table of Contents
- ❏ Magazine Review
- ❏ MTP's Reputation
- ❏ Cover Design
- ❏ Index
- ❏ Advertisement
- ❏ Author Name

How would you rate the content of this book?

- ❏ Excellent
- ❏ Good
- ❏ Below Average
- ❏ Very Good
- ❏ Fair
- ❏ Poor

How do you plan to use this book?

- ❏ Quick reference
- ❏ Classroom
- ❏ Self-training
- ❏ Other

What do you like most about this book? Check all that apply.

- ❏ Content
- ❏ Accuracy
- ❏ Listings
- ❏ Index
- ❏ Price
- ❏ Writing Style
- ❏ Examples
- ❏ Design
- ❏ Page Count
- ❏ Illustrations

What do you like least about this book? Check all that apply.

- ❏ Content
- ❏ Accuracy
- ❏ Listings
- ❏ Index
- ❏ Price
- ❏ Writing Style
- ❏ Examples
- ❏ Design
- ❏ Page Count
- ❏ Illustrations

What would be a useful follow-up book for you? _____

Where did you purchase this book? _____

_____

Can you name a similar book that you like better than this one, or one that is as good? Why?

_____

_____

How many MTP books do you own? _____

What are your favorite computer books? _____

_____

What other titles would you like to see us develop? _____

_____

Any comments for us? _____

_____

Fold here and tape to mail

- -

New Riders Publishing/MTP
201 W. 103rd St.
Indianapolis, IN 46290